Acknowledgements

This book is dedicated to those no longer with us, for whatever reason.

And also, with much love and gratitude, to:

My mum, who I hope doesn't read it! My sister Ruth and her family, Tamara, Sharon, Nick P. (RIP), Luke E., Matty P., Laura D., Shiv, Kiran G., Jerome R., Colin Goodwin, Michael P., Ralph H., Tony C., Darren from the 'Wood (YNWA), Banksy, Stoke Richard, James B., Alan McGee, Donny Chris, Joe, Alan, Josh B., Mick 'Bigbear' Hall, Pete L., Ken W., Dean (gas-head) G., Scott W., Mick (Diamondhead) Smith, Shesk, Monkeyman, Limousine, The Who (just to get a band of mine mentioned in the same sentence!), the staff past and present at City Roads, Barleywood, Clouds House, Milton House and the multitude of others who tried to help along the way – sorry it took a while – my agent David Luxton and of course my anonymous friends, you know who you are!

There are many others I could name. Please forgive me if you're not included here; you are not forgotten.

Also in loving memory of my dad, John Anthony Mason, for being with me long after you moved on to wherever it is we go . . .

Finally, in the hope she never has to write anything like this, to my beautiful daughter, Tabitha Honey Mason, who teaches me so much and one day, when she's old enough to read this, will still want us to go out to play together!

Love you, little bear.

It's often a thin line between fact and fiction. I
wouldn't know, I snorted it.

Prologue: The End

It is May 2006 on the Shakespeare Estate in Stoke Newington, exact time of day roughly five minutes after I've given a teenager on a stolen bike some money in exchange for some drugs that I hope will comprise my last ever hit.

A gram of heavily cut heroin and half a gram of equally fraudulent crack cocaine are being dissolved on the top of a discarded Coke can currently in the tremulous grip of the desperate unwashed hand connected to what remains of the rest of the mess that masquerades as a human being squatting at the top of the stairwell.

'Simon, you're gonna fucking kill yourself, mate.'

My audience of one suddenly seems a bit concerned.

'Doubt it, Dave, but if I do you can have my can of Special Brew. It's still cold.'

'Thanks, but I prefer Skol.'

'I've got a quid left over in my pocket, fucking take that if I go over and get yourself one of them, then, OK?'

'Ta, mate, nice one.'

The contents of the Coke-can cooker bubble and quietly hiss their disgust as they turn the requisite colour not too dissimilar to that of the nicotine-stained fingers now dropping the filter from a cheap cigarette into the tiny puddle of liquid self-hate rapidly cooling on the top of the can.

On the floor below us we hear a voice.

'Don't forget my fucking fags, you prick,' is the parting comment from whoever has been left shut inside as a door slams behind the prick in charge of buying the cigarettes and whatever else has been ordered to help alleviate the monotony of another day on the Shakespeare Estate.

I draw up most of the contents of the Coke can into my syringe

7

and spit on the back of my left arm in preparation for my attempt to obliterate myself from the monotony of another day in my life. This stairwell, a public toilet, a crackhouse, my old flat or a campervan in Spain, it makes no difference to me. I can't escape myself any more, so hopefully this hit is going to finally send me somewhere I might get some peace.

My audience is restless.

'C'mon, Simon, don't take the piss. You got most of that in your works, you've not left much for me, you greedy cunt.'

'I paid for it.'

'Yeah, yeah, true, but I sorted us out yesterday.'

'That was yesterday, Dave, and yesterday you got the bigger hit, a bigger hit of a lot less fucking gear too, mate, so shut the fuck up or I'll put the rest in my works and you'll get fuck all.'

'Dickhead.'

'Whatever.'

'You really gonna do all that in one hit? You're off your fucking head, mate.'

He's starting to really get on my tits, so I put my syringe back onto the filter and draw up some more of the shit-coloured fluid.

'I strongly suggest you shut your fucking mouth, Dave, and take what's left before I have the fucking lot, OK?'

'Proper dickhead you, eh? All right, get out the fucking way, will you?'

I am hopefully about to get myself permanently out of his way, everybody's way in fact.

There is a small abscess on the back of my left arm, slowly seeping blood, somewhere inside of which is the remnants of a vein that will hopefully be able to receive the blunt needle of the three-day-old syringe I am about to start prodding it with. In a life long since devoid of any hope, these few seconds of optimistic intrusion into the hole in my arm are as good as it gets. Think about that!

This is it. I hate 'god' almost as much as I hate myself but offer the scruffy twat a little thought as I beg for the elusive vein to show itself by flooding the barrel of my syringe with my poisoned blood and allowing me to release the belt I have wrapped around my arm so I can relieve the syringe of its contents and myself of the heavy burden of being alive.

Freedom is what drugs strongly suggested was on offer all those years ago. Freedom from feelings I struggled with then and still do now as I squat, trying to not puke prior to getting the drugs into my body. My inability to exist within my own skin in a world I have struggled to make any sense of is the double whammy to which eventually, after working my way through every other substance I could, only heroin seemed able to provide a solution.

Now, as I am about to bow out for the final time, I'm convinced that as I overdose and check out permanently my audience might possibly rifle through my clothes, take anything he can sell and leave me there for some other unfortunate resident of the estate to find. I accept this as par for the course but a small part of what remains of my soul hopes it's not a decent human being who'll discover me, someone who has no choice but to exist alongside all the scumbags like me who use their stairwells to inject drugs to try to avoid feeling like an utter cunt all the time.

Why do I feel this way about myself?

Do I actually know what I think about myself any more?

Who knows? Who cares?

Certainly not me as I rejoice at the miniature tidal wave of blood that suddenly washes up inside the barrel of my syringe and tells me the end is nigh. I release the tourniquet and prepare to take my final bow.

PART ONE

Do You Remember the First Time?

The first drugs I ever bought cost me three quid from a guy I met on the beach in Weston-super-Mare. He seemed to find the popping of my narcotic cherry an amusing experience, chuckling to himself as he took the cash I'd pocketed earlier during a rare winning streak in the amusement arcades. I crouched next to him as he skinned up, suddenly convinced that the entire Weston Constabulary were about to charge over the sand dunes, truncheons drawn, and attack us in some sort of hysterical, authoritarian, seal-clubbing-inspired frenzy before dragging us away to be questioned/tortured back at the nick.

Is a shit £3 deal of Lebanese hash a good cure for paranoia?

I didn't ask but neither did we end up getting battered to death by the local drug squad as I squatted alongside my 'dealer', keeping lookout while muttering, 'Yeah, man, that shit smells really good,' every few seconds as he skinned up.

He took several long drags before passing a soggy joint to me, grinning.

'Here, get that down ya. Have fun and enjoy the party. See you later, man.'

Unaware I'd been ripped off in tandem with scoring drugs for the first time in my life, I smiled back as I took the half-smoked spliff and watched him slope away along the beach.

I looked down at the smouldering joint, fleetingly wondering if I actually did want to enter the drug world. I found life confusing enough as it was but concluded that maybe if I smoked the joint I'd understand 'things' better. So I did, as rapidly as my lungs would allow.

Nothing happened for about 30 seconds, by which time my dealer had disappeared behind a sand dune. Had I been ripped off?

Just before this unpleasant and humiliating thought made itself at home in my mind, to be greeted by the paranoia already waiting there, waving a sign saying, '*Ha, ha, you're a fucking idiot,*' I started to giggle and my first drug-induced smile started to spread softly across my face.

Fuck you, paranoia, I'm on drugs now. What's the worst that could happen, eh?

I threw up.

Nobody had told me that would happen. Not the rock stars whose posters adorned my bedroom walls, nor the acne-encrusted goth hash dealer who'd just had my £3. Not that I'd have listened anyway. Listening wasn't a strong point of mine. I was a master of nodding my head in agreement just to fit in, but actually listening? It would be many more years before I could hear anything over the sound of the nonsense inside my head. Besides, I was on a mission now and the cannabis making its debut in my bloodstream told me I could see for miles and miles – oh, yeah. So listening didn't seem that important any more.

I'd begun my drug-fuelled quest for whatever the fuck it was I thought I was looking for, sitting on my own, stoned and happily confused in a cloud of hash smoke and a puddle of vomit.

I eventually managed to stagger home before the beach party I'd intended to go to had even started, grinning like the proverbial village idiot and stopping en route to throw up the cider I'd attempted to drown myself in earlier. I crept into the house and proceeded to make a sandwich using almost an entire loaf of bread, cold baked beans, tinned sardines and about a pound of cheese, as you do. Midway through my first ever munchie-inspired snack, I coughed up a bit of sick on said sandwich but continued to eat it anyway, as I was too stoned and paranoid to go back into the kitchen and make another one.

Sick sandwich?

Welcome to the future, Simon.

I was 15 years old, bored, uncomfortable and unsure of anything. Four years earlier I'd been shipped off to a Catholic boys' boarding school, which was apparently the best place to prepare me for life. My dad had been ill and he died not long after I went away to school. He had been a pilot in the Second World War, survived against all odds and found true love with my mum when he was in his 40s. He was my hero.

The two senior clergymen from the school who drove me home for the funeral were clearly under instruction not to reveal the awful truth awaiting me. They drove in silence at a priestly speed, then chose to stop at a motorway service station en route, leaving me sitting in the car outside, swallowing my tears as I worried about what had happened, while they enjoyed their lunch. In their defence, I don't suppose there was much they could have said.

The sight of my granddad walking towards me with his arms outstretched, looking frail and devastated, left me in no doubt as to what had occurred. He didn't have to say anything – he was crying and grown-ups didn't do that unless something terrible had happened. He bent down to hug me, triggering the first spasm of grief that left me hysterical as he gently escorted me to my parents' bedroom. There I found my mum and sister clinging to each other as they sobbed. When they saw me they both reached out as if beckoning me to join them in a human lifeboat that was being thrown about in a storm of unfathomable cruelty and despair – which was, of course, the truth.

There were family friends milling about, making endless cups of tea, all no doubt grief-stricken and wishing there was something they could do, but there is nothing you can do, is there?

I remember little of the next day or so. But at some point, my unrelenting thrashing about on my dad's side of the bed, clutching a photograph of him to my chest and wrapping myself in the sheets that still retained his smell, became too painful either for me to endure or for others to witness, so the family GP prescribed a sedative. It's what they did back then.

I have a theory that on some level an equation was made somewhere deep in the psyche of that distraught 11-year-old boy which roughly suggested that feelings can be avoided if there is sufficient medication to hand.

The fact you wake from the chemically induced slumber to confront the same problem a few short hours later is only explained in the small print that someone like me never reads.

It's just a theory, of course, but I'm entitled to it, eh?

The next thing I remember is seeing my mum kissing the lips of my dead dad as he lay in the chapel of rest. I couldn't move as the tears fell from my pallid, uncomprehending face onto the carpeted floor. This was not a place an 11-year-old boy should ever have had to visit. Not because taking me there to say goodbye was the wrong thing for my mother to have done but because losing my daddy was the worst thing that could have happened to me or any boy of that age.

I was 11 and knew only that my dad, my hero, my god, my everything was dead, gone for ever, and I hated myself for being too scared to walk over to the open coffin and kiss him goodbye like my mum had just done.

We vacated the chapel of rest, both still sobbing uncontrollably. I was consumed by an overwhelming sadness that already felt as everlasting as Christ and the heaven he apparently presided over. Neither of which my shattered 11-year-old heart could believe in any more – not that I was allowed to question it, of course.

I was returned to the 'care' of my school four days later, the badge on my blazer pronouncing the motto 'Let God Reign'.

Fuck that, quite frankly. I was soon far more interested in listening to what The Jam had to say.

When I was at home during the school holidays, my wonderful grandfather tried to be a father to me as best he could in his 70s, but he passed away within two years of my dad. A well-meaning family friend told me on the day of his funeral, 'You've got to be the man of the house now, Simon.'

I wasn't even thirteen years old and still had three years of boarding school to survive. I didn't feel like I had a house to be the man of, even if I'd known what that meant.

My school reports tell part of the story:

- Aged 11: Able and willing. Is a pleasure to teach, a credit to the school.
- Aged 12: Does well but needs to push himself a little harder.
- Aged 13: Could do a lot better. Is easily distracted. More effort required.

- Aged 14: Obviously doesn't want to learn anything. Is a constant distraction, disrupting the progress of others.
- Aged 15: We can only hope Simon changes his attitude and approach to life before it is too late.

The reason for this change is, of course, not documented anywhere. Those bastards might be evil but they aren't stupid.

A boy who'd lost his dad and grandfather within 18 months, whose favourite aunt had committed suicide, who'd witnessed a classmate drop dead in front of him at primary school and who now found himself placed in a school miles from his mum and sister would, I suspect, be classed as vulnerable.

The beast closed in, ready for the kill, sick with the pursuit of his thrill – me. There were late-night cigarette-and-whisky sessions in his office as he repeatedly told me he wanted to help. If I needed to talk about anything, I could trust him, he said.

'You're special, Simon, very special.'

We all know the fucking procedure now, eh? He followed it perfectly. He was, no doubt, an expert.

When you've lost the two most significant male figures in your life and the man who steps in to 'replace' them then proceeds to steal what little faith in life you have left, time after time, late at night while you lie paralysed with fear in bed, doesn't just create a 'hole' but also tells you on some level that you surely deserve to stay there.

A 'hole' in what exactly?

How the hell would I know? I was a child. I just knew that when I found something to fill it, I felt better. When something allowed me to escape myself I embraced it utterly.

Time passed slowly, very fucking slowly, but you knew that already, huh?

We formed the escape committee in desperation. Not to physically escape, as there were no locked doors or barbed-wire fences to cut. There was nowhere to run where you would not eventually be found and returned to face a wait outside the head's office, resigned to another whipping that apparently hurt him more than you.

No, the escape committee enabled our young minds to play with time, concerning itself purely with what we were going to do when we had served our sentence at school and would be free to do whatever we wanted to.

Or would we?

We assembled in the woods by the old bomb crater, a symbolic reminder that there was indeed 'a war on, you know'. Them and us.

Them, the establishment: alcoholic, sexually repressed, angry priests; dysfunctional teachers who never left the kids alone.

Us, the kids: the escape committee.

We had no leaders but we had our tree in the woods. You took your place in the branches according to the length of time already served. The fifth formers perched high up like birds waiting to fly away. They sat amongst yellowing names carved into the branches by previous occupants, which reminded us that one day we too would be gone and perhaps happy and free. Younger boys sat lower down with spit and fag ash dropped from above in their hair.

We built bonfires to boil water for tea and to toast our contraband bread that we spread thickly with illicit butter and jam smuggled from the dining room. We smoked our cigarettes slowly, casually flicking the butts into the fire. No one who wanted to went without a smoke during committee meetings. We smoked and talked.

Henry talked about playing baseball while making his coffee – he was a Yank and didn't like tea. Malcolm was going into the army, so he said in between blowing smoke rings and burping. Andrew farted a lot and talked about playing for West Ham one day and the rest of us laughed because West Ham were shit . . .

Me? I'd lost any notion of what I wanted to be by now. If I had been able, I would have told the escape committee about the late-night visits – what he did and what he said afterwards. About the whispered warnings he gave that no one would believe me anyway, before issuing a balmy slap upon my ashen face and then silently disappearing out into the corridor, leaving me shaking and hating myself for being too scared, too ashamed, too fucking scared, to tell the escape committee or anybody else.

I didn't have to explain myself to the escape committee as we sat trying to be men, away from that red-brick building and the monsters who walked its corridors late at night. I just talked about the things I was passionate about – music and Liverpool Football Club, because both allowed me to escape myself better than anything else I'd found up to that point.

One day the beast was gone. We'd returned for our final year and vague explanations were given about why he was no longer present. The Catholic Church did what it did so often – protected its own and ignored the victims, or certainly did nothing to help repair the devastation the sick bastard had left behind.

They could have stopped him, reported him and prevented him from hurting others. They didn't.

Let God Reign?

No, thanks! I'll get stuck into the *NME*, cheap cider, hash and speed, if you don't mind, because unlike 'Christ', they actually exist. I can see them, feel them, buy them, plus they're more honest and reliable. I had to survive the final year at school, so thank fuck The Smiths had arrived.

Their first album pretty much gave me hope that, despite all that had occurred during my 'education', life was still capable of delivering moments of true beauty.

Did I think The Smiths were miserable?

Not a bit of it; they simply said everything I wanted to say but couldn't, and they looked so utterly cool at the same time. That album breathed life into me and for that I will be forever grateful.

Park Life

Back in Weston-super-Mare during the summer of my first spliff, my £3 hash, vomit, cheese, beans and sardine sandwich experience had given me something new to think about other than myself, how to lose my virginity and why Paul Weller was pretending to be French and had taken to wearing a beret.

How to score more hash?

I decided my best bet was to find some of the people the teachers at school had warned us about. The ones who 'had not studied hard enough, had failed their exams, would amount to nothing and were probably on drugs'.

Best advice I'd ever had from those bastards.

The unemployed people in Grove Park were to my desperate eyes a somewhat scruffy, slightly intimidating, mildly mysterious, exclusive group who frequented the park or the Italian gardens in the high street most afternoons, probably shortly after they'd got out of bed. They made doing nothing look like an art form as they lazed about drinking cider and Special Brew, listening to music provided by a tape recorder the size of a small shed. The fact that they all wore sunglasses convinced me they must be on drugs. The devil is indeed in the detail, or in the park in this case, with the best tunes, naturally. These people obviously had better things to do than go to school or work, and if this was failing I wanted some of it.

I'd never previously had the balls to sit with them. I'd often sauntered past and wanted to, but now they suddenly looked less scary and I wanted some more hash.

Needed, actually.

Walking into the park I saw Fergie and his mates looking drunk and bored. We nodded to each other and I assumed it was cool for me to sit down.

'All right, Fergie? Er, listen, I, er, need to, er, you know, score some dope, man. I've got money. Chris [beach boy] usually sorts me out but he's not in. Any chance of . . .'

'No probs, mate,' he said, eyeing my money. 'Here you go.'

He pulled out a peanut-sized lump of something wrapped in cling film.

'Three-pound-fifty, mate. It's a nice bit of rocky that. Skin one up, then.'

Problem: I might well have just scored my second piece of hash but I had never made a joint in my life and now, surrounded by seasoned dopeheads, I was on the spot.

'Er, tell you what, Fergie, I'll go and get a couple of beers from the shop. You can get a spliff together, if you want. Here, may as well use it all . . . if you want.'

He looked at me and smiled in a manner I could not quite fathom before handing me some change.

'Bob fucking Marley, you, eh? OK, I'll have a Special Brew. Make sure it's cold, though.'

'Yeah, yeah, of course.'

I headed over to the off-licence. The woman in the shop didn't even bother to look up as I placed the two gold cans on the counter; she just took the money and continued reading *The Sun*.

'Thanks . . . oh, and a packet of green Rizlas too, please. Long size,' I said, in my gruffest over-18 voice.

She remained engrossed in whatever nonsense was in the paper, placed my change on the counter and I headed back to the park.

Half an hour after sitting down with Fergie and friends I was unconscious, having smoked half the joint he had made and finished the can of Brew in just a couple of minutes.

Comfortable nothingness.

Result.

The rain woke me a few hours later, after everybody else had obviously relocated and left me to my nothingness, having also 'accidentally' taken my packet of ten Benson and Hedges with them.

I went and sat in the park shelter until I felt I could stand up properly, after which I headed towards the seafront and made my way home, a little unsure on my feet and of what to think about my new life. Obviously getting wrecked would take practice.

In the safety of my bedroom I fell asleep listening to *Quadrophenia* by The Who, delighted to discover that my favourite album now sounded different – it sounded better, it sounded like it had been written exclusively for me.

I was back in the park practising the fine art of passing out the next day and the next and then every day after that, weather permitting. The result of my endeavours was that the point of oblivion rapidly started to take longer to reach – a fact that didn't go unnoticed by my new mates, who were quick to acknowledge my efforts by, amongst other things, actually speaking to me without feeling the need to 'borrow' money and no longer 'accidentally' walking off with my fags.

I was 'in' with the failures and they were lovely – most of them, anyway. Hysterically eloquent in stoned logic, passionate about music, clothes and smoking dope, they looked cool, talked in a language that made sense to me, introduced me to bands I'd never heard of and never once told me I was a waste of space like the bastards at my school had routinely been doing for a long time.

What's not to like?

We built absurdly oversized joints, got stoned using chillums, bath bongs, bucket bongs, cider-bottle bongs, Ouzo-bottle bongs and hot knives. Sometimes we'd just eat lumps of hash when only a 'pure' state of total catatonia would do or we didn't have any fags, always with music to provide a soundtrack to the day's/night's proceedings.

If we were feeling sophisticated and were at Doug the Slug's flat, we listened to Miles Davis and the Velvet Underground while wearing sunglasses and chain-smoking all night. I felt part of something. Studying album sleeves while discovering new bands, or indeed new 'old' bands, getting stoned, drinking cider and trying to look cool while hanging out in the park seemed to be a necessity in order to survive the boredom of my seaside town, and the addition of cheap speed to my bloodstream soon provided an almost Olympian ability to talk utter nonsense while doing so.

We ranted against Thatcher and the 'System', the dole office and how much hassle you had to tolerate for your free money, not that many of us were old enough to be on the dole. The prospect of signing on became something to look forward to – almost as if it were the next rite of passage required to be a fully fledged failure and all that encompassed, which was by now the sum total of my ambitions.

Nothing really happened as the time passed, sometimes sedately, sometimes flushed with the linoleum sparkle of amphetamines. It didn't really matter as we were permanently stoned, in the process of getting stoned, or figuring out the ways and means to get as stoned as possible, as soon as possible.

It might sound boring and much of the time it probably was,

but because we were always stoned, it didn't seem to matter. Besides, if boredom is a necessity of youth and youth is wasted on the young, it seemed best to be wasted at all times.

I thought about a lot of 'stuff' when I was wrecked, although I rarely remembered much of it the following day. But of course that didn't matter either. I just got stoned, thought some different kind of stoned thoughts, then forgot them all over again. As long as there was a stereo, some vinyl, booze and dope, all was well.

Getting a musical education from Gil Scott-Heron, The Smiths, Lou Reed, Bob Dylan, The Waterboys and The Only Ones, while enthusiastically smoking yourself towards a state of utter catatonia was, without doubt, a whole lot more exciting than listening to some noncey priest telling me my life would amount to nothing if I didn't understand why certain sides of a triangle added up to . . . oh, FUCK OFF, I don't care.

I was with 'my people', some of whom I was convinced were surely destined for great things and might just take me with them for the ride. As I had no obvious talent for anything other than being skint all the time and generally a pain in the neck, I was going to have to attach myself to somebody or something if I was ever going to achieve my ultimate goal of escaping Weston-super-Mare.

Music and drug 'culture' seemed to offer a way out from what, in my stupefied mind, my home town had to offer, which was nothing – certainly nothing that interested me, anyway.

I signed on and signed up, my first ever giro spent on cider, a lump of hash and the latest single by The Smiths, as the rain fell hard on my humdrum town, my morning's shopping providing me and my mates with shelter from the ever-prevailing storm of boredom.

Was it really that boring?

You're asking the wrong person. I was too stoned and drunk to notice, really.

School's Out

I made it through the final year; I'd survived.

The parting shot from a teacher at school?

'Mason, you're a worthless piece of shit that's going to end up dead or in jail.'

Thanks for that and thanks for reminding me there's always someone I can hate more than I hate myself. Cheerio, Mr Teacher, you utter fucking bastard.

I wish I'd said that. I'm generally not one for regrets, but if only I'd said that to his face instead of bloody nodding in agreement with him.

Living in Weston-super-Mare?

DULL.

Going back to college to retake failed exams?

BORING AND REQUIRED DISCIPLINE.

As I had little choice in relation to my current location and lacked the motivation to do what was needed at college, it's not surprising that my appetite for getting stoned increased as I dreamt of escape and began to study.

I started reading everything I could get my hands on about drugs, the people who took drugs, the people who grew drugs and the people who smuggled drugs. My LP and singles collection starting to take in albums written by people clearly off their fucking tits on drugs, who clearly made music for people to listen to while similarly afflicted.

Weston-super-Mare was awash with drugs of all varieties due to the simple fact it was a popular location for two particular kinds of institution: nursing homes and drug rehabilitation centres. The first full of people full of drugs, nodding out as they waited to die;

the second full of people previously full of drugs, trying (or not) to figure out how to stay off the fuckers and live.

There was no shortage of prescription pills of varying colour and effect for sale and a relatively large displaced community of heroin addicts who'd been kicked out of rehab and decided to stay in the area and deal to satisfy the needs of other relapsed and now relocated junkies from all over the UK – the basic law of economics, never more evident than when practised between drug addicts, being supply and demand.

I stumbled through a few more seasons of failing to not be a failure: two college courses started, two college courses abandoned. My other failure friends didn't seem to care, of course, but my poor recently remarried mum was tearing her hair out and her new husband, although clearly in love with my mum and doing his very best to make her happy, was soon suggesting I join the army! I needed the discipline, apparently.

I discussed the possibility of joining the army and getting to drive a tank with my mate Tim. His response: 'What in god's name makes you think the army is going to let a fucking idiot like you have a tank?' was a very good question and one for which I obviously had no answer.

Things came to a head after my stepdad was punched in the face by the father of a girl who despite turning up for our second or third date with an industrial-sized box of condoms still managed to become pregnant.

My options, as far as I was concerned anyway, were clear: army training in the West Midlands or run away and take lots of drugs.

Hmmmmmmmm, let me think about that.

Join the army and quite possibly get blown to pieces by the IRA on the streets of Belfast or go and blow my mind to bits in London?

Doug the Slug had a friend, who had a friend, who knew someone looking for a flatmate in Kilburn, so after yet another unpleasant but probably well-deserved confrontation with my stepdad I got their address, packed a bag, scored some hash and speed, then fled.

London Calling, 1986

There are only 130 miles between London and Weston-super-Mare. It's just over two hours away on the train but a different universe entirely.

After snorting some amphetamines seemingly strong enough to have fuelled the space shuttle, I found myself drinking can after can of lager, speeding my tits off as the train pulled out of Weston station and transported me towards the new life that was possibly on offer in the metropolis. I was actually terrified, but six cans and a million light years later the speed had reduced any fears I might have had, while also reducing the size of my cock. Speed's good like that: big plans, big eyeballs, shrunken penis.

With a head short-circuiting with hundreds of new ideas every second and full of drug-induced attitude, I leapt off the train at Paddington, my eyes on fire, cheeks sucked in, fag at the correct angle, shades glued to my face and dressed to kill. Hey, ho, let's fucking go, indeed!

When you arrive in a strange and mesmerising new place, planning (I use the word loosely) to make it your new home, there are usually some simple things to consider. Locating the address you hope to stay at is probably one of them; most people may even consider it rather important. Snorting another massive line of nasty jaw-clenching amphetamine then heading into Soho and all that was on offer there is probably not the most sensible move.

I was 17 and speeding my face off; nothing really seemed to matter. I was in the big smoke and life, unlike my dick, was suddenly looking up.

The noises, the smells, the desperate, glorious energy became a beautiful sensory overload, sucking me in and, unlike the prostitute that would shortly spy me as I glided through Soho, sucking me off, too.

The neon lights, clip joints, police sirens, whores, homos and hustlers of mid '80s Soho and the wonderful array of multicoloured people, hustling, shouting and scurrying about, getting/having a life, all informed me I had arrived. I'd made it.

Yes! I've fucking MADE IT.

Me, me, me, me, me, me, me, me, ME.

I feel so alive – a sensation complemented by the total anonymity of being surrounded by strangers. No one in this city knows me, not one of the multitude of souls who call this home, but I am now a part of it, or at the very least I've got a chance to be, and for the moment that is more than enough.

Head tingling, back sweating, legs rocket-propelled by cheap speed, I shoot through the labyrinth and out into Piccadilly Circus, where I quickly change my mind about trying to shag a prostitute after being approached by the third street worker in as many minutes with fewer teeth than my granddad had.

'Maybe another time, baby?'

'Are you here tomorrow, love?'

She walks away laughing then coughs up a big greenie and deposits it on the pavement. 'Yeah, baby . . . every day, every day.'

Another line I think, no, insist to myself as I march through the streets, soaking it all up and sweating it out again, can after can of Stella reaching the parts that the beer that reaches the parts others don't doesn't reach either. The familiarity of various buildings previously only seen on television gives me the feeling of knowing exactly where I am, even though I've only visited London once before. More speed, more Stella, more, more, more LONDON.

I lose some money in the arcades in Leicester Square but don't care. I've won something anyway – more speed, more fags, more Stella. More, more, more.

It gets dark and the West End comes alive, more vibrant and seductive in a few hours than the hometown I'm escaping from could be if it existed for eternity. As I choke back the sulphate that's sliding down my throat, I fall in love with the greatest city on earth and instantly divorce myself from that place at the other end of the train tracks.

Weston-Super-WHERE?

I'm home.

Some time later I realised I was tired. Some more time after that I realised I had no fucking clue where I was or where I was going to sleep.

Sleep? Glancing at my watch, I saw it was 4.30 a.m.

I searched my jeans pocket to try to find the wrap of sulphate that had my friend's friend's address scribbled inside it. A short while after emptying my pockets for the tenth time I remembered that I'd chewed it and swallowed it when the last of my speed had become impregnated in it after I had been dancing – I use the term loosely – in some tourist hell-hole nightclub.

Unknown faces had stared at me as I tried to demand that the DJ play something by The Smiths. When my demands went unmet I'd proceeded to call him a stupid, fat, music-hating cunt and was then thrown out by the thugs in dinner jackets who had in all probability taken the remaining few pounds out of my jacket as they smashed my throbbing head against every stair in the process of wishing me a 'Goodnight, sir'.

I got a sinking feeling of Titanic proportions as I realised I was now totally broke with nowhere to go, no one to call and, worst of all, no more speed, alcohol or fags. My legs felt like they were melting, my new life disintegrating as the Technicolor explosion from the previous day's/night's drugs fizzled out and I in turn fell to earth, or Trafalgar Square to be more precise.

Here was the early-morning madness: people hanging out and waiting for a night bus, liquid eyes rolling around up-all-night faces just like mine. People beginning the start of the journey home after a night of debauchery, talking shit and searching out somewhere still serving a drink at 4 a.m.

Buses came and went, delivering the coming-down-but-wide-awake people back to redundant beds to stare at the ceiling for hours until sleep slowly, eventually arrived.

Home?

Seeing as I'd eaten the address of the home I'd hoped to go to, I skulked around feeling drained and disoriented, watching the night crawlers slope off and wishing someone would take me with them.

It felt scary all of a sudden, as the (lack of) speed started to slow down my body and mind, allowing reality and tiredness to begin to catch up. Fuck.

I perched next to one of the lions at the base of Nelson's Column for what seemed like hours in freefall. I thought about skinning up a joint but was suddenly far too paranoid, so I just sat there, jaws clenched, waiting.

Waiting for what? I don't know! I had no idea of what to do next.

Someone else did, though.

A shark circles in his car. Above us the rats with wings circle Nelson, his lions and the speed-wrecked, shipwrecked idiot below. No one knows I am here, but I am. Just about.

No doubt I am looking bewildered, lost and vulnerable, so the shark closes in for a thrill/kill.

'Hello, you look a bit lost, can I help?'

A bit lost? This guy must have been following me for years, right? Instinct, of a kind, kicks in.

'Got a cigarette, mate?'

'Yeah, sure. Are you all right? Can I help?'

'I don't know, can you?'

I think I know what he has in mind but this is not a situation I am prepared for, or maybe I am?

'Do you want a coffee, maybe go for a bite to eat, a chat?'

I've seen that expression before. I know what it means but I don't really care. I don't know how to.

We're in a car, an old car, warm and reeking of fags and stale spunk (which in retrospect was probably more fragrant than how I smelt by this point) as we head towards the river, looking for somewhere to get coffee. As we pass another McDonald's, I enquire as to where we're actually going.

'You said we were going to get some food, mate!'

'Oh, I thought I'd get you home first,' says the shark, revealing a salacious smile that suddenly leaves me in no doubt whatsoever as to his preferred early-morning fancy. His hand hovers above my knee.

'No! I want a McDonald's. Here! Look!'

I'm attempting but failing to avoid sounding anxious and this is akin to blood in the water in which a predator of his kind swims.

He places a hand on my leg and pulls over. I slip out of the front seat and into the safety of neon burger-land. Looking back, he is right behind me.

'Give me some money, please. I'm hungry and need to get my energy back up, you know . . .'

I try to avoid eye contact as he passes me a crumpled £5 note and disappears down the stairs to go to the toilets, leaving me in the queue.

I'm instantly out into Victoria Station, heart racing, leg muscles disintegrating but carrying me back out and away along Victoria Street, no longer scared but peculiarly encouraged by what has just occurred.

Maybe the streets are paved with gold after all? Or at least walked upon by dirty old men with more money than either morality or sense?

With the £5 note clutched tightly in my sweaty palm, I scuttle off towards Soho again, stopping only to buy cigarettes, chewing gum and orange juice, then float through St James's Park to eventually find myself back in Piccadilly Circus – the old main drag.

Sitting below Eros, with a freshly lit fag, I smile and go to make a call.

Our House

After a few calls to Weston I managed to get hold of the address I'd inadvertently swallowed the previous night and found myself on a Tube heading north to Kilburn.

Ten minutes' walk from the station along Shoot-up Hill and I was standing by the front door of a large semi-detached house with what resembled a refuse tip out front where the garden once was many years and student tenancies ago. Locating the doorbell, I drew breath, pressed it and waited . . . pressed it again and waited again . . . before I gave up trying to be considerate and left my finger on the doorbell until I got a response.

'Who the fuck is it? Fuck off, eh!'

Welcome to Kilburn, country boy.

'Hello, I'm looking for . . .'

A just-been-woken-up voice angrily interrupted me from somewhere inside.

'Who the fuck is it? What fucking time is it? If you're the landlord or Skinny Pete, Mr Boyd is not in. Now stop hassling me, I know my rights, man.'

'Er, I'm Simon . . . I'm one of Doug the Slug's mates from Weston. He said you had a spare room for rent and I've got nowhere to stay and I don't know anybody and I'm really tired.'

'Fuck off! Do you know what the bloody time is?'

'Er, yeah, look, I'm really sorry about that. I got lost on the way here, sort of . . .'

No response.

'Look, I'll pay rent and everything. I won't be a freeloader.'

No response.

'Listen, do you want to skin up and we can talk about it? I've got a nice bit of rocky here.'

The sound of a Golden Virginia-induced hacking cough followed by the resulting phlegm being flushed down the toilet indicated I'd possibly made a breakthrough.

I heard somebody half walk, half fall down the stairs. The door opened and there stood a thin, long-haired hippy with a grey sheet wrapped round a body that obviously hadn't seen a bacon sarnie in years. He looked me up and down, yawned and turned back towards the stairs. I took it as my cue to enter.

'Rocky, eh? Let's have a cup of tea and we'll get a smoke together and have a chat. My name's Rob. Will's not got in yet. Been out all night speeding his tits off somewhere, I expect. Come in.'

Yes! Yes! Yes! FUCKING YES!!!!!!

Rob farted and then padded up the stairs. I stumbled along

behind, holding my breath as I navigated my way through the gaseous residue of last night's veggie curry. We entered the kitchen to be met by another aroma – one unique to such an environment. A smell you will not encounter anywhere else. An odour so particular that it stays in the consciousness for ever. Anybody who has ever been a student, squatted or lived communally with other young men knows this smell. It's as much a part of the experience as taking drugs and staying up all night talking shit, putting Che Guevara posters on the wall, regrettable one-night stands, wearing shabby clothes and pretending to be left-wing for three years.

It's the aroma of the male student kitchen and to me it smelt like home.

Rob offered me a cup of Earl Grey and stuck out his hand. 'Right, then, let's have a look at this ganja.'

I handed it over and he proceeded to inspect it as if it were a precious gem, rolling it around his hand for a while before burning a corner with his Zippo lighter and sniffing the ensuing smoke.

'Ah, yeah, there's been quite a bit of this around lately. Right, do you mind if I get one together?'

'No, course not. Help yourself. That's what it's for, eh?'

As he proceeded to put seven Rizlas together, I surveyed the kitchen. Apart from several different-coloured moulds growing unchecked on the woodchip-covered walls, there was nothing but a poster of Fat Freddy's cat and a clock with no hands left to indicate anybody ever used this room.

Rob looked up and read my thoughts. 'Yeah, it's a bit barren right now but we're getting it together. Only moved in recently, you know.'

'Oh, right, when was that, then?'

'When we got kicked out of halls by the fascist scum – couple of years ago now.'

He finished building the longest joint I had ever seen, sparked up, smoked silently for a few minutes and then passed it to me. I pulled on it as he wandered off.

'I'll put some tunes on. What you into?'

'Whatever, mate. The Smiths, Velvet Underground?'

Rob returned and The Velvet Underground drifted after him into the room.

No, really, it's true. At least one of them apparently just had! The seven-skinner had almost finished me off. I felt absolutely fucked and was now clearly hallucinating – either that or Rob's flatmate had just walked in dressed entirely in black, strumming an acoustic guitar, fag hanging out of his gob and wearing a pair of Ray-Bans, singing 'Sweet Jane'.

Either situation was fine by me as my head hit the table and I began to mumble incoherently to myself while resting face down in a small puddle of my own saliva.

Somebody was poking me, almost shouting at me. 'Hello in there . . . Rob says you want to move in, yeah? Well, that's all right with me as long as you pay the rent and don't vote for Thatcher. Simple rules, man, yeah?

'Hello, anybody in there?'

I couldn't open my eyes but the voice continued . . .

'Look, I'm sorry if I've woken you up but you need to answer a few questions before we make a very important decision. I know it's early but if you want to take the room you have to understand the rules and now's as good a time as any to get things sorted, yeah?'

My eyes were still refusing to work but the voice was also refusing to leave me alone.

'Can I skin up, man? I'm a bit wired at the moment. Been up all night, yeah. Did some whizz, yeah. Went to the fuckin' Wag club. Fuckin' excellent, man, yeah. Have you ever been to the Wag? It's fuckin' excellent, man. Listen, I'll get some tea together and we'll have this chat, yeah?'

I was still face down at the table, eyes still closed. But the voice continued.

'Do you like The Velvet Underground? Fuckin' Lou Reed, man. Fuckin' excellent man . . . yeah?'

I opened one eye and tried to focus on the source of this babble.

'Oh, I'm Will by the way. Very pleased to meet you.'

Will wasn't even looking in my direction as he stirred in five sugars and spilt tea everywhere.

'Yeah, man, been out all night at the fuckin' Wag, man. Excellent, yeah? So, tell me, how's Doug the Slug doing in Weston? Heard he's moving back up here soon. Fuckin' excellent, man, yeah. Hey, have you got any skins? Need to get a reefer together, man. Been up all night. Did some speed and went to the . . .'

'The fucking Wag,' I interrupted.

Will turned to face me.

'Yeah, man, how do you know? Were you there? Fuckin' excellent night, wasn't it? I didn't see you . . . I was totally off my face, man. Did some speed . . . Have you got those skins I asked for? Right, kettle's boiled, let's get a cup of tea together, have that spliff, yeah?'

I pushed the Rizlas in his direction as he stared at the four mugs of tea he'd just made, obviously trying to figure who'd made the extra three, then giggling as he realised it was his doing. 'Woops, need to slow down here. You know, you seem pretty cool, so I guess the room's yours, man. Nice one. I'll show you where the social is, if you like. I'm going down there myself later . . . wankers owe me some money! How do they expect us to live, man? Good job I like amphetamines. Couldn't afford to eat every day, yeah? Anyway, welcome to the house. I'm Will by the way. Pleased to meet you, nice one.'

He finished rolling the joint, lit it and stood up and walked away, mumbling to himself. 'Right, new flatmate, that calls for a drink. I'll just have a quick nap, then we can get things sorted. See ya in a bit, yeah?'

Five minutes later he reappeared at the door amid a cloud of fag smoke, having wet and combed his hair back and now looking like a cross between Marty Feldman and a demented, undernourished vampire who'd just spotted his first neck in weeks.

'Fancy a line of whizz and a quick pint before we go to the social?'

It was obviously a rhetorical question, as sleep seemed to be off the agenda for that morning. I thought it sounded like a good idea given the circumstances and the fact Will was fumbling with a wad of notes big enough to club a whale to death with.

'Right, fuckin' excellent, yeah? Let's go. I'm buying.'

We headed out the door. Rob had gone back to bed, so it was just the two of us who approached his/our/my local, which was less than two minutes' walk away – well, more of a unwavering stride as far as Will was concerned. I staggered along behind him as he mumbled something about getting home later to finish some work before steaming into the boozer and striding up to the bar.

'Good morning, barman. Two pints of Guinness and two large whiskies, please. Oh, and one for yourself.'

It was shortly after midday and the place was mental already. This was definitely not Weston-super-Mare.

I've made it, I thought to myself as the first Guinness and whisky slid down the back of my throat, I've really fucking made it.

Master and Servant

Will was in the third and final year of his university studies, although when pressed on the subject he seemed reluctant to discuss anything about what exactly it was he had been studying.

'Yeah, you know, it's all utter bollocks, really. I can't really be bothered with it any more but it keeps the family off my back. They're expecting me to get a job soon, whatever that means, fuckin' yeah, no fuckin' way, man. Too much like hard work that, yeah, know what I mean?'

I nodded in empathy, although to be honest I hadn't really understood much of what Will had said during the previous few hours we'd been in the pub. It was all I could do just to stop myself from sliding underneath the table and eventually I had been forced to undo the belt from around my waist and actually strap myself into the chair, while Will had continued getting in Christ knows how many pints of Guinness with accompanying whisky chasers. His trips to the bar were the only times he actually broke off his 'conversation' at me – a barrage of mildly psychotic rambling that ceased for only as long as it took to demand more booze from the seemingly unfazed barman.

Just as I was about to slip into unconsciousness, Will informed me that we were ready to face 'the fuckin' brain-dead morons at the fuckin' social security office. Fuckin' expect me to live on twenty quid a fuckin' week, fuckers.'

'Listen, Will mate, I'm not sure if I can stand up at the moment, mate, you know? I've been up all night too, mate. I'm absolutely fucked, mate. I'm not really in the right frame of mind for the social. I really could do with some sleep, yeah?'

'Oh, right, well, that's a fuckin' pity, man. I didn't realise, see . . . fuck . . . Well, I don't think you'll be getting any sleep just yet . . . I put a little bit of speed in that pint you're drinking, mate. Fuckin' thought you looked a bit tired. Thought it would be a surprise, yeah?'

'How much speed, Will?'

'Oh, I don't know? A cheeky half gram or so . . . Just a little pick-me-up. You did look tired, yeah? Fuckin' sorry if I've fucked up but I did say we had to go to the social later. Are your teeth feeling a bit numb? Mine wobble a bit. Do yours? C'mon, let's get down there, yeah?'

As I stood to leave, the hairs on the back of my neck also stood to attention as I started to sweat pure Guinness.

It's all getting a bit intense.

'Are you fuckin' deaf as well as fuckin' ugly? I fuckin' told you three times already, my dear, I haven't spent last week's giro. I didn't fuckin' get it, it didn't arrive. Maybe the fuckin' postman stole it? All I know is it didn't come and I want my money, yeah? And so does my friend here. He's just moved to London from the countryside and hasn't got a fuckin' clue about anything. You know what they're like, don't you? Now, please, I've not been to sleep for a while cause I'm so hungry and I need to go shopping for food before it's too late, yeah, for fuck's sake.'

The woman behind the bulletproof glass pulled down the blind revealing 'This Position is Closed'. Will turned and looked at me with a look of total disbelief on his face.

'Did you fuckin' see that, man? I don't believe she did that. Right, fuckin'. . . oh bollocks, what's a man to do with these people, Simon? What shall we fuckin' do?'

I was having great trouble making out Will's words at this point due to a cacophony of screaming kids, and men hurling drunken abuse at each other or anybody else within spitting distance. The dole office was like a refugee camp for redundant cannon fodder, alcoholics and people with more kids than nicotine-stained fingers. It appeared, to me at least, that they were only issuing money to people who could swear in more than one dialect at a time, while simultaneously juggling mini-me children, cans of high-strength lager and a copy of *The Sun*.

Somewhere in the middle of it all was my new best friend in the whole world – Will – now screaming at the top of his voice.

'I don't know what to do any more. These people don't have a fuckin' clue, so I shall now retire to the pub, fuckin' quick-time! Simon, fuck these people. We need a drink.'

I nodded, unable to talk but most definitely in agreement as I followed him out of the dole office and back to the boozer, where we remained until we ran out of speed five minutes before last orders, or, to be more precise, when they refused to serve us any more because we were clearly too far gone – and, trust me, in that boozer that took some doing!

I had been in London just over 36 hours. A good start, I think you'll agree, and certainly more exciting than joining the fucking army, eh?

Up in Smoke

When all you own in the entire world is a large box containing crumpled editions of *NME*, cheap porn magazines, some records, notebooks full of bad poetry and a couple of changes of clothing, moving home is a piece of cake.

A mate drove my box up a couple of days later, returning to Weston with a letter to my mum assuring her I was fine and that I was living with some university students who were studying 'science' and probably going to become doctors. I also confirmed that, at this point, I had decided a military career was not for me.

Over the following weeks I found myself establishing a fairly leisurely routine: get up approximately midday, put on some tunes, cup of tea (PG Tips for me and Will, herbal nonsense for Rob), spliff or two, maybe a quick game of backgammon and then, funds permitting, an afternoon in the pub.

'Funds permitting' ceased to be a problem the night Rob and Will walked in the front door carrying four black bin liners, inside which was the sum total of their academic achievements to date.

Weed.

Lots of weed.

There was more dope than I had ever seen in my life, which, after some quick discussion, meant that the highly unlikely possibility of me ever getting a job became even less likely.

I had made a few acquaintances in the dole office and pub who were willing to take bits of weed off me on a regular basis and this earned me a tidy income on top of my dole money. The life of a small-time dope dealer suited me down to the ground. I considered it an honourable profession and any thoughts of further education or a 'proper' job went up in clouds of 'Kilburn Killer' home-grown smoke.

I also made one rapidly aborted attempt to sell some of 'our' weed outside the Golden Cross pub in Portobello Road, my street hustler shtick being rudely interrupted by an old Jamaican fella who, on witnessing me mooching up and down for a few minutes pretending to know what I was doing, called me over to him. As he sat on the steps outside his flat a few feet away from the pub, slowly cutting tiny slivers of squidgy black hash from a lump the size of a baby's fist, he enquired, 'Hey, son, how old are you?'

'Seventeen, mate. Wanna buy some weed? It's really strong, it's . . .'

'If you want to be 18,' he interrupted, 'I suggest you fuck off back to wherever it is they make idiots like you from, get me?'

I 'got' him.

Communal living obviously has its pros and cons. For me, the bin bags and cupboards full of weed and shelves stacked with books and records were more than enough to compensate for any minor annoyances I found with my flatmates. OK, I could have murdered a proper Sunday roast each week but Rob's lentil curry kind of grew on you anyway.

I devoured their respective album collections with unbridled enthusiasm, convinced I was getting a proper education while stoned out of my mind, sprawled on my bed. I skinned up on and pored over album sleeves, devouring previously unheard records by The Stones, The Velvet Underground, The Who, Dylan, Bob Marley, Peter Tosh, James Brown, Van Morrison, The Waterboys, Psychedelic Furs, Ramones, Talking Heads, The Only Ones, Iggy Pop, The Doors and The Clash.

Happy days indeed, then, and it was hard to see how it could get any better – until it did.

A mate from Weston phoned up one day and asked if I wanted him to get me a ticket for the Glastonbury CND festival.

Did I?

Do people piss on the stairs in the Kilburn dole office?

The Whole of the Moon

As Phil drove us onto the festival site a few weeks later and we found a spot to pitch our tents, we were almost immediately greeted/ambushed by a man/thing doing a convincing impression of a starving hyena that had just discovered the rancid carcass of a dead wildebeest, although he possibly smelt worse. He resembled an unkempt hedge, attached to which were some arms, legs and a face that looked like it had been battered with a hammer. He did, however, speak our kind of language and of course I immediately decided he was my new best friend.

'Get some acid that fuckin' works, boys. Nasty-bastard, peace-convoy acid!'

OK, if you put it like that it'd be rude not to.

Whatever he'd taken seemed to be working for him, so within thirty seconds of putting our camping gear on the grass we paid

£2.50 each for six pieces of blotting paper bearing an image of Superman. Our friend also had five grams of speed and two hundred and fifty or so magic mushrooms on him, so we bought those as well, just for starters. It was still only Wednesday afternoon, after all, and you've got to pace yourself at festivals, right?

Yeah, right.

The unbridled lunacy that was Glastonbury '86 inevitably had a somewhat weighty impact on me and even if I'd managed to stay straight for more than five minutes I'm sure my head would have been turned inside out regardless. For all I knew, the multitudes of weird and wonderful people now surrounding me could have been living in Somerset for the past couple of decades, ignoring the passing of time, shambling around their canvas city getting wasted, eating acid and veggie curry washed down with Special Brew.

Was I ready for this?

What was this?

I looked at the Superman blotter nestling in a tiny piece of cling film in my hand – 500 micrograms of 'nasty bastard, peace-convoy acid'.

I was almost ready for it but tucked into the speed, hash and cider first. I was saving Superman for Saturday night, after which, on Sunday, The Waterboys, the band I currently adored above all others, were playing. I was ready for that for sure.

For the time being, however, there was work to do. Someone had to be in charge of assembling the tents and someone needed to take care of Dr Octopus.

We eagerly unpacked the bong we'd brought with us, its combined parts comprising a three-gallon bell jar, a two-foot length of copper pipe, a huge roll of metal gauze and four long pieces of garden hosepipe. Truly a work of some considerable devotion and something we had been looking forward to christening with a mixture of teenage dopehead enthusiasm, pride and I think it's fair to say a little trepidation about how obliterated it would get us. I have to hand it to Gazza, he had surpassed himself with this basic but impressive bit of festival kit, which we'd christened Dr Octopus.

As Tim attempted to erect the tent and Phil went off to buy a few gallons of scrumpy, Gazza and I pieced together the good doctor, after which I slung it over my shoulder and headed off to find some water.

'Oi!!'

I looked around and saw a man with a face that made our acid-dealing hedge-person look like the poster boy for a health farm leaning out of a sizeable green marquee tent.

'Oi! You! Studenty-looking fellow. Bring that baby over here. Come on. Don't be shy. We won't hurt you.'

'I'm just getting some water together, man.'

'Well, there's a standpipe behind our house, here. Come on in. We're all from the moon.'

How could I refuse?

I shouted over to Gazza, who was by now struggling with the tent.

'Oi!' our new friend barked in his direction. 'Don't bother with that now. You'll find it easier after we've all had a go on this,' he continued, pointing at the good doctor.

I appreciated his logic and so scuttled inside the tent belonging to the people from the moon, taking with me our industrial-size bong and an appetite for smoking hash to match.

Two things rapidly became clear. First, that our hosts were not actually from the moon but in fact the more leafy suburbs of Andover and, second, that the good doctor was very good at its job.

Some time passed. I can't be more specific but just know that some time passed after our host produced a tennis-ball-sized lump of hash, bit off a mouthful and stuffed it into the top of the bong. Four of us took a tube into our mouths and sucked, coughed and sucked some more, as the bell jar filled with dense, green-tinted smoke. We sucked, coughed again and looked at each other for a sign . . .

'Fuck . . . . me,' said our host.

'Fuck . . . . me,' said Gazza.

'Fuck . . . . me,' said me. 'It works . . . .'

I started to dribble before crawling towards the entrance to the tent and throwing up everywhere.

'Marvellous,' said Gazza, as he joined me in projectile vomiting all over the grass outside.

We looked at each other, cackled, vomited, laughed again and then crawled back inside to rejoin our friends from Andover who were by now if not actually from the moon, quite possibly orbiting it.

Some time passed before any of us could move or string more than a couple of indecipherable grunts together and it was dark by the time we decided we might be capable of walking the 50 or so yards to where we'd left our other mates and our tent.

We staggered out expecting to see our solitary orange tent still standing, loosely speaking, in the almost empty field, but during the 'some time' we had been getting wrecked, about 200 tents, all seemingly of various shades of orange, had appeared. It took us a while to locate ours. Gazza eventually fell over it, reducing it to a crumpled heap and waking a startled Phil, who had already passed out after drinking what, judging from the puddle of puke outside the tent and the empty plastic container next to it, looked like many pints of possibly the most potent scrumpy in the world. I say this because I'm sure to this day that the puke-splattered grass had actually changed colour and died.

Somehow we managed to reassemble our little orange home, scrambled inside and, after eating the entire contents of our food stash for the coming weekend, passed out. 'An encouraging start to proceedings,' was possibly my final thought before disintegrating into my sleeping bag.

The festival of '86 was one of the last before the police were officially allowed onto the site. Hard as it may seem to believe for more recent festival-goers, there was a time when Glastonbury was policed pretty much by those in attendance and a few hired, almost friendly security/Scottish people.

Now, as anybody who has had the experience will tell you, it isn't exactly hard to procure a little something for the weekend, even these days. Back then it was hard not to. You could wander to certain parts of the site to score certain drugs: Yeoman's Bridge for speed, the entrance to the main arena for slivers of hash from a Rastafarian food stall, or up towards the King's Field for basically anything and everything else. Or you could just sit outside your tent and wait for 'room service'.

We all made plans and studied the festival programme to see what time certain bands were playing but making plans at a festival, for people like me at least, was akin to Neville Chamberlain waving his bit of paper in the air and promising 'peace in our time'. It might have sounded achievable to me, but to anyone with half a brain the notion was clearly ridiculous.

A more simian approach evolved: get up, have a piss/shit, maybe brush teeth, eat some crisps/biscuits for breakfast, smoke copious amounts of hash, then shamble about grinning at everyone in sight, trying hard to look as crusty as possible. Maybe locate the big blue cider bus while trying, unsuccessfully, not to lose all your mates and forget where you've camped, until you eventually pass out somewhere for a while. Who knows? You might even get to see a band.

Oh, Superman

It was going to rain. That much I was sure of, I think.

Nothing else was making much sense and it was purely by chance I was wearing suitable clothes for the imminent mud bath.

I was protected by a German army greatcoat and boots, peaked officer's cap, mirrored sunglasses and a liquid smile, nodding my head to music only I could hear in the process of trying to swap a bag of magic mushrooms for a traveller's horse. Someone asked if I was all right. I looked at them and smiled before lowering the sunglasses from my eyes. They walked away with an uneasy expression.

I laughed at the funny yellow and blue snakes in the grass – just another acid-crazed idiot sitting in a field of his own making.

The Superman was doing its thing and I was doing mine by feeling as far away from myself as I had ever been and at the same time being at the absolute centre of my own universe.

Me, me, me, me, me, ME and 500 micrograms of high-quality LSD.

So near yet so far away.

I knew it was going to rain, as there was wet stuff falling from the clouds.

'The clouds, man! Has anybody seen these clouds?'

Sure enough, the heavens opened just as the acid really kicked in, and I found myself alone with 10,000 other people standing in front of the pyramid stage. The Cure came on, a laser show commenced, and an even more impressive natural light show erupted above us as thunder and lightning ripped the skies and minds of the acid munchers below. Robert Smith was at least 500 feet tall, more lightning flashed across the sky, the thunder rumbled and my brain started melting.

It was money well spent.

I really didn't have a clue what the fuck was going on. How wonderful was that?

I drifted away from the stage and myself and went on a mission as the LSD occupied every particle of my mind, leaving me at peace with myself.

Some hours later, none of my mates would let me inside their tents and I couldn't remember if I'd brought mine with me.

'Slugs like giraffes everywhere, man, and did you know you have horse's hooves for feet, Tim?'

Apparently not.

It stopped raining, the clouds dissipated and there in the magnificent night sky was a full moon, the whole of the moon. I was lying down on the side of a hill, finally connecting with everybody in the whole world, or at least those of us watching a bank of cloud drift in front of that moon, the greatest show in heaven, on earth, for just £2.50.

What did I see?

I can't tell you that, you'd all want some.

Whatever it was, it left me feeling as at ease as I'd ever been. Tears rolled down my cheeks as I cried at the beauty of the heavens above me.

I wouldn't change the events of that night for anything. The fact that my first trip on acid would also prove to be the best was not something I could have known at that point; what I did know for sure was that almost as soon as it was over I wanted to do it again.

The Waterboys were playing the next day. I knew that for sure and I was going to get down the front to pay my respects and stand in front of the pyramid stage. The whole of the moon? The whole of the moon . . . I knew what he was on about now, or maybe . . . £2.50, £2.50 . . . fucking wonderful?

Hope, fantasy, good drugs, bad drugs and confusion?

Yeah, just add £2.50.

Sunday Afternoon

The next day I'm not really sure if I'm still tripping – hard to tell without taking time to allow reality to kick in like the Superman acid tab kicked in last night. Reality is, of course, every bit as potent as high-quality acid, just more expensive and with fewer 'fuuuuuuuuuuuuuuuck woooowwwwwww' moments, particularly if you live in Weston-super-Mare.

Unlikely I'd appreciate anyway, if pushed on the subject, which has the most profound effect on my dirty mind – reality or drugs. But I know which I now think I prefer, and I think therefore I am right, so maybe that's my answer? Maybe not?

I'm only 17. I know nothing but don't know that, and acid asks big questions at the 500-microgram-per-hit level. Cheap at twice the price, too! Cheap like me.

Meanwhile, hash, speed and warm beer have probably nullified any slim chance of actual reality disturbing me today as I wait for the band to come onto the pyramid stage and help me survive a bit longer in my world.

I'm waiting for the big music to come.

It's not a huge crowd yet but that doesn't matter, not to me anyway. I'm down the front waiting to pay my respects, waiting to hear 'The Whole of the Moon' – feel it like I'd seen it last night with the aid of the acid.

They walk on stage. He looks really fucking cool, sounds cool, is cool, not like me, although I live in hope. A hope that confuses reality and fantasy, good drugs and bad drugs, the confusion that I don't understand but think I do, of course.

'This is a Bob Dylan song . . . "Maggie's Farm".'

We hate Maggie, but again I don't really know why. My hatred seems to impress certain people, though. Good drugs, bad drugs and the people that take them impress me, so I take the drugs and the people and hate her. They take care of me with the big music as my small delusional world and the crowd that surrounds it grows bigger.

It feels like something special is happening right now, as more people are sucked towards the stage. Maybe the latecomers are just turning up early to see the next band?

The next band? That's a lifetime away, surely?

I don't know. I don't really care.

I don't really care about anything, but I think I do, often.

He's singing about 'surrender' – words that sound like they're meant for me but I'm not really able to hear. I listen but I don't hear. I'm at war with myself and surrender is not an option, not yet, not for a long time, due mainly to the fact I have no idea I have a fight on my hands and that the enemy is cleverly disguised as myself.

The cool person up on the stage sings about being my enemy but I am armed to the teeth and unwittingly prepared to fight for as long as it takes.

He keeps singing; I keep listening. He sings about man being tethered, but the acid disagrees. It tells me I'm free. Cost price: £2.50 a hit.

They play 'The Whole of the Moon'. I think I understand but it will be many years before I actually believe what I think it means to me, and a lot can happen in that time to someone who can't tell the difference between reality and fantasy, good drugs or bad.

I swallow another bit of Superman, just to stay safe.

Sunday afternoon becomes Sunday night. I find a tent that may or may not be mine. I neither know nor care. It's unoccupied and so I slither inside and melt into the ground, drift away to wherever it is a bit of Superman takes me, until the following day when I pack up my troubles, ingest the remainder of my drugs and leave.

I don't like leaving very much; I much prefer to arrive. But what else can you do?

Hope, fantasy, good drugs, bad drugs and fear?

Fear of what?

Amongst other things, of which there are plenty, fear of being left alone with just me and my feelings for company.

I made my way home, wherever that was.

Kill All Hippies

I unlocked the front door and walked upstairs feeling something was not quite right. Rob was sitting in the kitchen, skinning up as usual, the fifth side of *Sandinista!* still sounding a bit crap, as usual.

Will was not around, or so it seemed as we sat and smoked over a cup of Rob's latest foul-tasting herbal infusion. I might have just been to Glastonbury but I was not a hippy, so I got up to make some PG.

'I can't fuckin' believe you pay good money for that, man. What does it actually do for you anyway?'

I heard Will's voice but couldn't fathom where it had come from. Then again I hadn't been looking underneath the kitchen table, which is where my favourite student of the human mind, or whatever it was he was studying, was lying.

'Did you have a good time at Glastonbury, then?' asked Rob, not even looking up from his newspaper – *The Guardian*, of course.

'Er . . . yeah, it was . . .'

'Fuckin' unbelievable, you know,' Will interrupted. 'Fuckin' unbelievable that you can get 50,000 dirty hippies together in a bloody field at the same time without somebody in authority realising they could fly over in a plane, drop one reasonably sized bomb and immediately cut out 90 per cent of the waiting time at the dole office. Kill all hippies – apart from you, Rob, obviously.

Save us taxpayers a small fortune in benefit handouts.'

'Oh, for fuck's sake, Will,' said Rob. 'What the fuck has got into you this week? You really need to cut down on the amount of amphetamines you're doing and why are you still hiding underneath the bloody table? The landlord left two hours ago.'

'And since when were you a taxpayer anyway?' I added. 'And, yes, thanks, Rob. I had an excellent time. It's a shame you didn't make it, both of you. You would have enjoyed it. I took some acid too, it was . . .'

'Right! That's fuckin' it! I knew it! Didn't I say so, Rob, eh? Well, didn't I? I don't mind living with one fuckin' hippy, because I've known you a number of years and realise I will never make you see the error of your ways. You'll never change but I'm fucked if the balance in this house is going to shift too far towards peace, love, acid and soya milk. No! It will not happen. Simon, as penance, I insist that you go out and buy a large amount of amphetamines to prove you are not turning into some acid-gobbling, soap-dodging, tree-hugging hippy.'

'That's a bit strong, Will,' said Rob.

'Furthermore, I happen to know an honest dealer with a fair price. In fact, I'd better come with you and we can stop for a drink and a chat on the way back. I'll get my coat. Fuckin' acid indeed.'

Will scrambled up from underneath the table and disappeared into his room.

I looked at Rob, who was still engrossed in *The Guardian*.

'Thanks,' he muttered.

'What for?'

'Getting him out from underneath the table. He was starting to stress me out, really doing my bloody head right in, man. See you later.'

We went out to buy some speed. 'An honest drug,' according to Will.

When buying speed, it's often best to avoid being pulled into a totally mind-numbing, meaningless conversation with the dealer, who, more often than not, will be desperate to talk to anybody, about anything, at any time. Unless of course you enjoy that kind of thing or he's offering a freebie, in which case cancel any other plans you might have. I generally preferred a simple in-and-out job but I was with Will so this was probably not going to happen.

He knocked on Skinny Pete's door.

'Pete mate, it's Will, yeah?'

'No, I've nuthin', Will,' came the reply from behind the heavily bolted door. 'Come back tomorrow, Will. I'm busy catching up on some work for college. Go away.'

Will turned to look at me with an expression on his face like that of a man whose girlfriend has just eloped with his grandfather – shock, disgust, anger and incomprehension all mixed together. This was the only place he knew to score at the moment. He turned and banged on the door again, suddenly possessed, flapping his arms around and pacing up and down.

'Listen, you skinny Scottish moron, I am your best bloody customer by far. You cannot tell me there is nothing.' He shook his head, unwilling to accept what he'd heard.

Skinny Pete shouted back from behind the door, by now sounding agitated. 'Get tae fuck, you English piece of shite. I've got nothing till tomorrow. Now fuck off!'

'Will mate, leave it. Let's get down the pub instead. You could do with some sleep, anyway. We'll have some Guinness and chill out. You look fucking terrible, man,' I said, tugging at his arm.

'Scottish peasant. I'll find myself a decent dealer and then he'll be sorry. Fuckin' can't even do his fuckin' job properly . . .' Will raged as he flung himself at the door, kicking it hard then screaming in pain and hopping about on one foot.

'Scottish cunt!'

'English prick!'

We left.

Will was still ranting, hopping and cursing under his breath when we entered the pub 20 minutes later. A few pints of Guinness only made him worse. I'd not seen him cry before but he was weeping like a baby.

'It's not fair, Simon. I'm tired, I know, but I'm convinced that Pete has got speed. He just doesn't want to sell it to me. Why? Why? Why?'

'No idea, Will mate, really.'

I suggested to him that perhaps we might try again later but it was no use. Will was inconsolable and the Guinness simply made his self-pitying babble even harder to listen to. I needed to get home and sleep in a proper bed for the first time in nearly a week, so I made my excuses and left Will to babble at and depress the barmaid by himself – if having to work in that particular pub and regularly serve people like me and Will had not done so already, of course.

On reflection, considering the amount of speed Will was using, I suppose he was always going to be a safe bet to shatter the stoned tranquillity of our existence and, sure enough, the time came later that week.

Will still hadn't got his hands on any speed and he was not feeling too clever to say the least. He had locked himself inside his room and was playing 'Sister Ray' at ear-bleeding volume over and over again. Rob and I continued our half-hearted attempts to learn how to play mah-jong in the kitchen, while smoking a carrot chillum and doing hash hot knives. At some point in his life Rob had acquired a collection of ludicrous costume hats and I was now wearing my personal favourite (when catatonically stoned) – a red and yellow court jester's affair, complete with bells and pointed bits.

'Do you think he's all right in there, Rob? I don't know about you but that song's really starting to do my head in, man. Maybe one of us should go and check on him?'

'Uh uh, nah. He's been worse than this before. Last year he stayed up for five days writing an essay and got a distinction. He always goes a bit funny when he leaves the speed alone for a while . . . now, is this piece a dragon or a wind sign?'

'Maybe we should offer him a hot knife, chill him out a little. I'll go and ask.'

I stumbled up to Will's door and knocked.

'Will mate, do you fancy a hot knife?'

There was no answer. I knocked again harder.

'Will, are you all right, man? Rob and I are . . .'

'Agghhhh . . . no way, man. Get away from me, you hippy bastards.

You'll not get me eating lentils . . . . ever . . . . I'm gone now, man. Ha, ha, ha, ha . . .'

I opened the door in time to see Will clambering out of his window and dropping down into the garden below.

'Will, where are you going, man? Come back. I was only checking to see if you're all right. Rob! Come here quick. I think he's really lost the plot . . . Rob!'

He came into Will's room, looked at the open window and then looked at me.

'We'd better go after him, Mason.'

As that was the first time Rob had ever called me by my last name I began to think that the situation might be serious.

We gave chase, getting out onto the street in time to see Will disappear over the railway bridge on Minster Road, carrying a suitcase.

'Shit! He's got my suitcase. That's not good at all.'

I looked at Rob, puzzled about his apparent concern over a battered old suitcase when it looked like his best mate was going insane.

'Fucking hell, Rob! It's only an old suitcase. Will's not a well man, for Christ's sake.'

'It's got all the weed inside, man!'

'Fucking hell! Shit! We'd better catch him then, eh? Will, come back with that suitcase, mate. Will!'

It wasn't until we had rounded the first corner in pursuit of our freaked-out flatmate and I saw Will looking back over his shoulder before taking off at even greater speed that I realised I probably wasn't helping the situation by chasing after him while still wearing the jester's hat and Ray-Bans, waving a burnt knife while shouting after him, 'Come home and everything will be all right, Will. We'll take good care of you, honest.'

We didn't catch him. He jumped into a black cab that had pulled up at the lights. I never saw him again and, to make matters worse, we had run out of weed.

I spent the next couple of days smoking joints made from what I could pick up off the floor. By the third day I'd clearly gone insane and walked into the job centre actually looking for a job.

I got one, too. Mad, huh?

I went to work as trainee head barman in a posh hotel in Russell

Square, which could quite possibly have been the start of a decent career. A month later, after I'd drunk more booze than I'd sold, I was facing the sack. One lunch break I saw an advert in a travel agent's window offering cheap flights to New York, which quite possibly offered the start of something far more exciting. I had friends already travelling through the States on their gap year and trying to locate and join them seemed a much better idea than waiting to get sacked and signing on again.

Ninety-nine quid to fly to America with what remained of a month's salary to spend when I got there, or possibly having to move back to Weston?

On the Road

'Mum, I'm going to America next week.'

'Why? What for?'

A reasonable couple of questions for which I had no reasonable answer.

'Where in America?'

'Hollywood, I think. To be an actor,' was the best response I could come up with. 'It's on the west coast near Los Angeles.'

'What about your job at the hotel? When are you coming back?'

'When I make it, Mum.'

'What do you mean, "make it", Simon?'

Yet another good question.

'Er, listen, I'll call you again before I go. I've got some stuff to sort out in London first. Don't worry, I'll be fine.'

'But I thought you liked London. I thought you were training to manage a hotel. That's a good career, Simon . . .'

'I do, I am but . . . I'm taking some time out to . . . have a rethink. I'll call you later, Mum. Bye.'

'But you can't act, Simon!'

'Neither can Arnold Schwarzenegger, Mum, but he's done OK.'

My mum was not a fan of the aforementioned Hollywood star and so couldn't comment on his acting capabilities, but neither was she an idiot.

'But he was famous before he became an actor, Simon. He probably had money to pay for somewhere to live and acting lessons.'

'Then I'm going to ask for a refund on his behalf, Mum! Don't worry, I'll be fine.'

'But, seriously, what will you do for money there, Simon? And there's so many people on drugs and people who carry guns. It's dangerous in Los Angeles. I'm already sick with worry.'

'I'll be OK, Mum, really. I'm 18 now. I'll be fine.'

I hung up and thought briefly about people with guns and drugs in America, concluding that surely not everyone who took drugs also carried a gun? Besides, I'd been listening to The Doors a lot recently and figured I knew all I needed to know about America, really I did.

A couple of weeks later, as the 747 slowly crawled up into the sky, my fear rose with it. I was pinned to my seat until the opening salvo from my bottle of duty-free whisky and packet of Marlboro reds did its job and the fear subsided. The Waterboys made big music in the earphones of my Walkman, serenading my departure.

Eight hours and a lot of whisky later, I found myself standing in line at US immigration, Newark, New Jersey, nervously waiting for my turn to be interviewed. When asked the purpose of my visit I didn't think 'to go to Hollywood and become a film star' was the correct thing to say, so I informed the officer I was visiting an old teacher of mine in Boston for a short holiday.

I could feel myself shaking as she looked me up and down. Then, presumably judging me to be of no threat to national security, she proceeded to stamp my passport.

'Have a good vacation, sir.'

I was in the land of the free, home of the brave, with a bad hangover, possibly feeling free but not particularly brave. I had a few hundred dollars, some tapes for my Walkman, a copy of On the Road in my pocket and no idea what the fuck I was going to do next or indeed where I was going to do it.

Marvellous.

If you can make it here you can make it anywhere, right?

Trouble was, not that I understood it, but here, there or anywhere, I was always going to be there. If you know what I mean? And I still didn't really know what I meant by 'make it'.

Hotel California

How many drug-loving, work-shy English teenagers can you get into an overpriced, cockroach-infested studio apartment situated a 30-second walk from the beach in Los Angeles?

Depends on how many you know and how many the drug-loving, overworked official tenant of said property is prepared to put up with.

Quite a few, then, as it turned out.

A few days on the east coast had reduced my financial situation dramatically and as winter was approaching I made the decision to spend almost all of what little money I had left on a flight to LA, my thinking being that if I was to be hungry and homeless, it was better to be so in a warmer climate. I'd also heard that my two mates who'd flown over prior to my recent career change from 'hotel manager' to no job, no money, nowhere to live but no fucking way am I going home, were somewhere in California and apparently doing OK for themselves.

Another flight, another bottle of whisky and I was in LA. A few days after which and by some insane stroke of luck following a phone call to a mate back in England I discovered my two friends were living in a hostel in Venice Beach. I was currently 'living' in the back of a Volkswagen bus along with three other British guys I'd met in a pub in Santa Monica, all of whom were working as labourers for the owner of the bus. Despite having found their way from Mexico after following England to that summer's World Cup finals, then on to the black-market economy of the numerous building sites of LA, none of them had apparently managed to find anywhere to wash after eight hours' hard graft each day. They were lovely but they fucking stank to high heaven.

After three nights of listening to Yeovil Bob snoring and farting I'd more than had enough and thankfully tracked down my two friends, Julian and Pete, at their hostel.

Within a few hours they'd introduced me to an American they'd met while hanging out in a local amusement arcade and who currently rented a tiny one-bed apartment in Venice Beach. Within a few days of that, we'd all moved in with him!

Kevin, or 'Kevmate' to give him his quickly adopted moniker, as in:

- 'Listen, Kevmate, I'm going to get a job and pay some rent soon, mate, honest.'
- 'Kevmate, have you got a few spare bucks to get some weed, mate?'
- 'Kevmate, can I borrow the car, mate?' etc., etc.

was the official occupier of the apartment. It was his name on the tenancy agreement and usually his hard-earned dollars that paid the massively over-inflated rent suffered by people who considered it worth paying to reside in the by day tourist-heavy, by night crackhead-polluted enclave once home to such luminaries as Charlie Chaplin, Fatty Arbuckle, W.C. Fields, Jim Morrison and now Kevmate plus assorted 'fucking lazy, useless, drug-addled, bastard English knobheads', as he affectionately called his new found Euro-trash lodgers.

I couldn't have summed myself up better if I'd tried, though I'd maybe have thrown in 'sponging', 'deluded' and 'self-centred' as well.

By some ludicrous dictate, over the following 18 months the 'universe' provided that grubby, nicotine-stained room with a regular stream of equally grimy drug dustbins from Weston-super-Mare, all invited to stay for a night, all not managing to leave for many months.

Time passed, Julian and Pete left to begin university; I stayed to begin studying near-death experiences and drug addiction.

Venice Beach, 3 a.m.

He has a gun tucked into the waistband of his jeans, a brown paper bag containing a bottle of something that has obviously unleashed his inner demons in one hand, a small glass pipe in the other and a petrified 18 year old from Weston-super-Mare in his sights.

Oh, and, the 18 year old is out of his tiny mind on acid, which I think it's fair to say is not really helping on any level, as what remains of my LSD-saturated thought process tells my mouth to start laughing.

I'm also registering the fact that I might well have just shit myself, although it's hard to be sure as another wave of fear and LSD washes through me with equal vigour.

Three dollars for this? I almost think to myself and start laughing uncontrollably again, tears of no discernible purpose streaming down my cheeks, coinciding with the contents of my bladder emptying themselves onto the boardwalk below me.

Three dollars? Cheap at twice the price, I'd thought to myself as I'd swallowed the two tiny white blotters a few hours previously. I'd been fully prepared for the night ahead: 40 Marlboro reds, cheap booze, weed, music and an empty apartment.

What could go wrong?

Ha, ha, ha, ha, ha!

At some point I'd decided to go out for a stroll. Another bad idea of mine, or maybe it was the acid? Either way I'm left standing in a puddle of my own piss at 3 a.m. on a Tuesday morning, tripping my nuts off and laughing uncontrollably at a deranged crackhead with a gun in his pants.

I need to come up with something here, as I feel the current situation might not be going too well for me.

'Do you like The Doors?' is my best attempt to remedy the situation.

'What the fuck did you say, you dumb fuck?'

'The Doors . . . Jim Morrison? Do you like him?'

And then I start laughing again.

'Who the fuck do you think I am, you fucking fuck?'

I guess he doesn't.

I try again.

'Listen, man, I'm from Weston-super-Mare in England. I don't want any trouble, please . . . Cigarette?'

My hand is shaking as I pull the fag packet out of my top pocket and offer a smoke to my 'friend'.

He snatches the packet.

'Money . . . you got any money, you, you . . . where the fuck did you say you were from, you fucking fuck?'

'Fucking Weston-super-Mare, England. It's fucking shit,' says I.

'Have you got any fucking money, you stupid fuck?'

There is a crumpled $5 note in my pocket, I know, but I cannot convince my arms to move, stuck as they currently are, twitching outstretched in front of me in a 'I've-got-my-hands-up-please-don't-shoot-me' kind of stance.

'Give me some fucking money, you fuck . . . Are you fucking looking at my fucking dick, you fucking fag?'

Oh, Jesus!

His dick, not that I am in the least bit interested in it, is I assume concealed behind the gun that I am now trying to not look at.

'No . . . no, no, it's a . . . your gun . . . I don't like guns, mate. Please, I'm really not looking at your dick.'

He stares at me trying to not stare at his gun/dick. Then he starts laughing, which induces another bout of my own, by now totally hysterical, laughter, as I somehow manage to retrieve the $5 bill from my pocket and offer it to him.

'Jim Morrison?' says he.

'Yeah, do you like The Doors?'

He snatches the piss-soaked $5 from my hands and leans into my presumably ashen face.

'Jim fucking Morrison . . .'

Silence.

'He was a fucking stupid fuck just like you.'

57

And away he goes, leaving me standing in my puddle of piss, shaking like a leaf, laughing and crying in equal measure.

You gotta laugh or else you cry, right? Unless you're a stupid fuck like me on acid at 3 a.m. on Tuesday, Venice Beach, Los Angeles, in which case you do both.

Kevmate did his thing, which was basically work like a lunatic, come home, get wasted, pass out, get up and go to work again, and I did my thing, which was more or less the same minus the 'work' bit, unless you can call working my way through his record collection, getting stoned, wandering through Venice, watching people do what the people there do, a job.

I made friends with some British people at the only place I could get served a drink (it had become apparent that at 18 years old it was a lot easier to buy illegal drugs than get served a pint) and, incredibly, while drinking at the King George 'British' pub on Santa Monica Boulevard one night I accidentally accepted the offer of a proper job helping some of my new mates roof a multi-million dollar house in Brentwood.

I soon concluded that manual labour was not really my thing but buying small amounts of cocaine and weed, and selling it to the lads on the site most certainly was. My mate Jaffa, originally from west London but now happily ensconced in Santa Monica, did initially express some concern at the direction my career had taken but he was also painfully aware of my clear lack of ability in the building game and on several occasions had already prevented me from getting a clump from irate co-workers, furious at my lack of application to any task required of me.

'Fuck it, Simon, you'll probably do OK as long as you don't go silly. Stick with the pot dealing. That coke game can get messy.'

'Really? C'mon, Jaffa mate. I'll be OK.'

Thus I retired from the construction industry to concentrate on a more leisurely career path that did not involve getting up at 'death' o'clock each day to wander about a building site, pissing everybody off, and instead spent my days hanging out in the pub, sniffing coke and boring the pants off anyone who could bear to listen to my coked-up nonsense about becoming an actor.

One afternoon, between bouts of cocaine-induced self-centred musing, the thought occurred that I was actually missing my old mates. I called to tell them how great life out here was, how great I was and that they really should come and pay a visit to sunny LA, and a few weeks later I got an answerphone message from Weston which went something like: 'Simon . . . Jon and Gav here. Ha, ha, ha, we're coming to visit. Oh my god, we're coming over to LA, man. You'd better get us somewhere to stay, man. It's going to be mental! Ha, ha, ha, ha, ha! Call us. We're coming next week.'
Click.

Jon

He arrived to visit in the spring of 1988, wide-eyed and determined to see as much as of America as his dad's credit card would allow, so what better place to start than L fucking A, man?

Jon liked the good things in life and hard-earned family money meant he could have them. Money, eventually, would become part of Jon's problem.

He wasn't greedy or precious, far from it, but sleeping on the floor at Kevmate's apartment was all the slumming he was probably ever going to do and I assume that slumming it with a platinum credit card in your pocket never seems that bad, really.

Funny, great company, generous, handsome, music-loving (Bowie fanatic), Liverpool-supporting, drug-taking-and-buying daydreamer. Not surprisingly he was one of my best friends ever and loved by everyone who knew him.

I had been up all night with Cathy the Hippy, my neighbour, greedily shovelling coke up my rapidly disintegrating nose and talking complete shit, as you do. I knew my friends were due to arrive early but every time the thought of getting a few hours' sleep crossed my mind, a fat line of Charlie intercepted it at the pass and sent it scurrying to the back of my throbbing head.

Then, as ever, we reached the point of no return/no sleep and I knew I was going to meet them wired to fuck. Still, 'L fucking A, man!'

Driving like the coked-up lunatic I was, I managed to locate the airport, sort of parking before strutting around the arrivals lounge chain-smoking and looking dangerous – well, I thought so – until I spotted my two mates come shuffling through the gate, grinning like idiots on a day out at the seaside, which actually wasn't all that far from the truth.

We were all idiots in a way – harmless young idiots, of course. Some of the finest idiots a person could wish to meet, in fact.

'Mr Mason I presume?'

Gav offered his hand; Jon looked as excited as I'd ever seen anyone before or since.

'How's it going, Simon?'

Snuffle, sniff, cough. 'Bit tired actually, late night. Anyway, welcome to Los Angeles, boys. Come on. The car's parked in the red, white and blue zone.'

Jon immediately informed me he wanted to go to Magic Mountain amusement park. He'd just seen it on the telly and fancied a go on the big dipper. I inadvertently re-sniffed a lump of last night's cocaine that had been lodged in my nostril, thus providing me with a little more instant stupidity and reluctantly promised to take them as soon as they'd dumped their stuff at their hotel – Hotel Kevmate as it turned out.

The last thing I wanted to do was go to Magic fucking Mountain after spending the previous night polishing off a pretty impressive mountain of South American magic marching powder with Cathy.

Big dipper? No thanks. My head was fucked, my knuckles white and I wanted to go to bed. Jon and Gav were not going to let me, end of.

We left their bags at Kevmate's, where I took the opportunity to lick the mirror I'd been staring into and sniffing from all night, giving me a fleeting moment of energy that had totally diminished by the time I'd filled the car up with petrol. Soon enough we were sitting in the morning traffic chaos, heading north to Tragic Mountain.

The drive was horrible. Rush hour in LA is possibly the most ridiculous contradiction in terms ever. The only thing rushing was my blood pressure as the remnants of the coke short-circuited through my bloodstream. It was already 30 degrees outside. 'My' car (Kevmate had lent me the money. I was going to pay him back as soon as I got a job, OK?) had no air-conditioning, Jon and Gav were asking me all sorts of questions that although understandable and simple were simply fucking annoying and required thought I was incapable of achieving.

As soon as we got inside the park I found a bench and went to lie down and die, while the boys went off to play.

Magic Mountain? Feeling like shit mountain, more like.

They woke me when they'd had enough and wanted to go somewhere else. My little siesta had livened me up a bit, so I decided to call my friend James, an up-and-coming actor who lived in the Hollywood Hills and liked to hang out with 'Limeys'. Especially Limeys who had drugs.

'James, it's Simon. Listen, I've got a couple of mates over from England. Can we come over later and hang out, check out the Strip, maybe have a little party at yours?'

'Yeah, dude, that would be cool. I've got some acid, tequila and Quaaludes. Bring some coke, OK?'

'Jon, got any money?'

'What for?'

'Coke, Jon. We need some cocaine. Welcome to Los Angeles, man.'

Hollywood Nights

Later that night the four of us are cruising Sunset Boulevard in James's convertible Mercedes, soaking up the vibes and feeling like the coolest people to have ever come from our little seaside fleapit.

My deluded mind is suggesting I 'own' this city and my two

mates have come to congratulate me on my success and celebrate the fact I've clearly 'made it'.

Sniff, sniff, hurrah.

Somewhere amongst the arrogant, coked-up, self-obsessed nonsense of my scrambled head there may be a feeling of simple happiness because we are friends together having a mental night out in fucking Hollywood, fucking California, man but it's a shame I don't really know how to appreciate this fact without spending a small fortune on drugs that I probably don't need.

Need them or not, the acid starts to kick in and James thinks it's best we get home and out of harm's way, and the ever-present cops are starting to look really scary as we head to his place up in the hills.

Behind the safety of locked front doors, we continue our 'Welcome-to-LA-I-am-cool-as-fuck-party'. James wants to call some hookers but the thought of having to talk to a woman, let alone trying to have sex of some kind, is beyond what's left of my comprehension. I assume him to be some kind of freak until he informs us he'd only taken a quarter of his acid tab, seeing as the last time he'd tripped he got arrested for walking naked through the Hollywood Hills with a crossbow.

'Don't stress out, though, buddy. It was years ago. Here, let's do some more coke . . .'

His place has a terrace with a pretty impressive view out over the city. It looks good through unmodified eyes; under the influence of acid, cocaine, Quaaludes and tequila I suggest out loud that we are 'gazing upon heaven, boys'.

It's only the distant sound of gunshots that reminds us otherwise, unless Jon is correct and 'maybe Jesus owns an Uzi . . . fuck, this acid is really . . . . . . fucking . . . . . . fuck'.

He wanders off.

Gav soon seems to find the 110 channels on the elephant-sized TV more interesting than the panoramic view of the City of Angels, so it's left to James and I to talk total nonsense as we stare out into the night, toasting each other's profound but slurred meaning-of-life observations until the last of the tequila and coke is finished.

He stumbles off to bed just after sunrise.

'Hey, I guess your buddies found the spare room. See you later, dude.'

He walks straight into a closed door, laughs, does it again a couple of times then turns the handle and disappears into his room, still laughing.

Movement of any kind seems to be beyond me as the sounds of the city drift up and the early-morning smog forms its brown stain on the sky. I begin to drift off, still hallucinating slightly as I slump further into my chair, a sloppy smile plastered across my face. I sleep for a few hours until Gav suddenly comes stumbling out onto the terrace.

'Simon, Simon, quickly, come inside. There's been an accident. Oh shit, quick. It's Jon.'

He is half-whispering, smoking furiously and pacing up and down yet somehow still only appears mildly concerned.

'What's happened, man? Where's Jon?'

'I don't believe it, mate, Jon's . . .'

'What? What the fuck are you talking about, man? Is he all right? Where is he?'

'In the bedroom. Quickly, man, he's . . . shit all over the bed. It's everywhere, man – covers, pillows, everywhere.'

And, as I soon discover, it's all over the wall, the floor and, on closer inspection, Gav and Jon, too.

The two of them sit, covered in shit, on the bed of someone I just introduced them to, who's helped celebrate their first night in LA and who will probably be a little upset when he discovers the state of his silk covers and expensive carpet.

Jon has so far remained silent. Not a lot you can say, really. It's probably not the easiest situation to be in – waking up in a stranger's house the morning after the night he drove you round Hollywood in his expensive sports car, bought you dinner, shared his drugs and let you pass out in his spare room within hours of meeting you.

We stare at each other silently until I burst out laughing.

'For fuck's sake! Can't take you anywhere, you messy cunts. What happened, man?'

Jon starts to explain.

'It was the acid and the last gram of coke and the fact I've not slept for two days and I'm jet-lagged. I mean, it was an accident. I didn't think I was going to shit. I mean, I don't think I was awake at the time. The smell woke me up just now. What are we going to do? I mean, we've got to clear this mess up.'

Bless him, he's almost crying.

I stop laughing for long enough to take charge of the situation. It's not as if I'm too excited at the prospect of informing my American friend that – well, you know, what does one say in these situations?

'Awfully sorry, James old boy. The young fella seems to have lost control of his sphincter during the night. Shall we go out for breakfast?'

'Right then, let's strip the bed and, Jon, scrub that shit off the wall. Gav, you can do the carpet, it's not too bad. I'll locate the washing machine for the sheets and hopefully we'll get this cleaned up before our host regains consciousness. Oh, and for Christ's sake open the window. It fucking stinks in here.'

I go to find the washing machine while Jon and Gav get to work in the bedroom. Just as I'm discovering that James apparently doesn't have a washing machine, I hear movement from his bedroom. The turd twins obviously hear him too, because as I walk back into the bedroom Jon is throwing the sheets out of the window. Gav has apparently just got out of the shower to discover that Jon has the only available towel wrapped round his waist and is proceeding to try to remove it from Jon's torso as Jon slams the window closed. There's an ear-splitting bang as it comes off its hinges and hits him on the head, sending the two of them sprawling back onto the bed, naked and fighting over a shit-stained towel. The shit-covered sheets have got caught in the branches of a tree immediately outside the broken window and are fluttering gently in the breeze as I stand, still hallucinating mildly, tears streaming down my face as James comes strolling into the room.

'Hey, you guys want some breakfast? I'm just . . .'

Then there's silence – way beyond the embarrassing kind of silence.

'What the fuck? Jesus Christ! What the fuck . . .?'

I turn to face him.

'Sorry, mate, I can explain . . . jet lag.'

James actually finds the whole thing hysterical, as if Jon's little accident was some kind of ancient English ritual of appreciation, or maybe he's just mental and finds this kind of thing funny, like he finds wandering the hills of Hollywood with a crossbow on acid kind of funny . . .

Whatever, he takes us out to breakfast then drives us back to Venice Beach, where the boys' bags are waiting at Hotel Kevmate. I realise he'll be wondering whose luggage is sitting in the middle of the apartment.

'Let's do it again, crazy Limeys. Later, dudes . . .'

We stumble inside.

'Just as well we stayed at James's, eh, Jon? Wouldn't fancy your chances of staying with us if you'd shat all over Kevmate's bed to be honest. He likes his shit in the toilet!'

Kevmate gets home as we're smoking a bong and listening to *Live at Leeds*, possibly louder than it was when The Who actually recorded it.

I quickly load up another bong and drag him aside for a private chat to explain the situation.

'One week and that's fucking it. I swear to god, this is not a fuckin' hotel for freeloading Limey faggots from Weston-super-whatever-the-fuckin'-place-is-called. Jesus Christ, I must be insane. This is a one-bedroom apartment not the Four Seasons fuckin' hotel. Don't suppose you two have any more pot, do you? I'm so fuckin' stressed out I could shit!'

I glance at Jon and have to leave the room before I piss myself.

'Come on, Jonny boy. I'll show you where to buy weed in Venice Beach. You've got cash, I assume.'

'He fuckin' better had. I swear to god, the rent here's just gone up!'

I leave Gav and Kevmate to get acquainted and take Jon out to score some weed.

Predictably, the week's stay became somewhat longer, although, despite the overcrowding, all things considered we managed to co-exist quite nicely in a pot-saturated haze, barring the odd musical disagreement and squabble over whose turn it was to go out and score more weed.

Jon returned to England after a few months, Gav got a place with my mate Jaffa, and Kevin and I continued our residence in Venice Beach, interrupted only by the occasional girlfriend I managed to drag back to my lair, usually after a coke-and-alcohol-fuelled Sunday afternoon at The Mucky Duck British pub in Santa Monica.

Hey, Joe

You'd think that after the 'stupid fuck/puddle of piss' incident, for reasons of personal safety I would possibly have curtailed my late-night excursions on the streets of Venice Beach, maybe even learning to stock up on my basic night-time necessities in the same way normal people might stop off at a shop on the way home from work for whatever was required to assist their passage to bedtime.

Not a bit of it!

Clearly I was a slow learner and also a bit of a dimwit when it came to balancing the 'personal safety vs need to get right off my fucking tits' equation.

And so . . .

'Hey, Limey dude . . . you need some weed, bro?'

'Hey, Joe. Yeah, man. What you got?'

Yep, it's me and my latest best friend sourced from the never-ending supply of mental but welcoming drug addicts on the make I chose as company after Kevmate had passed out in a vodka/weed-induced state of release each night after putting in another 12-hour shift at work.

'So, listen, Limey dude, we gotta take a bit of a walk, bro. Old Jojo ain't got no bud on him right now but I got a brother a few blocks away holding some real kind heads at his crib.'

Which loosely translates as: '*Follow me into one of the scariest neighbourhoods in America so I can rip you off and score myself some crack.*'

But to my ears it sounded like a good idea and worth the risk because I needed to get stoned.

Off we jolly well go, then . . . dude.

Fifteen minutes of walking/trotting alongside my trusty companion later and I was waiting on the corner of Oakwood and California, which might sound pleasant/innocent enough but I can assure you unless your idea of 'pleasant' is standing in the middle of a gang-infested warzone, practically shitting yourself shortly after handing over $20 to someone like my friend Jojo and concluding that you have been at best ripped off or at worst are about to get stabbed/shot, it most certainly was not.

As my anxiety rose, I stumbled across the strange notion that I might well have been the first visitor from Weston-super-Mare to this particular corner of the American Dream at two o'clock on a Tuesday morning – a random and obviously completely inconsequential bit of mental avoidance of the exact nature of my current predicament. In layman's terms I was trying to make myself feel better – a process rudely interrupted by the sound of gunshots coming from the back of the building I was by now trembling outside of.

Fifteen minutes later and I was back chez Kevmate, scraping out the residue from the bong in an attempt to get a hit big enough to calm my nerves and hopefully put me asleep and out of harm's way for at least a few hours, when the door buzzer did its thing and buzzed.

Answering, I heard a voice say, 'Hey, Limey dude. It's Jojo. I got something for you.'

The same bit of my brain that had wanted me to stay waiting on that corner a few minutes ago immediately informed the rest of my brain that it was a stupid cunt for letting my feet carry me away from my best mate in the whole wide world who had now taken the time to come and deliver my bag of weed, and thus it would be bad manners in the extreme to not let him in to my apartment at 3 a.m. while Kevmate was passed out a few feet away.

Let's not be selfish then, eh?

'Come in, man. Did you get the weed?'

'Sort of, dude . . . sort of.'

'Sort of' was good enough for me. I pressed the buzzer to let him in.

For those of you who have no idea what a $20 bag of weed looks like, allow me to tell you what it doesn't look like. It doesn't look like an off-white pea-sized lump of crack, and that is what I was looking at seconds after allowing, in my opinion at least, my best mate in the whole wide world into the apartment.

'Jojo, that's not weed, mate.'

'Limey dude, listen. I can explain about the weed, bro. I'm still waiting for my man to hook me up with that but, dude, you fuckin' walked off and left me back there. I came looking for you but the cops were cruising about after some gangbangers got into it while I was waiting to get you your smoke.'

I was already feeling sorry for him.

'So what's gonna happen is we're gonna have a little smoke of this and I'll go back to see my man later. You cool with that, bro?'

Now at this point I'm assuming that most people would not have been exactly 'cool' with what was being proposed, maybe even making a straightforward request for their money back rather than accepting the offer to partake in a bit of casual Tuesday-morning crack smoking.

Wouldn't make for a very good book, though, would it?

'Yeah, OK, mate. You only live once an' all that, eh? You wanna go fir . . .'

Jojo already had his glass pipe in his mouth and was greedily sucking up half of 'our' crack deep into his lungs, holding a lighter over the top and slowly passing it over the rock, back and forth, back and forth, while gently sucking in the resulting smoke, first into the bowl of the pipe, then toking harder as the smoke disappeared in small swirling clouds into his expectant lungs. He held his breath for a few seconds before exhaling as his eyelids closed and his head tilted back, then . . . . . . silence . . . . . .

'Oh . . . Jesus H. fuckin' Christ . . . that's the good shit . . . the really good shit, dude.'

His eyes opened, straining in their sockets as he suddenly broke out into a sweat, his face turning a deep red as the blood vessels became engorged, before he jumped up out of his chair and hacked up a few mouthfuls of fluid from his battered lungs.

My turn.

'Suck it like a bitch's pussy, Limey dude. Shit's gonna take you higher than you ever gone before . . . Suck it like a fuckin' pussy. You are going to get so fuckin' high, bro.'

This last statement from Jojo was probably the only thing he'd said to me since meeting up earlier that was possibly true, not that I cared in the slightest as I finished my best pussy-sucking imitation, eyes closing as the drugs entered my bloodstream and I proceeded to have the best crack hit of my life.

I say that because it's true and if I was ever in the business of quitting while ahead, now would have been the best time to do so, but as Jojo was taking the pipe from my rapidly sweating palms and loading up what little remained of 'our' $20 worth of crack, all I could do was struggle to find words to describe the intense feelings of euphoria I had never come anywhere near to experiencing before.

Words failed me so I puked up in the sink instead.

Thirty minutes later we were back on the corner of Oakwood and California and I'd forgotten all about the $20 of weed Jojo owed me. I had far more important drugs to buy.

'The good shit.'

Six Months Later

'When am I coming down?' is the title of a track on The Godfathers album *Birth, School, Work, Death* and it was massaging my crack-obliterated brain as I sat on a bus that to me might as well have been going backwards for all the progress we seemed to be making in my attempt to get to the airport.

It's unlikely anyone has ever written a list of 'good' places to smoke crack cocaine but if they did I'm certain the back seat of a bus full of early-morning commuters in Los Angeles wouldn't grace the top ten.

The Godfathers didn't seem to care as I nodded my head from side to side, clutching the Walkman, packet of fags, passport and bag that constituted what remained of my 'life' in sunny southern California.

The headphones were held together by some sticky tape, as were the Walkman and sunglasses that currently made up my defence against the outside world – that and the last few rocks of crack I was in the process of demolishing while sitting, shaking and trying not to shit myself, on the back of that bus.

No one seemed to care, least of all me. I was way beyond caring by now. The City of Angels had now become the City of Chemically Induced Hell. Crack drills holes in the soul and buries you alive as you piss on your own grave.

The 'good shit' had fucked me up good and proper, reducing me to the pathetic, lying, thieving, psychotic mess who now sat twitching at the back of that bus, muttering to himself and cursing the lack of volume produced by the Walkman.

Not enough noise to drown out the noise.

The Godfathers asked when I was coming down.

'Who fucking cares any more?' replied the noise in my head.

Hotel Kevmate had been abandoned a few months previously as we had attempted to escape the by then daily ritual of both mine and Kevin's crack use. Yeah, that's right. I'd dragged him into my own private hell shortly after my excursion with Jojo. Within a matter of months he'd lost his job, had a nervous breakdown and sold his prized possession – an $8,000 motorcycle – for $1,000, which I'd managed to convince him would be enough to buy 'us' a decent amount of drugs that 'we' could sell on and possibly go into business with Jojo.

I don't feel I need to elaborate on how that plan turned out, do I?

To illustrate quite how fucking stupid crack addiction can make someone already as stupid as myself, I confess it was my idea to escape the 'confines' of Venice Beach and its attendant crack dealers by moving to another part of the city.

We moved a few miles closer to South Central Los Angeles, which to use an old English expression was a bit like shipping coals to Newcastle.

Within a few months of our move and after finding myself trying to break into Kevmate's room to get my hands on the stash of money/drugs I was convinced he was withholding from me, I sold my/his car and purchased a ticket back home. Which in my case meant heading back to a second-rate English seaside town in the middle of winter, the thought of which, regardless of everything else that was collapsing around me, would be enough to bring anybody down, wouldn't you say?

Can I recall saying goodbye to the man who had suffered my nonsense for nearly two years, put a roof over my head, bailed me out of jail, fed me, got me drunk/stoned and pretty much kept me alive as I tried to 'make it' in LA?

No, I can't, because I didn't bother to wake him up the morning I left. I had crack to smoke and wasn't about to share it with him or anybody else.

Crackhead cunt.

Me.

Peace Frog

I'm in the toilet at the rear of a London-bound 747, smoking a peanut-sized lump of crack, blowing the smoke into the bowl of the crapper in between chugging mouthfuls of bourbon. We're still on the runway and the stewardess is banging on the door, demanding I take my seat, ready for departure. My head is already at 35,000 feet.

'Are you OK in there, sir?'

'Just coming . . .'

I devoured my final pipe then staggered out of the toilet, staring her full in the face with a twisted smile before locating my seat and attacking the rapidly emptying bottle.

'We are now on our final approach. Please extinguish all smoking materials and fasten your seat belts, thank you.'

There was no need for me to fasten my seat belt, as it had been fastened for the entire duration of the flight, securing me in a comatose position. I'd drifted in and out of intermittent sleep before waking up and, not for the first or last time in my life, wishing I hadn't.

Tears full of whisky, crack, fear and self-pity ran down my face as I squinted out of the window, the faint early-morning English winter sunlight proving too much to cope with as I pulled my sunglasses down over my face and momentarily thought that one day, in another life, if I ended up in the same place, I would like to shake the hand of whoever was responsible for inventing them. Most probably some pisshead from the past who, one hungover morning, in a moment of booze-soaked inspiration, had given the world one of the most overlooked inventions of recent history. Forget the internal combustion engine, here's to Mr Ray-Ban or whoever the fuck it was.

Depositing my crack pipe in the vomit that a few hours earlier I'd deposited in the sick bag, I prepared for landing as best I could.

The man at passport control looked at my photograph again, then at the shivering wreck in front of him.

'Excuse me, sir, would you mind removing your sunglasses and turning your Walkman off, please.'

'What, mate?' I shouted.

'Walkman off.' He pointed to his eyes and ears.

'Oh, right, mate,' I shouted.

'So you are Mr Simon Mason, sir?'

'Yeah, that's me, mate. Why? Is there a problem?'

He looked at my photograph and then again at me.

'I don't know, sir, is there?'

'No, mate, no problem. Bit tired after the flight, you know.'

'Yes, sir. Welcome home.'

'Thank you, mate. Have a nice day.'

'You too, sir. You too.'

Shuffling away, I got about ten feet then puked all over the floor twice before making it into a toilet where I remained for nearly an hour, shaking, throwing up, shitting, crying and eventually realising I had no money to get back to Weston-super-Mare. So I cried some more as I found my way to the National Express coach stop, where

I scraped together the ticket money from a few concerned-looking passengers, promising I would repay them at some point back in Weston. Perhaps the sight of a frighteningly skinny, frightened young man, in T-shirt and shorts, freezing half to death in the December rain pulled on some heartstrings; either that or they just wanted me to leave them alone.

Eighteen hours after leaving LA I found myself standing outside my mum's house. The second she saw me she began to cry. We wept together for different reasons but in equal measure.

I was back home.

So You Wanna be a Rock 'n' Roll Star?

The next couple of weeks passed in an alcoholic blur as I retreated to the spare room at my mum's, withdrawing from the crack excesses of the previous months. Hash and whisky were my self-administered detox regime as I endured the horrific nightmares and mood swings that possibly scared my family and friends almost as much as they did me.

A copy of *Rock 'n' Roll Animal* rarely left the turntable of my stereo as I sat staring at the empty walls, bursting into tears seemingly at random, mouthing along to the words.

I'd told my mum and sister I'd been taking antidepressants while in the States, which, although plausible as an excuse for my current behaviour, still left them wondering what had been so bad as to necessitate their use in the first place.

Obviously I couldn't tell them the truth. To my mind that didn't seem to be an option, so I went to see the family doctor, who, after hearing my confession, looked at me over the rims of his glasses and told me to stop drinking so heavily, stop taking drugs, try going to a local Narcotics Anonymous meeting and perhaps get a job.

Sterling advice, no doubt, but not what I wanted to hear. I left the surgery and went to the Back-Bar pub to get paralytic.

A couple of hours later I was in full Jim Morrison mode, scribbling down my chaotic thoughts on a beer mat, feeling equally sick and sorry for myself.

Sweat pours from my face,
need to find a cooler place,
There's painful music, in my brain
sounds so familiar
yet seems so strange.

'Hey, it's Mr Hollywood film star himself. Mr Mason, long time no see. When did you get back?'

I looked up to see my mate Mike 'the Judge' coming towards me. I think I managed my first smile in weeks.

'All right, Mike? Want a drink?'

'Lovely! Pint of cider, please. So, come on, tell me all about it, superstar. You look bloody awful by the way.'

'Two pints of cider, two large Jack 'n' Cokes, please.'

'Bit early for that, isn't it, mate?' said Mike, nodding at the large Jack Daniel's already on the bar in front of me.

'It's a bit early for stupid fucking questions like that, mate. You wanna drink or not?'

'Just the cider. I've got college later, thanks. So, come on, what's been happening?'

So I told him everything and began crying again.

'I don't know what to fucking do with myself, man. I can't believe I'm sitting here in the Back-Bar, bloody fucking Christmas time, living at home. Mum thinks I'm mad, stepdad won't even talk to me, my sister's actually "grown up" and become a bloody copper, fucking doctor tells me to get a fucking job. What the fuck is happening, mate? Jesus Christ, another Jack 'n' Coke, please.'

There wasn't much he could really say to that, so he said nothing, until, looking down at the table, he saw the beer mat.

'What's that all about?'

'Nothing, just words, you know. Started writing stuff when I was in . . .'

My voice trailed away as I choked back another wave of tears.

I don't know why he said what he then said but he did and suddenly there was a glimmer of hope.

'My brother's looking for a singer for his new band. Can you sing?'

'Dunno.'

In all the years of mouthing along to The Jam and The Smiths, etc., I'd never actually listened to my own voice. Could I sing? Fuck knows. Jumping around, shouting to myself in my bedroom while 'playing' an old tennis racquet had always worked for me. Besides, not being able to act hadn't stopped me going to America to 'make it' as an actor in Hollywood, had it? And surely becoming a singer in a band couldn't turn out any worse than that had?

'He's rehearsing at Baz's this afternoon. I reckon he'd like these lyrics. He's mental as well.'

'Thanks. I'm not mental, I'm . . .'

'C'mon, let's go. We can get stoned with him if nothing else.'

What was it my doctor had said?

'Stop taking drugs, drink less and get a job.'

One out of three isn't bad going, I thought to myself as I suddenly decided I now had a job, one that potentially required lots of drinking and drug taking, if you were to do it properly anyway.

As for going to a local N.A. meeting?

Fuck that! I didn't want to stop taking drugs; I wanted to take more and figured that as long as I stayed away from the crack I'd be fine. Anyway, who wants to hang out with a bunch of washed-up junkies drinking coffee and talking about their sorry lives all the fucking time?

I vaguely knew the Judge's brother, Nick, having seen him play in a band in Weston a few years previously. He'd never given me more than a cursory nod whenever I'd passed him in the street and he never spent any time out drinking in town, so I didn't really know if I liked him or not – not that it mattered of course. Mike put me in the picture as we drove over to the 'rehearsal studio'. As he explained it, his brother Nick was currently happy practising his bass and getting stoned at his mate Baz's house, which was about as far as he would ever get in his opinion, mainly because he was a cantankerous bastard who, although he spent all of his time playing music, never actually listened to any. He didn't lack ambition or talent, which sort of put us on the same hymn sheet if you forget the talent bit. He just didn't seem interested in playing many gigs, having amassed a total of two in the past three years.

'I don't know, maybe you could give him a kick up the ass seeing as your own plans for world domination have been derailed recently? I should warn you about Baz, though. He's lovely but a bit strange. He has a habit of getting his cock out and demonstrating how far he can stretch his foreskin whenever he meets new people. Whatever you do, don't say yes when he asks you if you want to see his impression of a shower cap.'

As we drove, the part of my brain that was in charge of producing fantasy and/or bullshit flickered back to life, suddenly back in business after getting a thorough kicking in LA, and rapidly convinced me that I was now about to take my first tentative steps towards rock 'n' roll superstardom.

Baz with the magic foreskin answered the door after we'd been outside knocking for about 20 minutes. The sounds coming from inside had sounded like a lot of noise to be honest, but what did I know about writing songs? Maybe 'Jumping Jack Flash' also sounded like two blokes banging dustbin lids together at one point?

'Hello, Judge, come in, come in, and who might you be?' he said, nodding in my direction.

'Baz, this is Simon Mason. He's just flown in from the States and I think you and my brother should audition him.'

'He doesn't look very well, does he? What do you do, Simon Mason from the States? Take drugs for a living?'

'I, er . . .'

'He writes lyrics and sings a bit, Baz.'

'Right you are, well, come in. Let's go upstairs to the bedroom.'

I glanced nervously at Mike . . . bedroom?

'It's where they rehearse.'

'Oh, right, of course.'

The spare box-bedroom contained one drum kit, one prehistoric bass amp and one stoned-looking older brother who gave me his usual nod then proceeded to ignore me, turning to Baz, now seated behind his kit.

'Jazz, Baz, jazz . . .'

And they continued with the dustbin-lid song.

After about 20 minutes or so they stopped and Nick began to skin up while Baz went to make tea.

'So, Mr Mason, back from California then, where's the suntan?'

'I didn't get out much, Nick. I really like that song. What's it called?'

'Jazzbazjazz.'

'Oh, right, of course, yeah. Cool.'

'Simon wants to audition for the band, Nick. He writes lyrics and sings a bit.'

'Oh, didn't know you could sing. Got any lyrics with you, then?'

'Er, yeah.'

I offered the beer-mat 'song'. He glanced at the words, passed me the joint and began to play a heavy four-note descending bass line, which had the immediate effect of making Nick shake his head vigorously from side to side and shout, 'Genius . . .'

He obviously wasn't referring to my hastily scribbled lyrics, now discarded on the floor, so I guess he was referring to himself.

Baz came back in, rubbed his bollocks vigorously, then sat behind his kit. They both looked at me.

'You're supposed to start singing, Si,' said Mike.

'Oh, right.'

I closed my eyes, opened my mouth and shouted, trying to hear myself over the noise.

'Sweat pours from my face . . .

'Need to find a cooler place . . .'

And so it went for ten minutes or so – all of us doing our 'thing' over and over again. With my eyes closed, I could have been anywhere as I tried to create some kind of melody, which I clearly couldn't. It mattered not, because suddenly I was not a confused miserable (ex) crack addict; for those ten minutes I just forgot about the rest of the world and wailed.

There's painful music in my brain,

Sounds so familiar,
Sounds so strange.
The music in my head is playing loud, contorted and
twisted, burning sound . . .

'Sounds painful to me.'

The Judge obviously couldn't appreciate what was occurring and left the room. Nick and Baz looked at each other. Baz rubbed his bollocks again and nodded; Nick shrugged his shoulders.

'What are you doing tomorrow afternoon?'

I was half-pissed, very stoned and apparently now had a job, of sorts. Bollocks to the doctor. I felt better!

After a few more sessions at Baz's I thought it best to inform my mum of developments. As I was living upstairs in the spare room, it seemed right to keep her in the picture about my latest career change.

'Mum, I've joined a band.'

'Oh, right, as long as you get a proper job as well. Remember what the doctor said?'

'No, Mum, that is going to be my job. Nick reckons we'll be ready to gig in a few weeks. We're going to play at Piranhas nightclub in town. Everybody will be there; it's going to be great. We've already got our own vibe. Nick reckons we don't sound like anybody else.'

'Is that going to help?'

I said nothing; as far as I was concerned, imminent fame was just round the corner.

'Just as long as you get a proper job as well, Simon. You need a career and a pension for when you get older.'

You can safely assume my mum had never heard 'My Generation' by The Who. Music, or at least the kind of music I adored, was not her thing; she much preferred watching older people singing on *Songs of Praise* than the sound of angry young men proclaiming that they hoped to die before they got old.

My mum had plenty to feel aggrieved about. As a child she'd been evacuated from her Coventry home during the war, had to leave school at 14 to work in a factory screwing on toothpaste tops on an assembly line, been divorced and widowed by her mid 40s and was currently suffering from the early stages of multiple sclerosis. The reality of her life was that it had been hard but I never heard her complain. Her generation just 'got on with it'. Now it must have appeared to her she had a son clearly incapable of grasping reality of any kind, who was behaving like a lunatic and suddenly proclaiming he was Weston's answer to Mick Jagger.

I was about to respond further when the phone rang. It was Nick calling to inform me we had found a guitarist – something we'd overlooked up till now, not really having space in the spare room to accommodate one anyway.

'He's called Nigel and he wants us to go round his house and get stoned.'

Off out I skipped to meet the missing piece to our plans for imminent world domination – the fact he was called Nigel didn't seem to matter too much.

Nigel passed the audition, which as I recall involved the four of us sitting in his bedroom, taking turns on his bucket bong while listening to The Sisters of Mercy groaning away on the stereo for what seemed like days. It might well have been – it was hard to tell after the bucket did its thing.

At some point we made it back to the 'studio' and even though the bedroom was now completely full, we managed as best we could. We were now a 'complete' band, which was just as well, as we had a gig booked in a few weeks' time.

The Judge, our new 'tour manager', would come round and offer encouragement of a kind.

'Er, yeah, great stuff. Sounds a bit like The Velvet Underground,' being the most common remark – as generous as it was untrue.

'No, it fucking doesn't,' his brother would reply, which was true. 'Nobody else sounds like us.'

True again, though the fact that nobody hoping to 'make it' would want to sound like us at that point escaped us all. Besides, I had no idea what we sounded like, as I couldn't hear a thing.

Nick refused point-blank when I suggested putting a couple of covers in the set to fill it up a bit, stating, 'Nobody writes songs as good as mine, so what's the point? It would lower the tone.'

You can't argue with that kind of thinking, really.

We eventually had a set, of sorts, together:

1. Jazzbazjazz
2. Bitch City
3. Betty Blue Sky
4. Life like a Child
5. My Favourite Place
Encore.
6. The Music in my Head (beer-mat song)

We also had a name, purloined from a piece of graffiti I'd seen sprayed on a wall near the flat in LA. I had no idea what it meant but seeing as I wrote the words in the band, I insisted it was my duty to provide the name as well.

And so it was that as the gig approached we were as convinced as possible that everything was going to plan. My new best mates, Matt-lad, Luke and I went out fly-posting the town centre, snorting loads of speed and getting pissed while mixing up the wallpaper paste, as you do.

I coined the slogan that headed the posters:

End of a decade, Start of an era.
The best band you'll ever see in your life
LIVE AT PIRANHAS
£1.50

At that age, if you're about to front a band for the first time you have to believe in what you're doing or at the very least arrogantly try to convince anyone who'll listen that you do. Failing that, get utterly obliterated on booze and drugs prior to going onstage for the first time and just see what happens.

In order to do our 'unique' sound justice it had been decided that we had to hire the biggest and loudest PA system we could afford. During the soundcheck I gave the engineer an extra £5, telling him to 'make us sound like The Who, mate, all right?'

To which he responded, 'I'm a sound engineer, not a fucking magician, mate.'

It was then time for a quick trip to the off-licence with the Judge, my tour manager, to purchase a bottle of Jack Daniel's.

We sat in the dressing-room smoking bong after bong, a few well-wishers being granted entry as the Jack Daniel's was poured into my onstage pint glass, and then it was time to rock, or something like that.

The Judge, like all good roadies, had a torch and he lit our way from the dressing-room to the stage – all ten feet of it. Never mind, you have to do these things correctly.

About 150 people had actually turned up, most likely to enjoy the support band that night, a competent Blues Brothers tribute act who'd been gigging for years already.

Now they were 'my' audience and I was going to give them something to remember.

'All right, Weston? This is going to change your lives. One, two, three . . .'

Screech . . . thud, thud. Baz dropped his sticks as he also tried to count us in. I was suddenly feeling a bit light-headed.

The first 'song', I remember. When it finished, people were already backing away towards the rear of the club. By the middle of the third, people were leaving – a fact that I found totally perplexing. The start of the fourth song saw me clinging on to the mike-stand for dear life, my legs buckling, my head swimming in bourbon, enraged that anybody could walk out on the greatest rock 'n' roll band in the world.

I decided to 'speak' to my people.

'Yeah, fuck off then, you sad bastards. You don't know what you're missing. This is fucking rock 'n' roll. Go on, fuck off if you want. Hey, soundman, turn it up . . . Yeah, go on, leave, then. I don't give a fuck. I've got your money anyway,' I ranted, waving the wad of cash that constituted the door money in front of the rapidly thinning crowd. 'You don't know what real music is anyway.'

Clearly Bob Marley had not heard me singing when he famously said, 'One good thing about music – when it hits you, you feel no pain.'

Apparently, there were ten people left at the end: the four members of the greatest rock 'n' roll band in the world, my mates Luke and Matt-lad, the soundman, the bar staff and our tour manager.

I say apparently because by the time we'd reached 'The Music in my Head', our 'big-finish' song, the smoke machine had gone into overdrive, making it impossible to see anything. I fell off the stage before staggering away, paralytic, towards the toilets.

It's pitch black and I haven't got a clue where I am. I try to stand up but my trousers are round my ankles and I'm covered in puke and piss. As I fall forward, my head smashes against the cubicle door. I have a thought: I need to get out of wherever it is I am. Crashing around in the dark I miraculously find the door that is at the top of a flight of stairs, which I then proceed to fall down, stopping only when I reach the entrance to the club before somehow managing to unbolt the door as the alarm starts going off. Then I'm out into the deserted streets of Weston. I find the wad of door money in my pocket, smile to myself and stagger into a minicab office, where I demand to be driven home before throwing up everywhere again and being told, 'You must be fucking joking, mate! Not in that state. You can fucking walk. It'll do you good, son.'

'But I'm the lead singer in the best band in the world, man . . . You have to order me a cab!'

'I don't give a fuck if you're the singer in the fucking Rolling Stones, mate. You're not getting in one of our cabs in that state, now fuck off.'

'You'll regret this one day, you ignorant twat . . .'

I threw up again before staggering out into the rain and stumbling home, singing the beer-mat song at the top of my voice.

Club Tropicana

Strange as it may seem to those of you still following this tale of woe, I'd actually managed to become employed during the summer of that particular year.

If you think that seems nuts and somewhat incongruent with this story so far, how does being made head lifeguard at the local outdoor swimming pool sound? My appointment was possibly one of the most badly mismatched career/individual juxtapositions ever but it was one to which I brought all my 'life skills'.

So, lots of drug taking while thinking about myself and not much else, then!

Perhaps having heard that I'd just spent a while living in sunny California had persuaded the soon-to-be outgoing head of recruitment that I would possibly be a good candidate for the role? On reflection, I think the fact that the guy who interviewed me was a mate had swung it, that and I believe he wanted to shag my older sister and thought awarding me the job might further his cause somewhat.

Anyway, within days I'd donned the red vest and climbed onto my stool at the side of the pool. I don't think he ever managed to climb on top of my sister, not that I ever decided to ask, though. It's not like I'm a weirdo, eh?

Regardless, the job was mine, which pleased my mum, as she considered it a far more sensible occupation than my fledgling stabs at musical superstardom given that I was now officially employed by the council.

Yeah, I could swim but much preferred drowning in booze and drugs by this point in proceedings and it's a fucking miracle no one died while I sat, stoned out of my tiny mind, poolside that summer. Mind you, if you're going to recruit directly from the dole-office attendees in Weston-super-Mare, you've only got yourself to blame, eh?

The closest anyone actually came to drowning was my mate and fellow lifesaver/drug addict Jack who, after buying a few too many Valium from me prior to crawling up onto his stool at the side of the pool, had also decided to join me in a few blasts from the canister of Entonox gas we kept in the medical room.

Said gas is often administered to women during childbirth, so you can imagine its potency and perhaps our delight when, along with my new position of responsibility, I was given the keys to the meds room and that summer's supply of gaseous pain relief. Another mate was also keeping us supplied with a steady stream of Valium and a few other bits and bobs purloined from his ageing mother, who was currently dribbling into her lap in a nearby retirement home.

Jack and I were hurriedly deciding quite how much dribbling we were up for ourselves on that particular shift, concluding that two blue Valium and a few long blasts on the gas should be enough to keep us happy until lunchtime, before he shuffled off to keep a watchful eye on the few tourists who were already splashing about in the pool.

I headed down to the plant room to try to make a decision about quite how much chlorine I was going to pump into the pool that morning. This should have been a carefully considered ratio that no doubt had been previously explained to me at some point but it was a decision I often made based on other more self-interested motives.

My thinking was that the more of the eye-stinging stuff I pumped into the water, the fewer people there would be actually able to spend any time fucking about in it, thus reducing the chance of any fatalities while I sat catatonically overseeing events.

As the gas I'd just inhaled inflated my brain cells, it became obvious to me I was not really going to be fit for purpose for a few hours yet and I therefore pumped about three days' worth of chlorine into the system before stumbling back up to my perch.

An hour later the pool was more or less deserted aside from a few obviously sado-masochistic loons who sounded Welsh to me and were clearly happy to have their retinas burnt out as they cavorted in the crystalline water.

My attention was focused on a young 'friend' of mine called Becky, who had skipped college that day and decided to wear a typewriter ribbon instead of a swimming costume as she sunned herself a few feet away from me. Cheap sunglasses were just about preventing my eyeballs from sliding out of their sockets as the Valium/gas/eye-candy combination, along with the effect of some rarely seen sunshine, kept me rooted to my stool and I contemplated whether getting my head kicked in by my young friend's dad would be a price worth paying for further investigation of what was not actually being hidden beneath her pink bikini. Shortly after she rolled over onto her back to continue topping up her tan I had decided that yes indeed, it most certainly would and I was about to take her up on her request to walk her to the bus stop later when I heard the sound of someone's body connecting with the paving slabs that surrounded the edge of the pool, shortly followed by a splash as they then disappeared into the water.

Pete, another of my recently recruited best friends in the whole wide world, was at his post on the lifeguard's island at the centre of the pool. He had also recently paid a visit to the meds room but skipped the Valium and therefore seemed better able to respond to this sudden incident, as he leapt over the wall surrounding the lifeguards' post and began swimming towards the body that was about to resurface a few feet from where Jack should have been stationed.

All this occurred in just a few seconds, which is the same amount of time my befuddled brain took to figure out that the 'man overboard' was actually Jack and not one of the red-eyed, probably blind by now, Welsh tourists.

Jack resurfaced, giggling to himself, clearly not the worse for wear after apparently nodding out prior to his unintentional dip in the pool.

'Oh fuck, my head hurts, boss. I think I need to go to the meds room to have it checked out, mate.'

Taking the matter in hand, I sprang into full-on David Hasselhoff mode and escorted my still-giggling chum towards the privacy of the medical room, where I shortly concluded he was in shock and therefore in need of something to calm him down.

Pete joined us, as he was also clearly traumatised by this 'near-death' experience, and so I gave him a few hits of the gas before asking him to go and find some more Valium, as our stash was in Jack's soaking wet pocket and had thus probably been ruined by all the chlorine I'd earlier pumped in the pool we'd just fished him out of.

That'll teach me, eh?

A few weeks later we had finished the entire canister of Entonox and my stint saving lives and infuriating the parents of local college girls came to an abrupt end when a member of the public caught me smoking a joint on the sun terrace while conducting that morning's 'team meeting'. For some bizarre reason he felt it his duty to inform the operations manager, who fired me on the spot.

Still, no one had died, eh? Besides, now I could focus on my musical endeavours rather than young ladies in bikinis, of which there would obviously be plenty more when I became a famous superstar and had my own fucking swimming pool to play in, pumped full of cocaine rather than chlorine!

I Wanna be Adored

As far as I was concerned, my arrogant nonsense was as essential to the 'make-up' of all good rock 'n' roll stars as the songs they sang or wrote. The problem, not that I could see or hear it, was that I could not really sing or play a note. Yeah, I could possibly sling together a few words/lyrics that some people – mainly myself – thought were of real quality, but essentially I was a talentless idiot whose own perception of the sex, drugs and rock 'n' roll manifesto focused almost entirely on the drugs bit, with some sex thrown in if I could find anyone impressionable enough to listen to me banging on about myself and my plans for imminent superstardom during a post-coital joint – actually, if I'm being honest, probably during the sex bit as well.

Convincing myself that rock 'n' roll superstardom was surely my ultimate destination and anyone who couldn't see that was clearly mental became a full-time occupation. Perhaps if I'd spent anywhere near as long attempting to learn to sing or play an instrument I'd have collected a few more devotees for the ride. As it was, I continued my ascent to glory more or less alone, which actually suited me in some respects because I could now add 'outsider' and 'misunderstood' to the internal autobiography I was already compiling.

A night at the Bristol Bierkeller to witness a gig by The Stone Roses touring their soon-to-be-released debut LP confirmed a few things to me. The fact that I'd been unable to convince anyone else, either friends or bandmates, to come along with me only furthered my deluded notion that nobody else in Weston had their finger on the cultural and musical pulse I was so desperate to feed off. I also realised, perhaps most importantly, you didn't need to be able to produce a polished vocal performance, or in fact anything even remotely like one, to be the front man in the greatest band in the world.

Standing consumed with equal measures of awe, amphetamines, jealousy and Newcastle Brown Ale, then dancing, or at least trying to, as they reached the climax of their set with 'I am the Resurrection', I witnessed The Roses beautifully ascending towards exactly where I believed I not only deserved to be but also needed to be.

The next 18 months were nothing short of a drug-fuelled, delusional, 'style-over-content' campaign by yours truly, serving only to further convince myself that I had outgrown the confines of my seaside town and almost everybody I knew who lived there. Pretty much everybody who lived there and knew me simultaneously became convinced I was an arrogant, clueless cunt, not least the various poor unfortunates who had to share a rehearsal space with me and listen to me bellowing into a microphone demanding to be 'understood'.

When you consider the fact that almost everybody I'm talking about was regularly 'loved up' and off their fucking tits on Ecstasy, acid and dope, that's no mean feat on my behalf. I changed bands, but my delusion remained unaltered.

As the '80s became the '90s and the 'kids' grooved to a new sound, the loudest noise I could hear was the sound of my own voice informing everyone they'd got it all wrong as I trumpeted my disdain for acid-house music to anyone who would listen.

If The Stone Roses and The Happy Mondays, who I was by now becoming totally obsessed with, couldn't convince me I'd got it all wrong, then what would?

Oh, look! It's Glastonbury time again.

Everything Starts with an E

I started walking from Weston with my thumb out, soon hitching a ride right onto the site in a truck driven by a hippy collective going by the name of Green Deserts. Their mission, it soon transpired, was simply to put up a huge yellow marquee, smoke loads of dope, take acid, get pissed and eat veggie curry for breakfast, lunch and dinner. Perhaps they did have a more involved purpose but I didn't stick around long enough to find out. Within a short while of being dropped off and then asked to help out, I fucked off to sort myself out. I managed to 'borrow' a large plastic blue tarpaulin exchanged for five hits of Purple Penguin acid from my festival survival kit before locating a suitably picturesque spot by the side of the old railway track. I began to construct a temporary home using some freshly hacked saplings, which I bent, twisted and tied together in a oval shape before slinging the tarp over the top and nicking an old bit of carpet from the Green Curry Desert collective, or whatever the fuck they were called, to lay out on the inside. The finishing touch was a wood burner, 'loaned' in return for some more acid. Voila! I had built my first 'bender'.

Just as I was standing back, skinning up and admiring my newly completed abode, a television producer turned up and transformed my Glastonbury experience – like Keith Moon joining The Who, Bill Shankly arriving at Liverpool, or D.S. Burnside joining the cast of *The Bill*.

Yeah, that much!

'Oh, sorry, mate. You can't put that there. This area's for broadcasters, I'm afraid. You'll have to take it down and go somewhere else, I think. Over there somewhere.'

The hippy in me surfaced.

'You have got to be fucking joking, mate. Do you know how long this has taken me to get together?'

The main reason it had taken me so long was that I'd had no idea what I was doing, but I'd spotted some similar constructions being built on my way onto the site and had kept going back to look at the progress being made a couple of fields away, taking mental notes and walking back to my own construction. I possibly could have asked the hippy who was beavering away for advice but he was chanting to himself in German as he toiled away, was naked and looked a bit on the smelly side, so I kept my distance and observed.

The TV guy was talking to me.

'Well, who are you and what do you do here anyway?'

'I, er, I'm with Green Deserts, man. You know, we make veggie curry an' that . . . er, fancy a spliff, man?'

'Well, I have got a lot of work to do but I don't think a little smoke will do any harm. Actually, I think there's a lot of people here who are stoned, you know.'

'Oh, really? I hadn't noticed. Here, skin up, Mr TV.'

Dan, as I found out he was called, did indeed fancy a spliff, several in fact, and a couple of the cans of the Special Brew I'd brought with me and a line of speed. And over more spliffs and more Special Brew and speed we 'bonded'.

He then offered me a job! My kind of job! Working for him building similar constructions to the one I had just finished, because I was 'obviously an expert'. He promised to pay me out of the budget he'd been given to build a campsite for an outside broadcast crew who were due soon.

A few days later, he handed me a laminated pass that said:

ACCESS ALL AREAS.
DON'T EVEN TRY TO
STOP ME FROM GOING
ON THIS STAGE
OR WHEREVER ELSE
I FEEL LIKE GOING,
YOU DICKHEAD.

It didn't actually say that but it had that effect because nobody ever did.

I wore it proudly round my neck as I stumbled round the site going about my business wearing a ridiculous over-sized floppy hat that I thought made me look cool. My 'boss' apparently agreed.

'Yeah . . . Simon . . . the Cat in the Hat, you're going to be very useful, I'm sure.'

He was right.

Dan had a budget of £1,000 with which he had to construct his camp. I went to speak to my new mates in the travellers' field with a budget of £500. They in turn went to see their mates, who delivered all our requirements on a budget of £250.

The campsite was constructed ahead of schedule and my 'boss' Dan was cool.

But not as cool as the Cat in the Hat thought he was when some people from Weston saw me pilled out of my skull, riding a motorbike with Bez from The Happy Mondays sitting on the back, gurning away, en route to the travellers' field to do some 'business'.

The reason Bez was on the back of 'my' motorbike was the narcotic preferences of some members of his band. Certain drugs were needed that were not freely available to most people there, either backstage or out in the lunacy of the main festival site.

My 'fuck off, you prick, access all areas' pass had led me to the backstage area pretty much as soon as it had opened and it was here that I'd bumped into the 'percussionist' for The Happy Mondays as he mooched about doing whatever it is you do in those situations.

I guess that if you're a one man drug-dustbin, albeit in a band comprised of fellow narcotic black holes, currently enjoying mass adulation and the money that it brings, you're probably of the opinion that spending a few hours with some dickhead apparently on first-name terms with the drug dealers up in the travellers' field who always have the best drugs at the best prices could be interesting.

'Have they got any opium up there, lad?'

'Yeah, Bez. They've got everything up there. I've got a motorbike if you fancy a lift?'

And so it came to pass that in exchange for me escorting Bez up to meet the travellers and 'do some business', there was a large Happy Mondays 'approved' pill entering my bloodstream as I navigated the bike through the crowds, saluting the Weston contingent as we passed them.

By the time we returned to the backstage enclave Bez was my latest new best mate in the whole world and I had found a way to get hold of as many pills as I could shift, which, when you have a 'Hey, man, I love you, access all areas' pass hanging round your neck and you've been on the festival site getting to know certain people for over two weeks, is an awful lot of fucking pills.

An awful lot of some of the best pills to have ever been sold at Glastonbury – certainly that year and most likely ever since as well.

And so I entered the world of tour-bus wheeling and dealing, hopping in and out of what was left of The Mondays' mobile drug emporium after they'd been traversing the country in it for weeks as I went about my business. The upper front windows had a massive hole in them, the toilets looked like they'd been napalmed and there were empty baggies containing the remnants of more chemicals than the sewer system of an ICI factory strewn everywhere. A laminating machine that had been brought along to produce fake backstage passes was now in bits on the floor, alongside various expensively dressed but morally dubious northern narco-tourists, currently reduced to a state of MDMA-induced slush as they kept me supplied with the disco biscuits of the gods. Hallelujah, indeed.

By the time the festival ended I'd earned a nice chunk of cash, ingratiated myself with several 'important' music-biz people and befriended a member of the TV crew who had a room to rent in his London flat. We left the site on Tuesday and I moved back up to London.

Drug dealer to the 'stars'?

Only for as long as it was going to take for me to become one, of course. How hard could it be?

I also now thought acid-house music was actually not too bad at all providing you were whacked out of your mind on decent Ecstasy, which in London in 1990 was not exactly a difficult state to get into. In fact, as far as I and countless others were concerned it was harder to stay straight than not to.

Grateful When You're Dead

Twelve months later and imminent rock 'n' roll superstardom was remaining somewhat elusive for numerous reasons, which, if you have been paying attention so far, don't really need detailing again. Suffice to say my responses to the various 'Lead singer wanted, influences, blah blah blah' adverts and the auditions I attended after perusing the back pages of the *Melody Maker* every week had led to nothing.

I continually disparaged the rest of the world for being so out of step with whatever the fuck it was I thought I had to offer but maybe I should have read the adverts more closely. 'Lead singer wanted,' was what they said, not 'drug-addled, egotistical, deluded, tone-deaf annoying twat'.

Still, I had managed to live rent-free for over a year in London, which on some level a part of me considered a success as I chomped my way through countless pill-fuelled days and nights, extolling the virtues of my 'virtual' band to any poor bastard I cornered at any of the various raves I somehow managed to not get thrown out of. If you ever attended such parties back then, I was the long-haired scruffy idiot in the corner, dribbling into a can of Special Brew and trying to ponce a fag or a bit of hash from you, should you get within shouting distance.

Yeah, that was me. Sorry.

Speaking of being out of step with the rest of the world . . . Halloween 1990, Luke calls me to tell me we're going to see The Grateful Dead at Wembley Arena, that he's going to be up in London later and did I know anybody who might want to buy a few thousand magic mushrooms?

Buy mushrooms?

I'd never thought of that. We'd always picked our own.

Luke and I were sitting trying to 'organise' ourselves, mid pick, one year up on Nine Barrows Hill in Priddy, Somerset, when he pointed to the massive communications mast towering above us, maybe three hundred feet tall, as it stood making a strange humming sound between us and the slate-grey horizon beyond.

'Do you know what that is, man?'

'Yeah, man, it's a humming mast, electricity, super-spy snooper thingy . . .'

'Wrong, man.'

'What is it then, man?'

'Look at it again, see how it goes up into the sky against the clouds?'

'Yeah?'

'Well, it's actually a giant zipper and if you unzip it all the space will come in . . .'

I wet myself laughing. Maybe you had to be there, though.

I digress. Back to The Grateful Dead and what or who was or wasn't out of step with the prevailing cultural climate.

'I think we should put a couple of hundred in the pot. It's going to be a long night, man. Brew them up now and by the time we get to Wembley we should be fit for purpose.'

'OK, man, put the kettle on.'

The Judge, Julian and Jon were also along for the ride, an excursion that shortly found us all sitting on the Tube, laughing uncontrollably at nothing in particular. I was beginning to think we might have overdone it on the mushroom-tea front. We'd not even left central London and the orange, green and yellow colour scheme of the Jubilee line train carriage, which is pretty lurid to the straightest of minds at the best of times, never mind one with 300 fucking magic mushrooms swimming about inside it, was starting to really do my head in.

Luke was just about hanging in there, too.

'Luke mate, have some self-respect, man. Get a fucking grip, buddy. We have to change trains at the next station.'

'Why, man?'

'Because the elastic band that this train is attached to has now stretched as far as it can go and it is about to send the train and us shooting back into the tunnel the other way.'

The thought of which sent me to my knees as I collapsed onto the floor of the train.

'Really? Why?'

'Ha, ha, ha. Oh, I don't know why. Where the fuck are we, anyway? And why is everybody staring at us?'

'Simon mate, chill out, man. Hold it down, man,' said the Judge, trying his best to remain in some sort of control. Jon had not said a word for over an hour; he was just grinning and rolling his eyes around the underground universe.

Someone interrupted our little moment.

'You guys going to the show?'

An American hippy type came over. We stared at him, eyes on stalks.

'Might be.'

'Got anything to smoke?'

Luke and I stared at each other and then again at him before we both slid back onto the carriage floor, laughing hysterically, eventually deciding that, 'Yeah, we are. Yes, we have. Do you want some magic mushrooms?'

'Hell, yeah! How many you got, dude?'

'Millions and millions, mate. Millions and millions of the little fuckers.'

Our new friend Bruce from Atlanta happily joined us for the rest of the evening and, true to form, just like the old American hippy adage says: 'How do you know if a Deadhead's been staying at your home? He's still there!' he also moved into 'my' place for a while afterwards too.

As for being out of step and all that, if you can say that a few thousand people off their tits on drugs, dancing like lunatics for hours, was out of step in 1990, then maybe you weren't getting out enough. Different music, same agenda.

Who cares? The Grateful Dead were mind blowing, not that mine needed much encouragement by that point.

Caught by the Fuzz

My grateful American friend stayed at the flat for nearly a month before heading home, prior to which he contributed 200 hits of San Francisco's finest acid, handed over out of the blue as backdated 'rent' as he left for the airport.

Sean, my landlord/flatmate/provider of food/drugs/money, etc. came home from work shortly after Bruce's departure to find me lying in front of the gas fire, dribbling and mumbling contentedly to myself while playing a The Beloved album to the world, windows open, stereo on as loud as it could go.

He turned the music down.

'Simon, listen. I think it's about time you tried to earn some money, mate. You know I believe in you and that it's only a matter of time before you find the right band but, really, I can't see that it would do you any harm to actually have some cash in your pocket from time to time.'

Stunned into some sort of lysergic response, I endeavoured to deliver an appropriate reply.

'I know, you're right, Sean. Do you want some acid for your dinner?'

'No, thanks, I'm all right for acid at the moment. Did you hear what I said?'

'Loud and clear. I'll get some work tomorrow. I have a feeling that I can earn a few quid over the next couple of weeks. It's all about supply and demand, Sean. Now chill out, my man. I'm going to sort things out.'

'Where's your American friend, anyway?'

'Gone, Sean. He said to tell you thanks for letting him stay.'

'Bloody freeloading hippy bastard. Didn't he offer anything in the way of rent?'

'He gave me some acid.'

'How much?'

'Not much, er, a few. They're really good. Sure you don't want some?'

'No!'

'Yeah, man, hippies; you just can't trust 'em, can you? Turn the sounds up, please, mate.'

I take a train to Weston, 195 hits of acid in my bag. Matty is waiting at the station to pick me up and we go and earn some money by delivering my little pieces of Californian sunshine to the good folk of my hometown. I stay the night before heading up to Bristol to meet Luke, who also has some people for me to meet, and by the time he drops me at the bus station I've got a few quid in my pocket.

'Here you are, mate. Have a few on me. See you soon.'

I tear off a couple of strips and pass them to my pal.

It seems like a good time to take one for the road, seeing as I've finished 'work', so a tiny white blotter dissolves on my tongue as the coach pulls out of the station and heads towards the motorway.

If there is anybody else on the coach, I don't acknowledge them as I start to float around the back seat with an elastic smile stretching all over my face, thinking (sort of) that Sean will be pleased to see me later and pleasantly surprised when I actually buy him a drink or two. 'Fool's Gold' is doing its funky thing on my Walkman and as I slump in my seat I wish that the whole world could hear what I'm hearing at the same ear-numbing volume.

We – well, me and the captain of my spaceship – arrive at Victoria coach station a couple of hours, days or maybe even weeks later, I'm not entirely sure. Although it seems to take a long time to navigate, I finally manage to get off the coach and head out into the afternoon crowds with more than a spring in my step, my Walkman now giving me Primal Scream's 'Loaded' – very, very loaded.

I stop for a quick dance on the corner of Buckingham Palace Road and while I wait for the lights to change from purple to whatever, somebody taps me on the shoulder. I turn around to see two coppers standing in front of me. I am not prepared for this.

'Mumble, mumble, mumble,' says one of them, pointing at the headphones.

I point at myself then decide to put my hands up in the air, which might not have been the wisest move.

'Excuse me, sir, do you mind if we have a word with you? Could you take the Walkman off, please,' he continues, gesturing with tennis-racquet-sized hands.

'Fuck.'

Wrong word methinks as the music from the Walkman fades away to be replaced by the deafening boom of the copper's voice. I'm staring at the moustache bristling with activity above his foghorn mouth.

'Do you live locally, sir?'

'Fuck, yes, er, no, well, yeah, sort of over there [pointing south] in Lambeth, with my friend Sean. He's expecting me home for tea. He's a vegetarian, you know. Why? Is there a problem?'

They are both staring into my saucer-sized eyeballs while I am now visibly shaking.

'Have you got any drugs on you, sir? Bit of cannabis maybe?'

'Er . . . no, I, er, no, fuck, no, nothing really. I've just got off the bus, mate. Been to Bristol to see my best friend. He's called Luke.'

'Very nice, sir. Could you empty your pockets, please.'

I pull out my lump of dope and hand it to Plod. They have a look and a sniff and a smile.

'Nice bit of gear that, mate.'

'Er, thanks.'

'I'm arresting you on suspicion of being in possession of a controlled substance. You do not have to say anything but anything you do say may be used . . . blah, blah, fucking blah.'

The acid is battling with reality. It's getting hard to think straight. I think silence would be best here; the acid thinks otherwise.

'Yeah, my sister's a copper in Bristol, actually.'

'Shut up, you fucking prick.'

We're waiting for a police van to take the three of us back to the nick. I'm trying hard to make polite conversation with my captors. Well, one of them, good cop, a Scouser. Bad cop is the one with the overactive facial hair, which is too much for me to cope with, so I concentrate on his colleague.

'Yeah, she's been in for a couple of years, really likes the job, you know, capturing hardened criminals, protecting the public from muggers an' that, you know, real criminals.'

No response, so I keep digging.

'It's not a particularly big lump of dope, is it, mate? I mean for personal-consumption size obviously; it's not as if I had enough to start knocking it out for cash or anything, not that I would even if I did have, obviously.'

Silence.

'Liverpool are doing well, I reckon.'

'I'm an Everton fan, mate. I'm actually from Liverpool.'

'Oh, right. What about your mate?'

'Shut up, you fucking druggy twat.'

Bad cop is obviously keeping in character.

'Er, right you are, mate. This van's taking its time. Listen, can't we just do a caution-type thing and I'll be on my way?'

Fungus-face turns to me.

'Listen, mate, it's quite fucking obvious to me that you're on something a little bit stronger than dope, so we're going to go back to the station and find whatever it is, wherever you may have it stashed. Now shut your fucking mouth and start walking.'

He says something into his radio and we start to walk. It's all I can do to put one foot in front of the other and try to stop my mind from thinking about the firing squad they no doubt have waiting back at the station.

They begin to process me and within minutes start to search through my bag, almost immediately finding the stash of little white blotters I still have left. I have no clue as to how many there are.

'What's this, Mr Mason?' enquires Stalin-features.

I don't know why but I get the urge to be a bit honest.

'Acid, for personal consumption only.'

'Rather a lot there for personal consumption, wouldn't you say?'

'I like it. It's really good acid.'

'Right, lock him up.'

After three or four disturbingly long hours/days/weeks/years/fuck knows in the 'condemned' cell, which appeared to have blood seeping down its walls and nasty little creatures living in the toilet, I was beginning to think that the firing squad would actually be quite a relief, if only for the opportunity to have a final cigarette, my requests for which had so far been ignored.

Eventually good cop came to the cell door and informed me that the duty solicitor was going to be a long time coming, so did I just want to give my statement and go?

'Can I have a fag, please, officer?'

'Do you want to give a statement now?'

The best advice I could have received then or indeed at any time would be, 'Don't talk to the police when you're tripping.'

But I was tripping, very much so, and therefore was less able than usual to take the common-sense approach – something I was not about to receive any awards for in the foreseeable future anyway. Abject terror informed the idea that I had to get out of that cell and fast. Do a recorded interview with the police while on a brain-frying dose of LSD? I thought I could handle it without getting into too much trouble.

And so, on the promise of a roll-up and a coffee, I waived my rights to legal representation and offered myself up to two representatives of the lower end of the Great British legal system. By the time I finished my story my captors had added a couple more charges to the two I was already facing.

I somehow failed to understand that just because I didn't actually accept any money from my best friend in Bristol (whose name and address I now seemed to have forgotten) in exchange for the acid I'd given him, it didn't make it any less serious an offence. I tried to explain how it had come into my possession in the first place and made matters even worse.

'I was given it, in exchange for some dope and magic mushrooms . . . which I picked myself and I didn't dry them out . . . they dried naturally . . . it was the American from the Grateful Dead show that instigated this whole thing . . . he asked me for drugs . . . I was out of my head and just wanted to seem friendly . . . you know, hospitable like.'

'Do you understand what you're saying, Mr Mason?' said good cop, while Stalin beamed triumphantly at me.

I had now admitted to supplying a Class A drug, a Class B drug and shortly afterwards the possession of whatever they would find upon searching the flat – Sean's flat!

They kept asking questions I didn't understand at all until it all became too much for me to get my head round, so I just signed the statement and we went off to the flat, where three bags of dried-out mushrooms, some speed and about half an ounce of weed were discovered in my room. We then went back to the nick, I signed something else and eventually they let me go.

By the time Sean arrived home later, I was not feeling too well.

'Sean, for Christ's sake skin up, I've had a bad day.'

'Why? What's happened? You look bloody awful.'

'I'm not sure really, but I think I'm in trouble.'

'What kind of trouble?'

'The kind of a lot kind.'

Aside from the prospect of actually going to jail, which for an immensely annoying coward like myself was not something that filled me with joy at any point during the months preceding my trial, the most frustrating thing was that everyone I knew had an opinion on what kind of sentence I was looking at and would generally inform me of this whether I wanted to hear it or not.

When I say everyone, I am of course referring to the kind of people I knew. I should imagine that the vast majority of the great British public have no idea how many months/years of avoiding the showers and getting his head kicked in on a regular basis an idiot like me might have been looking at.

The opinions I heard varied from a few months to a few years.

The delivery of said opinions also varied. Some were offered with an almost tangible sense of 'Ha, ha, ha, you cunt, that'll learn ya,' while others were slightly more celebratory in their tone.

A few, however – those proffered by my friends – were delivered with a degree of compassion and it appeared I had not managed to totally alienate myself from the entire universe just yet.

Still, I was only 22. Just getting into my stride, really.

Eventually I got to have a meeting with my solicitor, the gist of which was, 'I think you may well be going to jail, Simon.'

Bummer! Or the impending likelihood of getting locked up for years with lots of bummers, more to the point!

Why I had the notion that the prison system was only populated by sadistic homosexuals just waiting to drill me a new asshole, I have no idea. Maybe I was just getting it confused with my school?

My brief was talking to me as I wrestled with mental imagery most likely informed by the rape scene in the seminal British movie *Scum* more than anything else. He talked while I was mentally getting fucked in the ass in a potting shed, sort of.

He had received a written transcription of my interview with the arresting officers; it did not make good reading.

'You told me that you had taken some acid a couple of hours before getting arrested.'

'Yeah, I was off my face when they interviewed me.'

'Why didn't you tell them? They would have had to delay the interview and had a doctor visit you, by which time there would have been a duty solicitor available. I mean, you've really made things difficult for yourself. What the hell were you thinking of?'

'I assume you've never taken acid, Mr Needham?'

'No.'

'Thought not. Listen, surely as this is my first offence I won't go to prison? Can't you persuade them that the acid was for personal use? How many did they find?'

'Thirty-five.'

'That's one a day for about a month, more or less.'

'Do people normally take that much acid?'

'John Lennon did more, in fact.'

'But you're not John Lennon.'

101

He had a point. Not that being a rich and famous rock star would have made any difference, of course. Other than the fact I'd have got a decent fucking lawyer.

'Listen, Simon, unless we can prove you were unfit for interview at the time of questioning, you're in trouble. I'll request a copy of the interview tape; in the meantime, have you had any luck getting a job?'

'Earnt a few quid at Glastonbury a while back but it was all cash-in-hand, so to speak.'

'Nothing we could mention in court, then?'

'Er, no, not really.'

'I'll be in touch. In the meantime try not to get arrested again, oh, and maybe forget about all this music-business nonsense and try to get some proper employment.'

'Right you are, Mr Needham.'

It was obvious to me that my legal representation had no idea what I needed to do and had clearly not recognised my latent genius. I mentally crossed him off the guest list forever.

Almost immediately discarding his advice to get a job, I decided the best thing for me to do now was to actually join a band, become famous overnight and get a decent lawyer. I just had to find one desperate enough to take me on.

I lived in London, I could get my hands on really good drugs. I knew a few people in the music business! How hard could it be?

Of course I'd also require a manager and so approached a mate of mine whose appetite for imbibing chemicals and alcohol was of a similar, if not greater, size to my own. As he was an economics student when not purchasing considerable quantities of Ecstasy, cocaine and weed, he seemed the obvious choice. It helped that as well as having the constitution for excessive familiarity with the drugs he took, he also generally tolerated me constantly lurking about his flat, trying my hardest to convince him, despite no real evidence, that I was about to become a rich and famous rock star and therefore a potential source of income as opposed to the generally flat-broke, freeloading source of coked-up bollocks that could not be trusted to be left alone anywhere near his stash of drugs or money. Fortunately for me, the music business acquaintances

I introduced to him spent sufficient cash to make my presence worth the regular occurrences of 'misappropriation of company stock' whenever I drifted in and out of the area.

Perhaps the fact we'd known each other for years, spent time in LA together, both worshipped The Stones and The Who and shared a similar obsession with making serious amounts of cash while being as off our tits as often as possible might well have helped my cause somewhat.

That's a bit like being friends, isn't it?

The actuality that I was still stuck at the 'imminent stardom' stage with little more than a deluded fantasy that I was about to make it was probably softened by the fact that he smoked, sniffed and popped more of his products than most of the people he supplied them to.

As far as I was concerned 'we' couldn't fail. Unless I went to jail that is.

My solicitor had suggested getting a 'real job'; I suggested to Julian we start our own record company.

He liked the idea and so a few weeks later we purchased a company name off the shelf, Probation Records Ltd, had our business cards printed and ordered a company seal from the solicitors.

At our first 'business' meeting, while I was hoovering up a line of coke the length of a small child, laughing at my cheekily named enterprise – 'Can't wait to see the look on my solicitor's face!' – I was wondering if it was a good time to tell my 'manager' that the band I'd claimed to be ready to make a single with had recently thrown me out. I'd persuaded them to leave their jobs/girlfriends/flats in Weston on the promise of wages and somewhere nice to live/rehearse in London. A squat with no furniture, hot water or electricity in south London and having to go busking to earn their wages hadn't exactly enamoured them to either me or my plans for world domination and I was sacked before we'd even managed to create any music to have musical differences over.

I chose to remain tight-lipped on the subject for the time being and continued demolishing my own 'wages' with another line of the celebrity sherbet.

One night we threw a party to cement our partnership and when asked I told our guests that the other lads were too busy in the studio to attend but wanted me to be there to 'fly the flag', so to speak.

A sign saying 'I am an utter cunt' would have been more appropriate, however the booze, coke and pills I was 'taking for the team' disagreed; I am a genius dontcha know?

We all got absolutely fucked to bits and towards the end of the evening Julian and I struck up a conversation with a bloke who had been dishing out some powerful pills to our assembled guests. A short while and several not very short lines later we'd agreed on a price for 200 of the little beauties. I'd given him my number and he promised to call the next day, as we/I continued to congratulate ourselves/myself all night long.

'You're safe, mate. Nice one, geezer . . .'

'You two are safe an' all. Proper gents, blah, blah, blah.'

As you do.

But then we had a change of plan.

Later

We are all in a black cab heading to north London, sniffing coke and drinking champagne as we go. The sun is out and we are feeling indestructible. Our sweaty-looking new best mate is nodding his head up and down as he changes seat for the sixth time.

'You fuckin' mad bastards. Probation Records, mental. Funny fuckers, ain't ya? Listen, I'll have to pop up the road to pick up when we get there, yeah. Have you got the cash?'

This is our new best mate. He's safe – a proper geezer. He was at our party. We look at each other then hand over the wedge.

The cab pulls up outside a tower block in Holloway.

'Keep the meter running, mate. I won't be two minutes.'

He jumps out of the cab and heads off into the estate.

'So how do you know this geezer, Julian? He seems pretty cool, nice bloke. When did you meet him? Fucking top geezer, yeah?'

Julian stares at me and I get that sinking feeling again.

'You mean you don't actually know him, Mason?'

'He's a friend of yours, isn't he? Well, isn't he?'

Ten minutes later

'I thought you'd invited him, you fat cunt. Oh my fucking good god, two fucking grand. I thought you knew him . . .'

'Don't fucking blame me, you twat. You wanted to come up here with him . . .'

'You gave him the money.'

'You told me to . . .'

'You're supposed to be the fucking accountant. This side of things is your responsibility, you fat cunt.'

'You're supposed to be a pop star but I don't see any sign of a record deal on the horizon, you talentless prick.'

The truth hurts. I try to compose myself.

'Why didn't you go with him?'

'Why didn't you?'

'Cos I thought you knew him.'

'No, I thought you knew him . . . prick.'

And so on.

The cabbie interrupts our little discussion.

'I don't think your friend is coming back, gents. Do you want me to go back south? The meter's still running. I hope you didn't give that bloke all your cash, as this fare has cost you a small fortune.'

Fucking black cab drivers – know-all bastards.

Later still, back at the 'office'

'Well, we're not going to run out of roach material for a while,' I say, while throwing the still unopened box of business cards at Julian, who is hoovering up the last of his Charlie and muttering incoherently under his breath.

'Two thousand fucking pounds! You are an idiot of the highest order. I can't believe I let you talk me into this.'

Chop, chop, chop, sniff, sniff, sniff.

'I don't know why you're still having a go at me. What the fuck am I going to tell my solicitor? "Oh yeah, good job, stayed away from people who took drugs but not people who fucking robbed all mine. Yeah, Mr Needham, I got ripped off trying to buy 200 Es. Sorry about that."'

Chop, chop, chop, sniff, sniff.

'So what are we going to do now, partner? It's not as if somebody's about to walk in and give us a pile of cash.'

The doorbell rings.

'Get that, will you? It's a customer who wants an ounce of weed. You can deal with her. She's also someone who thinks they're going to make it in the music business. Possibly not a fucking idiot like you but who knows? You'll get along famously. I'm going down the pub. Actually, I'll let her in on my way out. Oh, and obviously we are no longer partners. You're on your own, pop star.'

I lick the cover of the CD case Julian has just finished using and roll a joint, a big neat one, and wait.

White Lines

'So what do you do for a living, then, Juliet? Here, smoke some of this. It'll knock your tits off.'

'Er, well, that's a good question. I've just changed careers, actually. I used to work in PR but all of a sudden it seemed really boring, so I've gone into the music biz. It's fab!'

Not the description I'd have used at this point but I carried on listening and racked out a few lines of coke to show some solidarity with my new 'friend'.

'Oh, yeah. I'm in that game, too. What exactly do you do?'

'I run a recording studio and I'm hoping to set up a record label soon.'

I was smiling now and quickly added two more lines to the as yet untouched couple on the table.

'Oh, really? That's great. Where's the studio?'

'Oh, it's amazing! It's built inside a nineteenth-century prison in east London. I don't really know the first thing about the music business. I like The Cranberries, though. Do you?'

'Fucking love 'em. Here . . .'

I offered her a rolled-up note and gestured to the powder.

'Oh, wow! Don't mind if I do but isn't it a bit early for this?'

'This is the fucking rock 'n' roll business, Juliet. It's never too early.'

'So yah, I used to work in PR but I've been put in charge by my uncle, who's a property developer. He fancied a stab at the music business – rediscovering his youth, I suppose. He's incredibly wealthy, ha, ha, ha.'

After one of the most annoying fits of laughter I'd ever had the misfortune to hear, she continued.

'The place was about to go into receivership. The last owner practically ran the place into the ground – had a drug problem, ha, ha, ha. I've got to try to drum up some investment money and turn it around in the next few months. Wow, this pot is excellent . . . I haven't seen you here before, what did you say you normally do?'

The Lord truly works in mysterious ways. Ha, ha and indeed ha.

'Oh, me? I work in the music business, too. I've just started a record label, funnily enough. Would you like some more cocaine? Perhaps a little drinky winky, too?'

'So, yeah . . . sniff, sniff, sniff . . . the label's really going to take off . . . sniff, sniff . . . we just need to finalise things with the bands we're trying to sign and get some studio time sorted. Sniff, sniff . . . here, have another line. Let's make it a fat one. Feel free to skin up by the way.'

'Thanks, don't know how to actually, ha, ha. Would you mind? What's the label called?'

'Not at all, Juliet. It's called Probation Records Ltd.'

'Yeah . . . sniff, sniff . . . wow! That's an amazing coincidence, what with the studio being inside an old prison. It's an amazing place; you should come and see it some time.'

An hour later and we were sitting in her office chain-smoking skunk spliffs, snorting more coke and working our way through a £45 bottle of brandy.

'So, Simon, I'm a bit of a hippy at heart, actually, and believe in fate throwing people together for a reason. I need somebody who knows what they're doing to get involved here – someone like you, maybe? Trustworthy, reliable and prepared to work hard, someone who can see the bigger picture.'

I don't think I've ever been described so erroneously before or since. It's funny how quickly life can turn around, eh?

We decided we needed a name for our new partnership. With my court appearance looming I felt strongly that we needed something with a certain ring to it and so THE GOOD HONEST MUSIC COMPANY, incorporating PROBATION RECORDS LTD, was formed.

A couple of days later and I had my own office, a share in a potentially successful 25,000-foot studio complex, a credit account with a luxury cab company and a somewhat disbelieving, pissed off ex-business partner/manager.

My solicitor was suitably impressed when I gave him the news, informing me that any trial judge would look favourably upon my endeavours to become a respectable businessman and this might well save me from a custodial sentence. He thought I was joking about the name, though.

I was feeling rather pleased with myself and obviously another celebration was in order – a big celebration.

Juliet had been talking to various City types concerning the possibility of obtaining the serious financial backing needed to improve the studio facilities. She knew how to deal with these people. I thought they were all utter wankers, which was as good an example of 'if you spot it, you got it' as you'll ever find. However, we needed the money and as I had chosen an office down in the bowels of the building, I didn't have to talk to any of them. Instead, in the search for cash I made a few calls to more of my kind of people.

'So, come on over and have a look, Scottie. I've got a wicked venue down here. You'll love it, mate. Oh, and could you bring a few bits and pieces with you when you come? Yeah, yeah. Nice one, mate. See ya soon.'

Scottie arrived later that afternoon accompanied by his entourage and the requested bits and pieces.

'How the fuck did you get this gaff? I always thought you were a bit of a chancer, Si, but fuck me . . . You've come up with the goods 'ere, ain't ya? This place is mental – fucking perfect for doing parties. What ya got lined up?'

'Well, Scottie, my good man, that's where you may want to get involved. You see, we don't actually have any cash to speak of right now and obviously this place costs a few quid to run . . . Here, sit down, skin up. What do you think we should do?'

We smoked a joint, had a few brandies and were soon as thick as thieves, so of course if I needed a few 'dollars' to cover me for a while then, 'Well, that's what mates are for, ain't it, Si?'

Who was I to argue? Actually 'Who am I?' full stop, would by now have been a question I'd have struggled to answer.

We decided to hold a couple of events the following month. Scottie would naturally take care of publicity and security and all the implications therein in the meantime.

'Here's £500, Si. Tide you over for a few days. I'll be in touch. Probably bring some people over during the next couple of days to have a butcher's at the place, all right?'

'Yeah, nice one. Here, let me call you a cab. Where you going? Fancy a quick line before you leave?'

Juliet was confused.

'What exactly does your friend want for his £500, Simon?'

'Ah, you see, Juliet, that's the difference between your people and mine. We're a little more informal down here, know what I mean?'

'No, not really. I hope you know what you're getting into.'

Scottie moved into my office a couple of days later, bringing with him the various colourful elements that constituted his crew. They were scary but I felt safe enough and if I didn't I just snorted more coke or popped another E.

If you're going into the promotions world, you have to have a little muscle on the firm and suddenly we did – lots of it. Unfortunately we had no brains to give instructions.

While they were busy moving in, I was making phone calls to everybody else I knew who might be prepared to get financially involved in my budding empire – more drug dealers and petty criminals, mainly.

Over the next few weeks a lot of 'interesting' people came and went, and deals were set up for big parties we intended to host within the complex. Expensive brandy was drunk, expensive drugs were taken and costly executive taxis ordered on my expense account

TOO HIGH, TOO FAR, TOO SOON

delivered a stream of people with cheap morals and an even cheaper view of the law to and from 'my' studio. We even had a few bands in to rehearse, although I have absolutely no fucking idea how that happened.

To my mind, I was empire building, taking the piss out of the criminal justice system, refusing to accept the government's social persecution of anybody remotely interested in having a good time. Nobody could tell me different. I had the passion for it and a vision I really believed in – at least when I was coked up to the eyeballs anyway, which was pretty much all of the time.

What could possibly go wrong, eh?

I'd never asked too many questions about how much money we needed to re-fit the studio. My job was to get bands in to rehearse and provide the cash to keep us afloat until 'Her Upstairs' got the nod from her City friends. I never had any reason to doubt her resources; I assumed she knew what she was doing, as she did I.

Oh, dear!

Juliet walked into my office one night, crying.

'There's no money coming. The investors don't want to know. What are we going to do? This is the end before we've even got started!'

Two fat lines of cocaine later, we had other ideas.

'We're not done just yet, Juliet. We've got the parties coming up and we're going to make a fortune, trust me!'

'But everybody is on the guest list. How are we going to make any money like that?'

Bless her, eh?

'That's what I've been working on down here in my office, babe. You said you wanted someone you could rely on, eh?'

'But your friends all look like people off *Crimewatch*, Simon. I'm worried about the kind of things you've been doing down here!'

'Well, Juliet, your "friends" haven't exactly come up trumps, have they? Don't worry, babe, we can just keep throwing parties every week and pay for the studio upgrade as we go. C'mon, girl, we'll have a

110

quick rethink, figure out what needs to be done first, then . . .'

'They want us out of the building by next weekend.'

Fuckingfuckingfuckingfuckingfuckingbloodyfuckinghell.

'Who are "they" exactly, Juliet?'

'The owners of the bloody building. They know we haven't found the investment money and they don't like the look of the people they've seen coming in and out. They think we're dealing drugs or something. They wanted to call the bloody police, Simon. What have you been up to down here?'

Sniff . . . bollocks . . . sniff . . . sniff . . . sniff . . . sniff . . . sniff.

Luke walked into my office.

'Scottie's on the phone for you, Si. He's not coming in today but he needs to talk to you about his party.'

'Tell him I'll call him back later.' (Much later as it turned out.)

'Can't you talk them into giving us a little more time? Surely they can't just throw us out? Don't you have a contract, Juliet?'

'No, I can't; yes, they can; no, I don't.'

She walked out, sobbing. There wasn't much left to say.

Luke tried to cheer me up.

'Listen, man, this isn't your fault, really. Maybe Scottie's party will go ahead anyway. We're bound to make a bit of cash there. We can have a holiday and go and chill out somewhere hot, have a rethink, kind of thing.'

Juliet came back in.

'The owner of the taxi company has just been on the phone. Wants to know when you're going to settle the account, Simon.'

'How much do we owe him?'

'*You* owe him two and a half grand. It's your name on the contract and luxury cars on account don't come cheap, "mate".'

The phone rang again. It was my solicitor with the date of my appearance at the Crown Court. My case was due to be heard the following week. You've got to laugh, eh?

'Luke mate, have you got any cash on you? I need a drink.'

'Yeah, man, let's go to the boozer. We need to come up with a plan.'

We hit the optics with a vengeance and then my mobile rang – it was Juliet.

'Simon, there was a man from Southwark social security here asking for you. I've sent him to the pub. I don't want to know what's going on any more.'

As Luke and I were the only people drinking in the pub at 11.45 a.m. it didn't surprise me that the fat, bald and, quite frankly, rather tawdry-looking bloke who entered walked right up to us.

'Hello, are you Mr Mason?'

'Mmmm . . .'

'Oh, good. I'm the secretary of the local entertainment committee, east London social security. We have your main room booked for our staff Christmas party. I spoke to your colleague Mr Scottie last week. I've brought the deposit money for the venue hire.'

I stared at him and smiled my best smile.

'One thousand pounds cash – half the total cost – is that correct?'

'You'd better come back to my office, er, what did you say your name was?'

'Oh, Dobson, Simon Dobson. Pleased to meet you.'

'The feeling's mutual, I can assure you, Mr Dobson. Come down to my office; I'll write you a receipt.'

And so it came to pass that the only document ever to receive the official Probation Records company seal was a receipt for one thousand pounds cash from the man from the dole office.

After showing Mr Dobson out I walked back past Juliet's office and saw her clearing out her desk. This seemed like a good idea, all things considered.

I dumped all the Rizla packets, empty brandy bottles and crumpled wraps of paper into the bin, made a phone call to Flight Bookers, closed the door and rejoined Luke in the pub, crawling on all fours past Juliet's office on the way out.

She had in all probability known for some time there was never going to be any money coming and that things were destined to go wrong thanks to unrealistic expectations and too much drug-induced bullshit.

'Luke man, I'm going to go away for a while, just booked a flight.'

'Where are you going, man? What about the court case?'

'Look, mate, I don't fancy jail, really. It'll do my head in, so I'm going back to Los Angeles, see what my mate Kevin's up to.'

'Is that a good idea, man?'

I shrugged my shoulders.

'It's marginally more attractive than getting banged up and bummed to death.'

'Yeah, but you won't be able to come back.'

There then followed one of those cinematic silent pauses.

'You can come and visit me; besides, what have I got to lose?'

A tear rolled from my eye at the same time as a cocaine-encrusted bogey slid out of my nose – a perfect illustration, largely, of why things were the way they were. It goes without saying that I couldn't see the relationship between the two as I choked back the tear and snorted the coke-bogey back up into my battered nose.

Luke and I went out drinking for the rest of the day and night until we both ended up at a friend's in south London.

I met someone that night, someone who demonstrated love for me in a way I'd never previously experienced but someone who I'm sure regrets ever setting eyes on me. I have no idea where they are these days but I can only hope life is treating them better than I did over the following few years.

We spent the week or so prior to my flight to America together and the night before I left for the airport she blindfolded me and walked me along the street to a nearby park.

'Wait here,' she whispered in my ear.

'OK, you can take the blindfold off now.'

As I removed her scarf from my eyes, a firework shot up from the grass in front of me and exploded into the night sky.

'Good luck, Simon. I'll miss you.'

I think this may well be the most romantic thing I've ever experienced and she deserved so much better than me. Everybody did but few people suffered as much.

I flew away to America the following day; it would have been much better for her if I'd never returned.

San Francisco

A remarkably sober, yet anxious and confused me was waiting to pass through US immigration while trying to figure out how I'd spend the rest of my life on the run in America. The welcoming embrace and offer of accommodation from my Deadhead friend, whose parting gift of a sheet of acid months earlier had played a significant part in my current predicament, seemed as good a place as any to start considering my options.

'OK, Bruce, I'm in a spot of bother here, mate. I'm going to need a place to get my head together and think about what the fuck I'm going to do next.'

'Yeah, brother, not a problem. Wanna get high? Smoke some weed, do you want any more of that LSD, dude?'

I considered my reply carefully.

'Not right now, mate. I need to get some sort of plan together, you know? I'm in a bit of a situation here, so I'll need to keep a clear head, mate. I'll skip the drugs for now, eh?'

And if you believe that you're a bigger fucking idiot than I was.

Two hours later I was tripping my bollocks off at a party inside a warehouse the size of a small continent, at which there were some of San Francisco's finest drug aficionados, more varieties of chemicals than there are notes played in one of Jerry Garcia's guitar solos, a forest of cannabis plants and yours truly, who had by now been reduced to a gibbering incomprehensible mess, slumped in a corner as he tried to explain to his audience of curious Californian hippy friends exactly what the fuck he was doing there, while simultaneously trying to convince himself that he had not, in fact, just made the biggest in a seemingly never-ending line of big fucking mistakes and bad decisions.

'Dude, that's far out, man. You mean you can never go back to England?'

'Not unless I want to go to jail, mate.'

'Dude, how long would they put you away for?'

And that was exactly the right question at the right time, because I didn't have an answer. I needed an answer.

A wave of acid-fuelled clarity suddenly made my decision for me.

'What time is it, mate?'

'Dude, it's like nearly tomorrow. Why?'

It was already tomorrow in my solicitor's office back in London, where a few seconds later he received an incoming call from some drugged-up lunatic in San Francisco.

'Ah, Simon, I've been trying to get hold of you. Where the hell are you? I've got some good news at last. I've finally received the tape of the interview you gave to the officers who arrested you; it's completely inadmissible.'

'I'm in San Francisco, Mr Needham. What do you mean it's inadmissible?'

'Well, I've only had a written transcript until now, the contents of which, as I've told you already, did not entirely help us; however, I've finally got the actual tape of the interview and at the start there is something not previously disclosed.'

'Uh huh . . .?'

'At the very start of the interview they ask you when was the last time you took some of the LSD they believed you to be in possession of and you tell them clear as day two hours ago!'

The LSD battering my synapses in San Francisco did a backdated, triumphant, cosmic high-five to the LSD that I'd gobbled on that bus ride prior to getting arrested in London, and the following morning I was on yet another flight, demolishing a bottle of bourbon while slumped in the back row of the plane carrying me home from my 48 hours of 'exile'.

Two days later the case was thrown out of court and I walked away with little more than a slap on the wrist, a short while after which my best mates got attacked and I very nearly got thrown off a roof.

Gangsta, Gangsta

There is a building in Earls Court, possibly many in fact, that have flat roofs upon which you will find a small wooden structure housing the water tank(s) for the properties below. Amongst the various dead pigeons and rodents that had made that particular 'shed' their final resting place, on a rainy summer night many moons ago you would also have found a dead cert for the title of 'most terrified, very annoying, crap low-level drug dealer in the world'. Me, in other words.

How did I end up sitting waist deep in freezing cold water a hundred feet above the streets of west London with dead vermin for company?

Once again, not surprisingly, drugs had been instrumental in the lead-up to my current predicament, where it now looked likely that I might find myself incorporated into the tarmac of the streets a hundred feet below. Those potentially responsible? The very angry former 'employees' of my former musical empire who wanted their £500 back and were battering the door of Alex's flat to pieces with the same blunt instruments they would surely soon be applying to me.

What was it Juliet had said?

'What exactly does your friend want for his £500, Simon?'

My response?

'Ah, you see, Juliet, that's the difference between your people and mine. We're a little more informal down here, know what I mean?'

The time for being informal was clearly over, unless you consider getting a proper kicking then being thrown off a roof an act of casual familiarity.

The door failed to keep the lunatics out, disintegrating at exactly the same time that my bladder stopped working.

'He's gone out the fucking skylight. He's on the fucking roof. The cunt's on the roof.'

The more observant of you will know that to have been the truth; however, had they said, 'The cunt's in that tiny wooden shed that surrounds the water tank that only a painfully skinny, drug-addled dickhead could possibly squeeze into,' I would not be writing this book.

But they didn't say that and I am.

What they actually said when they clambered up onto the roof was, 'He must have jumped onto the next building. The cunt's got away.'

I spent a further two hours shaking like a leaf while listening intently for any noises emanating from the flat below before managing to convince my limbs to work. I then slithered out from my shed of shit and crawled on all fours towards the skylight, from where I could hear what I hoped were friendly voices below.

'Mason, you are a cunt of the highest order. They've taken fucking everything – coke, pills, money, even the fucking telly. I can't believe this! Why are you such a fucking liability?'

Good to be alive amongst friends, eh?

'Sorry, I didn't think that was going to happen, Julian.'

'They pulled a fucking shotgun on me, you cunt!' said Matty, who was clearly not best pleased at having had his evening's drinking in the King's Arms interrupted after his 'shift' in our 'shop', dishing out the 'stock' we now no longer had.

'What happened anyway? How did they find us?'

Matty was racking out a line of coke that covered half the length of the table we were now sitting around. I presumed this was from his personal stash, seeing as we'd just been liberated of everything else.

'Scottie brought some fucking lunatic with him who'd only got out of jail today – proper fucking basket case, big scar right across his face. They just strolled into the boozer, calm as you like, and asked to speak to me, took me outside, then pulled the fucking shooter out.'

Half the line disappeared up his nose without him missing a beat.

'So I'm left standing downstairs, coked and pilled out me nut with some cunt waving a fucking shotgun at my face demanding to know where you are.'

The rest of the coke went up the other nostril.

'So what the fuck am I supposed to do? I can't fucking believe this. They've taken fucking everything, you utter cunt. You fucking stink of shit by the way!'

'I'm sorry, mate. Any chance of a line?'

He stared at me with a look that suggested I had more chance of winning Sports Personality of the Year than getting some of his bugle up my nose.

'Where were you hiding anyway, Mason?'

'In the shed on the roof where the water tank is. I thought I was going to die.'

'You'd probably be more use to the human race if you did,' said Julian.

'Thanks, mate.'

'So what are you going to do about all this fucking . . . mess? Scottie wants his money back – from you not us. He said we'll get our stuff back when you pay him back but I assume that, as per fucking normal, you've sniffed more coke than you've managed to actually sell?'

They knew me well.

'I, er, I'm going to have to work it off, chaps, if that's all right with you?'

I got the 'Sports Personality' look again.

'I suggest you fuck off back to that poor cow in south London who has the misfortune to be sharing her house with you and thinks you actually love her, while we speak to Scottie tomorrow and see if he's calmed down enough to consider not fucking killing you and more importantly maybe giving us our stock back once I explain that you do not work for us any more.'

'What about his £500?'

'That's your problem, you stupid prick. Knowing you, you'll probably manage to convince her to lend it to you until you're a famous rock star on Top of the fucking Pops.'

An event that was also about as likely as me being Sports Personality of the Year.

Matty tried his best to force a smile in my direction as I slouched out of the flat, walking straight through what remained of the front door, and crept into the wet London evening. My nerves were so shot to pieces, I found myself shaking and twitching uncontrollably as I tried to disappear into every shadow and shop doorway en route to the Tube station and the relative safety of my girlfriend's flat in south London.

When I say 'girlfriend', what I actually mean is the latest in a line of people willing to suffer my bullshit, neediness, delusion and empty promises because, for reasons I still cannot fathom, she perhaps saw something in me that went some way to explain why I was the way I was. She loved me with all her heart and I eventually, over many years, smashed that beautiful soul to pieces. I am truly sorry.

I got the £500 from her and true to form also persuaded her to go and meet Scottie, along with Julian and his 'minder' in a bar in Camden, to hand over his cash. Scottie, to give credit where it's due, immediately returned what had been removed from the flat, down to the last pill.

'Honour amongst thieves' was a notion that had clearly passed me by as I continued my journey, destroying people's faith in me with empty promises. There was an ever-increasing collection of hurt and profoundly disappointed people left in my wake, a fact that was by now impossible to ignore.

I continued to take drugs and upset people in equal measure but the drugs I was taking were not really working any more. By which I mean they were not hiding me from the shadow that followed me about, pointing its finger accusingly to highlight my shortcomings in just about every area of life.

Hash, speed, alcohol, magic mushrooms, LSD, cocaine, Ecstasy, whether taken individually or, if circumstances allowed, all at the same time, no longer gave me relief from the almost constant internal suggestion that I actually was the utter waste of space most people by now thought I was. My ego still thought differently but my compete lack of self-esteem concurred with the opinion of the rest of the world, and the void created by this dichotomy of self-obsessed inner turmoil needed to be filled with something.

I needed help but had no idea how much trouble I was in, and so I continued to believe that if I could get people to feel sorry for me until such time as I'd 'made it', I'd be OK.

What exactly did I need?

Perhaps some therapy to help me resolve the issues I carried from my schooldays, the loss of my father, the crack-induced madness in Los Angeles, the excessive use of LSD, cocaine and Ecstasy, my inability to feel like I could connect with another human being? Perhaps that might have helped?

Maybe I should just have followed my doctor's advice from a few years previously?

'*Stop taking drugs, cut down on the drinking and get a proper job.*'

I'll never know because, as much of what remains of this story will inform you, I took up none of the above options. Instead I took up something that at first seemed to make the need for any such choices completely redundant.

I wanted an instant solution to the problem of being me. Heroin did the trick very nicely indeed, thank you very much, so I took that up instead. As you do when you discover that, amongst other things, it kind of negates the need to take anything else. Not that I did stop taking everything else; it just changed my priorities.

Heroin soon came first and if that sounds like too casual a statement to reflect someone 'deciding' to use a drug any normal person would run a mile from, well, the thing about heroin is it initially convinces you that you are making a choice each time you embrace it and throws a blanket over the reality of what is actually happening.

The handful of people I already knew that used it didn't seem to be having too bad a time, not that I was interested enough in anyone else's life to have made an accurate report of the ins and outs of their smack addiction. Besides, I wasn't stupid enough to get in any real trouble with it. And if I did? Well, I was going to be a rock 'n' roll star and be cool like Keith Richards. He'd managed to create albums like *Exile on Main Street* while off his tits on skag, so it couldn't be all bad, eh?

Truth is, at the start, aside from a bit of puking, I couldn't find anything about heroin I didn't fall completely in love with. Not a thing, because it did what I needed it to do, which was everything that I could not do for myself.

Many people have tried through music and verse to describe their experience with heroin; mine was simple – it 'allowed' me to be me.

What did it feel like?

It felt like the answer, like a pharmacological light bulb going on above the head of an idiot stumbling through life, clueless as to the best way to exist, until I opened a door into a world where everything suddenly was as it should be.

Remarkable as it may sound, my new devotion to smack remained a secret at first and the people I sold drugs for continued to tolerate me thanks, I suspect, to my association with my latest set of 'clients' and the endless parties our business dealings gave us access to.

The musical climate was changing again and 'we' were all going to make lots of money and possibly become famous.

I was actually totally convinced.

Part Two

Deal

I'm at home in Camden, it's cold and wet outside, nobody wants to go out to play and neither do I. I'm staying in with a roll of tinfoil and a £20 baggie of 'solution'.

The phone rings but I can't be bothered to answer. I don't need anything or anyone else right now.

It keeps ringing until I am convinced someone must have died and even then I answer reluctantly.

'Yeah, hello?'

No one had died but as a result of answering that call I soon got the opportunity to witness musical history come alive right in front of my eyes.

'Simon, it's Phil. Listen, mate, can you come down? I've got a band on tonight, driving me mad for a bit of . . .'

'Yeah, yeah, careful what you say on the phone, mate. What do they want, how much?'

He talks to somebody.

'They'll have whatever you got, mate. Listen, they're a bunch of scallies from Manchester so, er, you know . . .'

I knew.

'Yeah, OK, listen, I'll be about 30 minutes, put me on the list, yeah? Are they any good?'

'Well, just about every fucking A 'n' R man in London's trying to get on the list, so something must be up. I'll see you in the office when you . . . Listen, mate, he's coming, all right?' he snaps at whoever is bothering him at the club.

'Sorry, Simon, the fucking singer's driving me mad. See you in a bit.'

Thirty minutes later I'm in a cab with fifteen little plastic bags hidden in my socks inside my new Puma trainers.

On arrival I walk straight to the front of the line where the guy holding the guest list is arguing with someone claiming to have a plus five; he settles for a plus one.

The promoter sees me, ushers me inside and downstairs to his office. It takes nearly five minutes to go forty feet as the place is absolutely mobbed, boiling hot and therefore just about perfect for what is about to happen onstage.

This is my world and I love it. I have a place here, a sense of purpose. I want to be here and because of the little baggies I have on my person other people want me to be here as well. I'll settle for that; it's a win/win situation.

'So, do you want to leave this with me and I'll sort out the band when they get back here from the hotel? They'll be here in 20 minutes; sounded shit hot at the soundcheck, though, just signed to Creation.'

'You reckon it's worth sticking around, then?'

'Yes, mate. Listen, here's the readies for this little lot. You'll need this pass tonight, too. I expect you'll have as much business as you want later. I've gotta go and sort out the rest of their rider. You don't sell bottles of Jack Daniel's do you? Fancy a quick line before you go?'

Obviously.

I make my way up to the bar as the coke slides down the back of my throat. You cannot move for bodies as I look around the room to see everybody else looking around the room to see who else is here.

'Oi, Simon, got anything . . .?'

I grimace at Hugh, who's shouting at me from about three feet away. Fucking idiot, why don't people think before they announce to the world you're a drug dealer? Probably because they're already coked up to the eyeballs and wouldn't give a shit if you got nicked anyway. You get money and the occasional good night out, not respect when you're in the little plastic-bag business. Sometimes you get a night you will never forget, no matter how messy things become.

Hugh is now standing next to me, sweating and babbling into my ear while trying to shove a screwed-up bundle of notes into my hand.

'Here's 60, mate. Bloody hot in here, how are you? Seen anybody else? Is it any good? Have you got more? I think Barry wants something.'

'See you later Hugh, I'll be around.'

He's already squeezed his way towards the toilets, still babbling to nobody in particular.

'Hey Simon, you got . . .?'

'Hey Simon, you got . . .?'

And so it goes on until the stage lights go down and the band start up.

The singer stands still, staring at the crowd, holding a star-shaped tambourine that we will never hear over the wall of sound that follows.

It sounds like a Carpenters song for about five seconds until the fuzzy-haired drummer hits the floor toms and both guitars kick in. It is deafening and demands our attention. There is nothing else going on in this room now, no way you could talk to anybody or even think about going to the bar. I am rooted to the spot, can't move even if I want to.

I'm not sure if they're going to play a set or come into the crowd and start punching people. The immediate effect of what I'm witnessing, however, is about the same as getting a punch in the face. The song unwinds and grabs me by the head, bass reverberating through my stomach, guitars screaming into my open mouth and I can't take my eyes off the singer as he continues to just stare through us all.

We are invited in and the entire room does indeed shake along with him. They give us no option. None whatsoever.

A dingy pub in King's Cross, me and THIS band, in my world, the only world that matters. I belong here, out of my tiny mind, properly drugged up, other people's screwed-up money in my pocket, a witness to something special, still secret from the masses.

They deliver their set, by the end of which there is no doubt in my mind they won't be playing tiny venues like this much longer. I've seen hundreds of bands but this lot are clearly special. I have to meet them; we are clearly meant for each other.

There is no backstage area to speak of at this venue. Instead there's a thin corridor about 20 foot long leading to a tiny changing-room which in turn leads out onto the stage. There are about a hundred people all trying to push themselves towards the dressing-room – no way through, pass or no pass.

Hugh is shouting at me again from the other end of the corridor and between us stand another 40 or so Hughs. I can't be bothered with any of them and with only one mangled sweaty baggie left in my pocket I figure it's time to go. There will be another time to shake along with them.

Up in the Sky

Hugh's face is pressed up against the video entry screen downstairs and as usual he is shouting into the microphone.

'Simon, Simon, it's Hugh and Barry. Hello, hello, Simon, it's Hugh . . .'

'Yes, Hugh, I can see you, come on up.'

Buzz, click and slam.

Creation Records are holding a night at the Albert Hall, 'Creation Un-drugged', with a party at the Forum after, which will no doubt be attended by all the usual suspects and Hugh therefore thinks we should all go along.

By the time I've retired to the privacy of my bedroom to get 'prepared' for a night's work and Hugh and Barry have also sorted themselves out it is too late to go to the Albert Hall, so we head up to Kentish Town. Passes are sorted, VIP area located, crumpled bundles of notes pressed into sweaty palms, drinks paid for, nonsense talked, heads turned back and forth, nothing interesting happens, par for the course.

I head off to the toilets to sort out the bundles of screwed-up notes in my pockets. I am sweating profusely as I count and fold the proceeds of the night so far before tucking it away in the sole of my Pumas, leaving enough to get a few drinks in one pocket and the remaining goodies in the other. Suitably adjusted, I rack out a huge line, snnniiiiffffff . . . ahhhhhhh . . . then unlock the door.

And there, standing in front of me, is the singer from the band I fell totally in love with in King's Cross.

I don't say anything as I'm gagging slightly. I bend over the sink to splash some water on my face and when I look up he's checking himself in the mirror, obviously liking what he sees.

'Your band are the fucking business, mate, swear to god, man. Saw you in King's Cross, fucking blew me away, mate. Seriously mental, mate, you lot are the fucking business.'

'Nice one, what's yer name?'

'Simon, pleased to meet you, fancy a line?'

'Fucking right, mate, mad for a bit of Charlie me. Hey, lads, Simon here is going to sort us all out with a bit of Charlie.'

'Nice one, mate.'

'Nice one.'

'Sound . . . mad for it.'

I hadn't noticed the other three standing there. Well, you wouldn't, would you?

We go back into the cubicle, split open a bag, carve four lines, sniff, sniff, sniff, sniff, nod approval, shake hands and become best mates, although I seem to have somehow 'lost' a rolled-up £20.

'Nice one, Si.'

'Yeah, sorted, man, proper bit of Charlie that. Got any more?'

'Yeah, a bit. Sixty a gram, mate. It's fucking spot on, though, no shit cut into it, mate.'

'How much cash you got, lad? C'mon, Si, do it for fifties, man, eh?'

'Shut up knob'ead, you ain't even in the band. How much money have you got?'

Knob'ead pulls out a rolled-up twenty.

'Here, Si, take this, give us a bag an I'll sort out the rest later. C'mon, let's have it proper mad tonight.'

I take my £20 back, hand over a bag and for some reason don't mind in the slightest. It doesn't matter; it's just rock 'n' roll.

We head upstairs to the bar, where Hugh, noticing my new friends, slithers up, patronises them for a minute then takes me to one side to discuss credit arrangements for the evening. I quickly hand over a bag and wave him away like the annoyance he is. I'm trying to make a good first impression here.

I return to continue paying homage to the singer.

'A 'n' R men, all the fucking same, do you know what I mean?'

'Yeah, man, fucking dickheads the lot of 'em, apart from ours, of course. He's cool.'

'Of course. Want a drink, mate?'

'Nice one, Si, large Jack and Coke.'

He shuffles from side to side, never still for a minute, energy pure and impure, nodding at people he doesn't know and doesn't really want to, as long as they know who he is. He doesn't give a fuck. I like him.

I give him my mobile number and promise to catch up with them the next day to deliver some decent weed to their hotel. They leave together as they have a photo session in the morning to which I am invited although they don't know where it is yet.

'Sorted, no worries, man. I'll call ya. Nice one for the Charlie, geezer. See you later, Simon, see you later.'

There doesn't seem any reason to stay, so I head out to get a cab.

I am wired but somewhere in my head is a feeling of being in on something really special. Right in, part of, involved, made it.

I don't get the call the next day so I choose to turn up early for their gig at the Marquee. I am waiting outside when a minibus pulls up and out steps the band. The singer sees me, bowls over and we walk inside together. I get an AAA pass from the tour manager and do my duty, sticking around to hear the soundcheck, where 'I am the Walrus' gets cranked up to levels not heard since (the) who knows when? It was loud, fucking beautiful and fucking loud.

That done the brothers have an argument about who's staying at what hotel and why the older of the two always has money and the singer can't get by on his daily allowance. Seeing as he doesn't have to give me any money for his drugs I figure he's doing all right really, but it ain't about that. He is the fucking star of the show and why the fuck does his older brother have more money all the time?

'Cos I write the fucking songs, knobhead, publishing money. You'll get yours when the album comes out.'

I sort the bass player out with some dope. He pays for some Charlie too, and I leave the backstage area to its sibling argument. There are touts asking for 50 quid outside, 50 quid for a band that have yet to release an album. People are paying too and by showtime there is not a ticket left for any amount of money.

Inside is a furnace. If the devil does indeed have the best tunes I guess he insists on serving them up at the right temperature.

They come on and it is glorious. They are untouchable and they know it, the crowd knows it and as I stumble past Richey from the Manics I think he knows it too.

They finish with 'Walrus', by which time I have decided that no matter how out of my brain I get tonight, I have witnessed something I will remember for the rest of my life.

The show is over but the rest of the night has only just begun. The backstage rider is rapidly demolished, so we go back to their hotel. Them, the girls, the boys, the white line, the cigarettes and alcohol and the Cat in the Hat.

I get home sometime the following afternoon, get the foil out and sit down to smoke some smack. As the brown powder melts, smokes and sends up its relief, I wonder how much foil you would need if you ever found a way of chasing the sun. I smile a stupid smacked-out smile and slide away, thinking I should get a band together.

Glastonbury, 1994

This needed to be a big one for me and Pete, as, for various reasons, money was not as plentiful as it should have been. There was no shortage of hard cash but our 'finance department' were regularly insisting there should be more of it heading their way, considering the amount of product being moved.

Either our business 'loans' had been too plentiful and not collected on time, which was probably not true, or we'd been taking far too many Class A drugs that we should have been selling, which possibly was. Regardless, we needed to expand operations if we were to continue 'in post' and earn more cash over the summer months.

The flat Pete and I were now renting in Notting Hill cost nearly 300 quid a week. Factor in taking taxis everywhere, giving away whatever amount of coke/pills was often required to persuade a female to remove her knickers, plus the undisclosed narcotic 'slush fund' and other assorted sundries that contributed to having a good time all the time and our outgoings all added up to a tidy sum. Getting messy cost money, basically.

Did we slow down on our own personal intake? (That's the personal we told each other about and not the personal that was, well . . . personal!) Of course not! It was fucking summer, man. We were having the time of our and possibly your lives.

We decided that this year the festival service we intended to provide would require, amongst other things, a marquee of our own that would need to be manned for at least 72 hours non-stop for the duration of the weekend. If you are going to be at the centre of such things at Glastonbury, it's no use pitching a two-man tent in a hedge miles away from your people and being in a coma for the duration, is it?

As for the 'other things' and how to best distribute them, that was very much my department. Over the previous years I'd made some very useful connections on the site, which meant we could get in undetected and then get even further in to make our wares available to the great and the good in the backstage area. So now it was just our basic camping equipment and our 'set-list' that needed sorting out.

We visited an army-surplus store to try to buy a decent-sized marquee but ended up leaving with a 15-man green tent – not quite what we'd been after but it looked pretty good when we'd eventually erected it against the hedge behind the pyramid stage. We then purchased the biggest portable stereo we could find and about a million batteries, a couple of rugs, some lanterns and a small wood burner, as an afterthought. We also got a couple of sleeping bags, just in case.

I phoned Keith the Bastard and after a bit of haggling secured the use of a four-berth caravan to serve as an office/secure place to stash 'things'. This would be parked a safe distance from the backstage area, up in the travellers' field. Most importantly he agreed to meet us outside the festival in Pilton village and get us and our 'equipment' in – for a price of course. We also rented four long-range walkie-talkies, two expensive mobile phones and, after a few lines of coke later that evening, nearly managed to book a helicopter to take us off the site on the Sunday from the backstage compound. At the last minute we failed to secure the necessary deposit money, seeing as our cash was ring-fenced for the rest of our weekend's shopping list.

The finished list?

- Nine ounces of very decent Colombian cocaine, into which we cut an ounce of baby's teething powder, creating an ounce of 'free' Charlie for ourselves and other 'important' people who might need bringing onside, thus leaving approximately 252 grams of coke to sell for the weekend, which felt about right.
- 500 very strong Es (speckled doves, if you must know)
- 100 hits of acid
- Half a kilo of weed
- Nine ounces of Indian Hash
- Two ounces of amphetamine
- Three bottles of Chivas Regal
- Four crates of Stella
- 400 Marlboro Lights
- 20 packets of Rizzla
- Digital scales
- 1,000 little plastic bags
- Toilet paper, ten rolls
- Chewing gum

There was also some other stuff neither of us admitted to having, which was:

- Heroin
- Tinfoil
- Bicarbonate of soda

- A large spoon
- A Blur CD

As lists go, for a long weekend in the countryside it looked adequate. Maybe could have done with a few more pills, but hey, we'd survive.

On departure day our festival equipment was packed into a large blue holdall, chucked into the back of a hire car and along with the tent then driven very carefully from the flat in London to a pub a few miles from the festival site, where we were met, as agreed, by Keith, who wanted payment there and then.

'Keith, give me a little while to get a fucking drink, then I've got to get this lot backstage and put this fucking tent thingy up. Bastard thing weighs a tonne, mate. Your "wages" are packed away somewhere in the middle, anyway.'

Keith smiled his bastardly smile, 'Oh, no problem. I've got an on-site security jeep here. Come on.'

I didn't get to have my pint; Keith was suddenly in a hurry.

We drove, lights flashing, pulses quickening, straight through what seemed like the whole of Avon and Somerset's finest who were manning roadblock after roadblock, then numerous other festival security checks before getting onto the site and driving right up behind the main stage, where Keith deposited us in a corner of the field 150 yards from the main backstage bar.

Fuck jumping the fence!

We (Keith) had our 'hospitality area' erected in half an hour, finishing just as my mate Mike appeared. Mike's job was to issue backstage passes to those who, for whatever reason, had secured the 'privilege'. I gave him what he wanted and in return he gave me what I needed to do my work.

An hour later we were suitably attired with the requisite AAA passes to ensure our safe passage through whatever backstage areas we would need to travel and were back in the Jeep, driving across site to see the caravan, where we spent a few hours unpacking, drinking, sniffing, rolling and talking about the weather forecast, which according to the Bastard, was looking good. Personally, given the amount of drugs we had in our possession, I wasn't too bothered what the weather was going to do. It seemed unlikely that I'd notice.

On the Monday there were still three days to go before the general public were allowed in and six before the only band I was contemplating going to see were due to play. I considered them the only band that really mattered at this particular point in time and also believed we were now mates. This was partially because I actually believed they liked me as a person, which gave me some much-needed self-worth or at the very least made me feel important as I attempted to cling to their coat-tails, and partially because just maybe they were? The truth of course was, as was often the case, I would have liked them either way. I had a habit of mistaking people tolerating me as a sign of friendship.

Pete and I congratulated ourselves repeatedly before both excusing ourselves to have a bit of 'personal space' to 'chill out' a little more, which involved him going for a wander to possibly try to locate some tinfoil from somewhere and me not having to because I had brought some of my own, which I wasn't prepared to tell him about at this point in proceedings.

How do people know how and where to score the best drugs at a festival?

Dunno, never asked 'em, never had to. I always took my own and this time people seemed to find out where I was pretty quickly just by word of mouth – gurning, spittle-flecked word of mouth mainly.

After I had sorted myself out, there were other people who also needed to be looked after in order to allow things to run with the minimum risk of interruption.

Always, always, always, sort out the head of backstage security. He will most probably be Scottish, not really into drugs but aware that many of his staff that weekend will require something to keep their eyelids apart. You give him as much speed as he requires, and when his workforce are pretty much all from Glasgow, that's a lot of speed. This is a narcotic loss-leader but you can now be sure you are unlikely to get nicked and your punters will also feel safe when they are reclining in your hospitality area, racking out lines, swallowing things or attempting to roll a joint while coming up on a . . .

'Fuck me! This pill is strong!'

If, as you are always quick to inform new punters, your product is as good as you say it is, they will come back, usually with friends who also want some and therefore hoping to get something free for introducing them to you. That's how it works – always has done, always will.

And so it did.

The people came, the sun shone, I wore a leopard-skin top hat and looked stupid but didn't care as various pop stars, attendant crews and liggers mooched around backstage.

We saw them; they saw us. Our hospitality area often had people waiting outside to get in as money and plastic baggies changed hands. People told us they loved us; we took their money and thanked them as they left with their little plastic bags. Hundreds of little plastic bags, hundreds of idiotic, smiling, drug-fuelled platitudes such as, 'Mate, you're the fucking best dealer at the best festival in the world.'

Yeah, I know.

Any sign of paranoia?

Not really. The Scottish security guards were doing their job just fine and we felt well looked after as we looked after our punters well.

How much money was there?

Who was counting

No idea, I wasn't counting; making money wasn't really the point as far as I was concerned.

My friends from Manchester arrived and I made sure I was the first person they saw as they fell out of their bus.

The singer saw me, left his girlfriend to put up her tent alone and came back to mine, where I gave him his festival survival bag and packed a chillum full of skunk weed just for starters. Like a good rock star, he smoked it in one big hit and the next twenty minutes turned out to be the longest period of time I ever spent with him without hearing him speak.

Pete called me on the walkie-talkie and I shut up shop to get re-supplied back at the caravan, leaving my rock 'n' roll star to wander about trying to find his head, the rest of his band and the stage he was shortly due to perform on!

Trip to HQ over I waved my AAA pass to just about everyone within a five-foot radius then got myself onto the side of the stage to wait and pay homage.

I watched from less than 20 feet away as they went through their set, smiled back at the singer as he walked off at the end and signalled for me to follow him. I didn't want to follow him; I wanted to actually be him. This is a good indication as to how incredible I thought his band was that day and how little I thought of myself on a regular basis if I didn't have enough drugs in my system.

I gave him some drugs. He didn't bother asking if I wanted any money; I didn't bother asking for any.

Within minutes he was surrounded by people demanding a moment with a proper rock 'n' roll star and offering praise and adulation. I was surrounded by people wanting drugs on credit until we were all back in London. We both did what was expected of us.

Towards the end of the afternoon, those seeking 'something on tick till we get back to London, mate' start to outnumber those with cash in their hands to spend.

What to do?

I am a dealer. These people are the customers. We are all on way too much E. So it's a yes, then. We love each other anyway, so it's no big deal.

The Scottish security guards passed by to say hello just as I was counting some money.

'Ye all right, mate?'

'Yeah, cool, mate. You wanna line?'

'Nah, that stuff turns ye intae a cunt, laddie.'

'Oh, OK.'

It occurred to me at some point on the Sunday afternoon that the backstage area of Glastonbury this particular year was probably the coolest place on earth. Or maybe it was the effects of all the money and drugs?

Hope, fantasy, good drugs, bad drugs and the people who take them? Whatever it was, it was fucking amazing. The sun shone all weekend too, until eventually the plastic bags were gone. Shortly after which so were Pete and I, but not by helicopter. Still, you can't have it all, can you?

Manchester

We are out raving in Hulme, in what remains of the partially demolished shopping centre, which at this precise moment in time is inhabited by a few hundred utterly smashed to pieces, northern, pill-munching lunatics, a number of whom are sitting next to me on top of the roof of a derelict shop, perhaps once the destination for kids sent out to get their parents 20 Embassy or a pint of milk. Neither item, nor anything remotely resembling a newspaper, is currently on sale should you venture up onto the aforementioned roof and discover the Cat in the Hat holding court with his fellow rooftop ravers, informing them that he is the 'official chemist' to the band currently touted as the biggest thing to come out of their hometown since The Roses, and, as such, they can be assured that his chemical wares are of an appropriate strength. It is also no secret that his current 'employers' enjoy more than a passing acquaintance with the celebrity sherbet and happy pills.

Tonight's ad hoc festivities are really just a precursor for tomorrow's trip up to Glasgow and the inaugural T in the Park festival, where, no doubt, thousands of Scotland's indie kids will soon fall in love with the glorious rock 'n' roll wall of sound produced by Manchester's finest.

'Where am I anyway?' says I to the blonde pillhead gently grooving along to whatever it is the DJ is conducting affairs with 30 feet below us.

'On a roof, you daft southern twat.'

'Yeah, I know I'm on a roof, babe. That's why we're all sitting down, isn't it? It's too dangerous to get up and dance.'

She gets up and shakes her dungaree-clad ass to the music, seemingly oblivious to the possibility of being crippled for life or killed should she fall from her current perch.

'What, babes? Gi's another of them pills, Mr Cat in the Hat on a Hot Tin Roof, or whatever the fuck you're called . . . Come on . . . fuckin' mad fer it, me.'

We were all, of course, utterly fucking mad for it, whatever 'it' was, which currently, in my case anyway, was the possibility of getting the occupier of those dungarees out of them at some point before meeting the band the next day for the drive to Glasgow.

She gets her pill – two, in fact – as does her equally cute mate. Speckled doves – possibly the best concentration of MDMA ever pressed into tablet form. I don't care about not getting any money in return. I have plenty more and am going to make a small fucking fortune over the next few days as I endeavour to fuel the supersonic train of my favourite band, its entourage and whoever else requires my services as we go on the rampage in Scotland.

'Hulme, babes.'

'What?'

'You're in Hulme.'

'No, I'm not. I live in London – that's home.'

'Ha, ha, ha, you silly southern cunt. I said Hulme, not home. Fookin' love this tune, me. Bye.'

And off she goes, wobbling along the roof and back down into the party pit below.

Never mind, I didn't like her that much anyway and, besides, I've got to try to locate the flat I'm staying at tonight, inside which I have stashed the rest of my 'work' for the upcoming trip, which makes it kind of important that I don't get left up here on the roof in Hulme, or wherever the fuck I am.

I know where I'm going tomorrow, though, and the van that's taking us there is leaving in a few hours' time. There's clearly no fucking chance in hell, or Hulme to be more precise, that I'm going to get any sleep, so, leaving my vantage point, I crawl along the spine of the roof and go in search of my 'boss'.

'He's got off, Si. Told me to look after yer and make sure you don't get fookin' robbed of all them pills. Gi's one, eh?'

The singer has indeed 'got off' but his mate Sid seems happy enough to look after me for the next few hours before we finally end up back at the flat, where I avail myself of more than a little bit of something to keep my eyes open. It's going to be a long drive and an even longer weekend.

Mad for it?

Are you kidding? I was made for being mad for it, just as long as I'd got my own private stash of instant nothingness about my person, of course.

As I close the door to my room and begin bagging up my coke for the impending day's work, I pull some tinfoil out of my pocket, roll up a tube, sprinkle some smack onto the foil and chill until the band arrive in the van a few hours later.

Supersonic?

Our white transit van has come to a non-scheduled stop due to the soon-to-be-ex-driver of the aforementioned vehicle having neglected to notice that it required diesel, not petrol, if its passengers were to be delivered to Glasgow on time that day.

'You're fookin' sacked as soon as the fookin' AA get here, you stupid cunt!'

We are on the hard shoulder of the motorway, a mile past the petrol station that was the scene of the mistake.

The passengers have decided they require something from the Cat in the Hat's bag while they continue their game of Frisbee and wait for the AA to arrive. The owner of the bag is trying to figure out how long he might be spending in jail should its contents be discovered by anyone other than the band and its entourage, most of whom are now throwing a small orange disc back and forth across the busy lanes of the carriageway we are no longer travelling along.

'Come on, Si. Fookin' sort us out a line, eh? Do us a pill, too, while ye're at it, eh?'

And so it goes on.

I do what I'm there to do. I had hoped, however, to be in the more rarefied air of a backstage compound when doing so, rather than the fume-heavy environs of a motorway hard shoulder near fucking Carlisle, but you know, when it comes on top, and all that!

I conclude that if in fact it does 'come on top', the voracious appetite for chemicals of the Manchester (City) Frisbee team, currently going through some impromptu practice, would probably be sufficient to ensure that everything contained in my weekend kitbag was consumed at the first sign of the Old Bill stopping to say hello. There are ten of us present – OK, nine. The fucking driver's sacked and he's getting fuck all. We are, of course, all mad for it; it won't be a problem.

Thankfully for me and the bank balance of the people from whom I'd 'borrowed' my weekend's refreshments the AA man arrives before any members of the British transport police pull over and start sniffing about. We are already sniffing rather too much and looking more than a little lively for it to go unnoticed, and I am convinced it is only a matter of time before Dibble turn up.

Yes, I'm paranoid! So would you be if you'd not slept for 36 hours and had your fingerprints all over the contents of that fucking bag.

'What stupid dickhead put petrol in a diesel? This van is going nowhere. I'm going to have to organise a tow truck. How many of you are there?'

'Nine!'

'Right, well, I can take four with me now. When's the gig? The tow truck can take the rest but it'll be a few hours. We're very busy today.'

I immediately start recalculating if there will be enough of us left after the band leave with the AA man to consume my goodies should the Old Bill turn up while we wait for the tow truck.

The man who writes the songs makes an executive decision.

'Right, obviously I'm going with the AA man now, cos I'm in fookin' charge and I've got press interviews in three hours' time. Simon, you're coming with me for obvious reasons.'

I don't hear his explanation as to why he chose the other two passengers, as my ego has just exploded. Within seconds I'm sitting inside the AA truck, opening the bag and racking out long lines as we travel along the motorway again, leaving the bemused and somewhat pissed-off Frisbee players to continue their game until the other tow truck arrives.

Fuck it! They needed the practice!

Thankfully they were much better at playing songs than they were at Frisbee.

'You are my personal chemist this weekend and as such you need to remain within 20 feet of me for the duration, OK?'

Snnnnniffffffffffffffffffffffffffffffffffffffffffff.

'Of course, it'll be my pleasure.'

'It's your fookin' job, Simon!'

Oh, yeah, so it is. Nice work if you can get it, too, eh?

We are safely ensconced in a room in a Glasgow hotel, making final preparations before getting a taxi to take us to the festival, where my 'boss' is about to make his entrance and begin the by now regular occurrence of being told what he already knew.

'Your band are fucking top, mate. You're gonna be massive, want a drink?'

'You ready yet, Mr Chemist?'

Snnnnniiiiiffffffffffffffffffffffffffffffffffffffffff.

'Born ready, boss. Let's go.'

The weekend's festivities are already in full swing as we navigate the 'normal' people queuing to get their passes issued and gain entrance to the backstage area. We obviously don't have to stand in line or give our names – well, my boss doesn't and a cursory 'He's with me' is sufficient to secure me the AAA laminate that is now being pressed into the face of the security guard standing between us and the excesses of the VIP area that contains my employer's 'people' and therefore my 'people', too.

There are roughly 100 yards of grass between us and the bar, inside which are the vast majority of label bosses, A/R men, promoters, press, music journalists, assorted 'cool' people and other nefarious individuals who make up the rock 'n' roll fraternity. It's absolutely heaving in there.

As we swagger towards the assembled masses, I remain, as requested, a few feet behind the chief, whom I fully expect to shortly be mobbed by the professional well-wishers, arse lickers and maybe even some people that genuinely like him before he even gets to the entrance of the marquee.

There is suddenly a minor stampede of such people, who have clearly spotted him as he approaches. I fall back a few more feet, not wanting to cramp his style, so to speak. There then follows a moment that on some levels sums up the whole sorry business very nicely.

I am instantly surrounded by a drug-hungry scrum, all of whom are clearly more interested in speaking to me than going into full-on 'You're a fucking genius' mode with my employer.

My boss is briefly bypassed and left to get his own drink, while I deal with the mob that surround me but not the writer of one of the greatest debut albums of all time.

'Hey, Simon, really good to see you, mate. You got any . . .?'

'Hey, Simon, thank fuck you're here, no one's got any . . .'

'Hey, Simon, can you do us some tick until I get to a cashpoint?'

'Hey, Simon, do you accept cards?'

Me, my ego and my bag of tricks have arrived. Tonight, I'm a rock 'n' roll star.

Except, of course, I'm not.

Snnnifffffffffffffffffffffffffffffffffffffffffffffffffffffffffffffffffff.

Or am I?

Who fucking cares, anyway?

I care, I just don't know that I do, or indeed, how much.

Twenty-four sleepless hours later and ten thousand of Scotland's indie boys and girls are demanding that the Manchester (City) Frisbee team, now up to its full complement thanks to the arrival of the singer, take to the stage and prepare to deliver in person what the music papers have been frothing about since the *Melody Maker* put them on its front cover just a few months and a lot of hysteria ago.

The inside of the huge marquee feels like a sauna, a massively over-populated sauna heavily pregnant with expectant fans swimming in alcohol and quite possibly some of the contents of the kitbag belonging to the Cat in the Hat.

The Cat in the Hat, meanwhile, is standing centre stage, out of his mind, riding a wave of MDMA and soaking up the inebriated fervour of those gathered in front of him. Footballs and supercharged Scottish people are tossed about in the seething maelstrom that, for some strange reason, the band's manager had decreed needed a bit of geeing up before his charges take the stage.

That's a bit like saying Mount Vesuvius could have done with a bit more lava pre-eruption but when offered the chance to get onstage and preach to the converted for a few seconds before the gig I wasn't exactly about to say no, was I?

'OK, Scotland, are you ready?'

The reply is affirmative.

'Yeeeeeeeeeeeeessssssssssssssssssssssssssssssssssssssssssssssssssssssssssssssssss ssssssssssssssssssssssssssssssssssssssssssss!'

'OK, then, let's fucking have it for the greatest rock 'n' roll band in the fucking world, the Manchester (City) Frisbee team!' Or words to that effect.

I am sent reeling by an invisible wall of energy, sweat, drugs, booze, smoke, sex, desire, hope, hormones and a few footballs, as behind me five people walk onstage, tune up, turn on, feed into and return with interest that same wall of energy.

I couldn't move, talk or think anything other than, THIS IS WHAT IT FEELS LIKE!!

This is what I need.

This could be enough.

I am almost crying as the singer taps me on the shoulder, my moment of pretend rock 'n' roll superstardom over. The chief is already into the first few bars of the opening song and he's earnt the right to shake along with his people. I might well have contributed in some tiny way to the hysteria of the masses, certainly those who have VIP passes and are now gathered at the side of the stage, but it is not my church they are demanding to inhabit nor my sermon they are clamouring to hear.

What I could just about make out, in that moment of 'borrowed' adulation, battling to make itself heard over the noise of the people and the music they are screaming to be swept away by, is a voice inside me that says, *'You are a clueless, fraudulent, desperate cunt and if they all knew what you were really like, they'd fucking hate you.'*

It takes a huge line of cocaine and another pill, sniffed and swallowed before they finish the first song, to drown out that voice and I can then also celebrate as they obliterate every last soul assembled and we all sing along and really feel like we are going to live forever.

Do I have enough drugs to last that long?

The heroin in my pocket tells me I do and that's why I now have it with me at all times.

Holidays in the Sun

All this hanging out with rock 'n' roll stars was getting stressful, so maybe I needed a holiday? I could plan the next move in my still imminent but definitely going to happen assault on the music business. Surely success was just around the corner, what with my industry connections?

Yeah, right! Probably just around the same corner as the teenager on his BMX I was looking for once again as I stood suffering from 'food poisoning', waiting for him and his instant cure.

Of course I'd told myself it wasn't going to happen to me. I had convinced myself I was an opiate tourist, just passing through rather than setting up camp. Addiction was for people with nothing to live for, not those on the cusp of living forever!

Despite providing a remedy for the self-obsessed nonsense that masqueraded as my thought processes and subsequent 'feelings' by completely removing me from them and thus providing an instant cure to the ever-present guilt, shame, lack of self-worth and other assorted nonsense fuelling my internal conundrum of how to cope with the above and function in the world, smack addiction was not going to happen to me.

That's the lie – the root of all the other lies that follow sooner or later. The lie you choose to believe because, despite ever increasing evidence to the contrary, the denial is so beautifully wrapped up by the opiates caressing you as they glide through the bloodstream. You actually believe that you really do just have a touch of flu or perhaps a slight case of food poisoning as you wake up again after a few months of convincing yourself, 'I'll have a day off it tomorrow, won't be a problem. Yeah, tomorrow, of course, that's it. Tomorrow, after I manage to get the things I need to get done today sorted out, the first of which is to get some heroin to deal with this fucking food poisoning.'

My secret affair with heroin didn't stop me using other drugs, though, and cocaine in particular fuelled my belief that fame and glory were soon going to be mine for the taking.

Hugh, however, had not seemed particularly convinced about the prospects of my pending superstar status during the previous few days we'd just spent demolishing my stash, not that I much cared what he thought all the while he'd been pulling crumpled £50 notes from his wallet.

'Yeah, H, my band's going to be called Limousine, mate, yeah . . . sniiffffffffffffffffffffffffffffffffffffffffffffffff . . . Limousine, man. It'll be really cool when we're waiting in a posh hotel lobby and some man shouts, "Car for Limousine," and it will be a big fuck-off limo, do ya know what I mean, Hugh? Do you get it, man?'

Sniff, sniffffffffffffffffffffffffffffffff.

'Ambulance for Limousine the way you're going, Simon.'

Sniff, sniff.

'Hey, that sounds fucking great, Hugh, that's what I'll call the album. Nice one. Here, have a line on me.'

We were sitting in my flat in Notting Hill at 'we've just run out of coke o'clock' on a Sunday morning and Hugh and I had been awake since going out clubbing and rubbernecking at Smashing on Friday night.

'All back to mine after, everyone, eh?'

My 'friends' had been happy to accept my hospitality, of course, particularly those with no money who were clinging on to those that did. Now, however, it was just the two of us sitting there, smashed to fucking pieces, as I wondered how he did it, just coke, coke, coke all weekend. He must have been wired to fuck.

Me? Well, I had a few baggies of instant solution/instant denial in my bedroom next to an industrial-size roll of tinfoil and a bottle of Valium. I was coked up, wrapped up, smacked up and arrogant as fuck in my drug-addled state as I insisted to Hugh that I would soon find the band I was looking for and fuck everyone who thought I was just a drug dealer. 'I'll fucking show you all soon. Success is just round the corner, you fools!'

Eventually I managed to kick Hugh out then phoned a dealer who sold my kind of drugs and went to wait on a corner for the teenager on a BMX who ran them about. I scored and returned home.

Just as I was nodding off, dreaming my opiate-assisted nonsense, Pete came crashing through the front door and into my bedroom with the man from Peckham and Gazza.

'Wake up, superstar. We're going on holiday!'

'What the fuck are you talking about? What holiday? Where? How?'

'It's booked. Saw an offer on the telly last night. We're going to Kos for a week. Come on, get your passport and pack a bag. We've got a plane to catch!'

'You're joking. Fuck off, I'm knackered.'

The three of them were standing in my room, grinning, bags in hand and obviously not joking. Within an hour we were all sitting in a black cab on the way to Victoria to catch the Gatwick Express, which was halfway to the airport before I realised I had left something important in the cabinet by the side of my bed. Fuck!

I dug around inside my pockets and my spirits rose a little as I discovered a small plastic baggie amongst the coins inside. The coins were spent on Kit-Kats at the airport, the chocolate quickly discarded, foil cleaned, tube rolled and within five minutes of take-off I was in the toilet, greedily sucking up my in-flight meal.

I had been nodding out inside for half an hour and dribbled all over my white Manchester (City) Frisbee team T-shirt before being disturbed by a knock from the stewardess. I opened the door.

'Are you OK, sir?'

She took a good look at me and shook her head but didn't wait for my answer.

'I think you'd better sit down and try to get some sleep . . . sir.'

Heading towards my seat I passed Pete on his way to the toilet I had just vacated.

'You forgot to brush your teeth, mate,' he muttered as we passed.

Digging out a small mirror from my wash bag, then licking off the specks of coke that covered most of its surface, I had a look at myself, but not in any kind of thoughtful, self-reflective manner, of course. Fuck that! My front teeth were covered in black heroin tar, I had speckles of cocaine all over my nose and my eyes looked like one was trying to kick fuck out of the other. I was a mess and therefore clearly in need of a drink or three.

Beverages ordered, I dipped a napkin into my brandy and ginger and proceeded to try to wash my face and scrape the crap off my teeth before we got to our destination and had to face the authorities at the airport, the location of which I was by now unable to remember. I had no idea where the fuck we were going but wherever it was I hoped they served heroin with whatever other local delicacies they might have on offer.

I then passed out for the rest of the flight and indeed most of the journey from the local airport to our apartment, where I almost immediately passed out again.

Kardemena, on the Greek island of Kos, was once a beautiful little fishing village, possibly up to roughly the same time that my beloved Liverpool Football Club were kings of English football. They had clearly declined in tandem, as it was now also shit.

In case any of you were wondering as to how/why someone from Weston-super-Mare became a fan of a team based hundreds of miles away, the answer is not as obvious (or not) as you might think.

Shortly after my dad died, my mum's cousin took me to Highfield Road, then home to Coventry City Football Club, who were at that time about as average a team as you could find. My dad and I had watched football on TV together but he didn't support any particular team and I was still trying to figure out where to place my flag, so to speak. I went to school near Coventry, who were in the First Division. My family home was near Bristol, and City were also troubling the middle section of that table on a regular basis too, so as I sat watching the match, still devastated by the loss of my daddy a few months earlier, it was suggested to me by my grown-up friend that I should choose a team to follow.

The Sky Blues were in the process of actually beating Liverpool, the then regular champions of Europe and the old First Division, although judging from the lack of atmosphere coming from the home supporters you could have been forgiven for thinking they were waiting for a bus rather than closing in on a memorable victory over probably the greatest British team ever seen, before or since.

The away end, however, was a different spectacle altogether. Thousands of Scousers waving flags and scarves, dressed in expensive, uber-cool tracksuit tops, singing songs, taking the piss and looking like they were having the best day out of their lives as they watched their idols fall to a 1–0 defeat.

As I gazed upon both sets of fans, a decision was made. I was a Red!

No offence to the Sky Blues but I think it's fair to say I had enough misery to cope with already and King Kenny and Co. looked a better bet to provide some regular, much-needed happiness in my life than the men in blue, despite that afternoon's victory.

Considering I eventually succumbed to the lure of instant gratification provided by drugs, I'm both surprised and grateful I didn't give in to the urge on that wet and cold afternoon in Coventry to go with that day's victors, instead making a choice better suited for what followed in the '80s, which proved much kinder to me and my inner glory-hunting twat as well, at least as far as football was concerned.

I digress.

I walked along the strip, looking for the others, as by the time I'd woken up they had gone out, leaving me a note informing me they would be drinking by the beach. I hadn't now risen because I'd had enough sleep – if only! My coma was disturbed due to the fact my body needed more heroin. Not that I had a problem with it, of course. Certainly not while I still had some left anyway, which, ten minutes after waking up, I didn't, as I tossed the screwed-up Kit-Kat foil into the bin by the side of my bed and decided to have some breakfast.

The 'most important meal of the day' consisted of the last few mouthfuls of duty-free brandy from the bottle at the side of my bed and the line of Charlie somebody had kindly left out for me, or more likely forgotten about earlier.

Stumbling down into the town I found a strip of 'British' bars, all of which were occupied by families of tattooed, moustachioed, sunburnt, pram-pushing holiday-makers; the men folk didn't look too hot either as I mooched in and out of various restaurants called The Black Swan, The King George or The Red Lion, all serving proper 'home-cooked' British food.

If this wasn't hell already, the first spasm of flu/food poisoning withdrawal suddenly sent me lurching into the nearest toilet to puke, from which I emerged 25 minutes later.

I shuffled away to locate my friends, or more precisely Pete and the contents of his toiletry bag, inside which I was sure he would have a remedy for my ills, stricken as he was with the same strain of food poisoning/flu/denial as myself.

The boys had found a bar called The Bubble, which its Greek owner thought hysterical.

'You know, lads, bubble and squeak, innit?'

We sat and drank in sunglasses and silence, watching the parade of footie shirts go by. Fuck me, England's finest were all there: Carlisle, Stockport County, Rotherham and obviously loads of really ugly overweight bastards wearing Man United shirts, which I despised the most as I tried to not hate myself too much for leaving my stash of heroin back in the UK.

The Mancs were an ugly distraction from my nasty predicament, whereas Pete was the solution. He went to the bar and I slipped off after him.

'How much gear have you brought with you? I forgot mine, mate. I'm out.'

'Me too.'

The world stopped instantly as my inner despair became outwardly obvious.

'Don't fuck about, Pete! You must have brought some with you, you've got a habit.'

'Oh, and you don't, Si?'

He's a cunt.

'I've got a few Valium, mate, and a bit of methadone.'

He's God.

'Besides, it's not like we've got a real habit, is it, Si?'

Told you he was similarly afflicted, didn't I?

I accepted his offer of a beer and returned to my seat. Fuck it, I'll be all right. It's not as if I'm a junkie, is it?

Six hours later I staggered out of the bar and headed back to the apartment, hoping in vain that some heroin might have magically appeared on the screwed-up piece of Kit-Kat foil I'd binned earlier. I then proceeded to tear my luggage apart as I waited for Pete to return and give me some methadone. My search brought me half an E and three blue Valium, two of which were swallowed on the spot. A tear ran down my cheek as I sat on the bed wondering if I could get an early flight home.

All I could see when I closed my eyes were the contents of my bedside cabinet at home. My stomach turned over again as I threw up, disgorging the pills I had just taken. I quickly picked them out of the puke and swallowed them again.

Desperation sent me scurrying back to the bar to try to persuade Pete to hurry up and sort me out, which, bless him, he did but the ineffectiveness of the tiny amount of methadone he could spare to relieve my discomfort left me with no choice but to neck my remaining Valium and hope the next day might not actually be the worst of my life.

The rest of the night became an alcoholic mess. Little was said by either me or Pete as we watched Gazza and the man from Peckham actually laughing and having 'fun'. I hated them equally. The finale of the first evening of our holiday found me bent over the toilet bowl, puking my guts and cheap booze into the sewers of hell.

Four days and nights were then spent either in bed or in a Valium/alcohol-assisted puddle on the beach, getting over my 'touch of flu', before I woke up on day five of the holiday starving and tired but willing to get out and see something other than the toilets as I resurfaced from my first proper heroin cluck convinced of a few pertinent ideas.

The first: that it was, of course, going to be my last, which I informed my fellow travel companions about at great length; the second: that I would only use heroin on 'special' occasions from now on, which I told nobody about.

There were, of course, plenty of other utterly ridiculous ideas rattling around inside my head, one of which was that we needed to hire scooters and go in search of the lesbians!

At some point during my convalescence, Gazza had heard that there was 'a fuckin' lesbians convention going on, on the other side of the island . . . or something like that, I dunno, I was drunk . . .'

He had not discovered any attractive, single – or married for that matter – women so far during his evenings spent making a drunken idiot of himself while trawling the local bars and he was now sure that the law of averages dictated there must be a few bisexuals amongst the Sapphic sisterhood apparently gathered together for the 'Greek leg of the world clam-jousting tournament', as he so delicately put it.

Fuck it! What else were we going to do? Go and look at historical artefacts?

The following few hours saw us trying to ask local farmers if they knew where the lesbians were staying.

'Sir, sir, excuse me, you speak English? Er . . . the "Lesbos", you know, er, Lesbos' Hotel?'

The local Greek farming community had clearly not been invited and needless to say we never discovered if Gazza's information was correct or just the result of too much cocaine, vodka and wishful thinking. Instead, we trundled around all day, trying to act like 'normal' people, eventually finding a quiet beach bar where we settled in for a drink or ten.

Someone had some Charlie left, which was dispatched during the evening's revelry, and so by the time the bar owner asked us to leave, we were all wired enough to not entertain for one second the idea that perhaps we should not have been driving. Miraculously we got back to the apartment in one piece, which was more than can be said for the chicken that the man from Peckham ran over on our way home.

The final couple of days were spent on the beach, where we met some English girls who, incredibly enough, had also just spent their holiday recovering from flu/food poisoning and were now keen to help us spend the last of our cash getting wasted in The Bubble. In keeping with the prevailing attempts at normal British holidaymaker behaviour, some drunken sex occurred during the course of the final evening. It doesn't really matter who got laid and who didn't, does it? OK, I did, and it was probably the best three seconds of her life, which was also roughly the amount of time it took me to steal a bottle of whisky from the duty-free shop at the airport for the journey home the following morning. A journey that was relatively uneventful if you don't include the man from Peckham losing his passport for an hour prior to boarding, throwing up into his lap five minutes after take-off, then spending the rest of the flight unconsciously slopping puke all over himself.

That was 'normal' holidaymaker behaviour, wasn't it? It must have been, judging by the manner in which the flight attendants took one look at him and left him alone. We obviously pretended that we didn't know him.

Pete and I arrived back at our flat hungover to fuck but seemingly fully recovered from our recent bout of 'illness', a fact we chose to celebrate by immediately going out to score some heroin together.

We both had a habit again within days and naturally continued to pretend that we didn't, and as long as we had other drugs to sell it seemed a bit unfair to trouble each other with our little problem anyway.

It's My Party

There are nearly 1,000 people lining up outside the Leisure Lounge club in Holborn, London, demanding to be admitted to celebrate the launch of what is about to become the UK's fastest-selling debut album of all time.

There are ten lines of cocaine racked out on a toilet cistern inside the club. The entourage of the band who created said album are demanding to be admitted to the cubicle while the Cat in the Hat is trying to hide the remaining ounce of coke upon his person before opening the door. He then has to go to the club's entrance and figure out how he's going to make up the money already spent on the coke, which he vaguely promised to make freely available to the singer and his mates. This is a grandiose gesture that had he not just been handed a guest list from the band's record label with nearly 900 names on it might have had the desired effect of making him seem indispensable from this point on, to band, label and crew as we collectively swaggered onwards towards rock 'n' roll superstardom together, or something like that.

Snnnniffffffffffffffffffffffffffffffffffffffffffffffffffffffffffffffffff.

The Mancunian mafia banging on the cubicle door wanting their free drugs as promised clearly don't appreciate the situation and are already threatening to relieve me of my duties and my drugs and take control of the situation themselves.

'C'mon, you silly cunt, sort us out, will ya? Fookin' mad for a bit of Charlie here, eh?'

'Yeah, Si, c'mon, where's them drugs you promised us? Fookin' Cat in the Hat, or what?'

'Sort it out, lad, eh? Let's fooking have it, eh?'

I open the door and slither out as five agitated northerners descend nose first into the cubicle to squabble over the remaining powder while I stagger towards the main entrance and the throng scrambling to get inside the club.

Big Ray is on the door. He has the guest list upon which are the names and plus ones, twos, threes and fours of pretty much everybody who is anybody in the rock 'n' roll business at that time. There are also the names of plenty of people who have nothing to do with the industry but know someone who is, various tabloid journalists and of course all the people I invited personally to shake along with me and my superstar mates.

The people who are not on the guest list and therefore expected to pay for the privilege of hanging out with me are lined up separately and have already been told the club is full. The ounce of coke they were theoretically going to have paid for is shortly under attack from all sides as my guests enter the VIP area into which I have already retreated and am now trying to hide while I figure out how I'm going to pay for it along with the 200 pills I also promised free of charge to those deemed 'cool' enough to be admitted into the 'very' VIP area.

The 'very' VIP area has two full-sized, very expensive snooker tables in it, upon which Primal Scream and their mates are now holding court, spilling drinks, chopping out lines and generally not treating a snooker table in the manner to which it is accustomed.

'Eh, Si, gi's some pills, mate. C'mon, where's the free drugs, eh? Where's the drugs? Do us a gram, will ya?'

And so on.

I get a message from the front door to say that the club is now actually full but there are still 150 people outside whose names are on the list and who are really not fucking happy they cannot get in. The band's label are also not happy about this at all and want to know why I've fucked things up. I have by now swallowed three of the pills, while the rest are currently tickling the brains of the Scream's snooker team and other assorted indie boys and girls already frugging away round the tables. The potential paying guests have got bored of waiting outside and fucked off, leaving me to pick up the entire tab for what remains of the 'free' drugs.

The rest of the 'biggest night of my life' is spent locked inside a cubicle in the women's toilets, on my own, with a rapidly vanishing bag of very expensive 'free' cocaine before I manage to escape unnoticed from the venue at 'Oh my fucking god, what have I done o'clock' and have to walk home because I've no money to pay for a taxi, let alone an ounce of coke and 200 pills.

There is a message on my answerphone the next day from the owner of the club wanting to know how I intend to pay for Primal Scream's snooker session, which has resulted in the destruction of both tables.

The various music press reports about the party, however, are positively glowing.

I was not invited to help 'promote' any more band-related events ever again, nor, as I had hoped, was I seen to be indispensable in their imminent rise to fame. Apparently my guest-list fuck-up had kept the tabloid journalists locked out of the event and thus prevented the wider public from witnessing the mayhem inside, something the label bosses had hoped might make front-page in the red-tops and help boost already impressive album sales.

Surprisingly, I was not approached by either *The Economist* or the *Financial Times* to explain my personal business strategy, although a reporter from the *News of the World* did camp outside my flat for a few days, doorstepping me and asking me for an 'interview'. In true tabloid tradition, 'I made my excuses and left.'

It was time to start trawling the 'Musicians Wanted' section of the weekly music press again; I obviously wasn't cut out for the promotions game but continued lurking about helping people stay up all night as we celebrated 'Britpop' and all that entailed.

Some of those nights were fantastic; many, just like the bands involved, were not so.

Limousine

One morning I got home from another long night of bribing people with free drugs to talk to me to discover an answerphone message asking me to call somebody who appeared to know me. I had no clue who the person was but they managed a band looking for a singer and apparently the band was good – really fucking good. Returning the call still left me clueless about who I was speaking with but I pretended to know them and we arranged to meet in a rehearsal room the following day.

I made my way over to Camden, wanting something special, soulful, passionate, expecting nothing of the sort and personally capable of giving even less. I found a loud, odd-looking three piece. Loud was, of course, very good.

The drummer looked like Animal from the Muppets, which was OK for a drummer of his obvious ability – in fact, OK for a drummer full stop, really. The bass player was perfectly thin and looked like he needed to get some sleep but threw all the right shapes and his fingers were bleeding. The guitarist, initial drawbacks aside, by which I mean he reminded me of Peter Sutcliffe and was about ten feet tall, could play like a man possessed. What he was possessed with I could not fathom, nor did I really care; he could clearly make his guitar do things I was mightily impressed with as he ignored me for half an hour before the bassist suggested I try to sing a melody over the magnificent noise they'd been creating at an equally wonderful volume.

Visibly nervous, I produced a crumpled piece of paper with some hastily scribbled lyrics on it.

Suddenly I had the peculiar feeling that if I fucked up now I could kiss my notions of being a pop star goodbye. These guys are seriously good and you only get a chance like this once in a lifetime, I thought to myself, as I closed my eyes, waited for my cue and gave it my all.

Are you on board with us, riding through a night that is
never long enough,
Got a first-class smoking seat,
Take a good look
See what I see . . .

Surprisingly it sounded all right – to me at least; I don't know what the others were thinking as they had their backs to me and were looking at one another, trying to keep time. We carry on:

It's easy, follow me driving through the night with the
Limousine,
I feel the earth move, under my feet; take a good look see
what we see.

I was trying to bond and although the guitarist still refused to acknowledge my presence, the other two were now looking in my direction and nodding their heads. We worked on the song for a while before I felt my throat starting to dry up. I hadn't sung at volume for a long time, I was nervous and running out of lyrics in my head. I also wanted to know what they thought.

'Er, listen, guys, I really think you've got something. This song fucking rocks, man, but to be honest I need a drink. Anybody fancy a pint?'

Less than an hour's work and I wanted to go to the pub.

Bass player, Mr Skinny with bleeding fingers, replied.

'Yeah, sweet. We've gotta be out of here about now anyway. I could murder a pint. Anybody got any money?'

Of course I had money for beers and bonding. I also had cocaine at home, which was where we ended up after a couple of drinks and what was almost an acknowledgement that I sounded all right. I say acknowledgement; it was, in fact, the presented opinion that I didn't 'sound as bad as everybody else we've tried today'.

I took this to be at the very least a foot in the door, a door that opened a little bit more when I got more cocaine out.

I played the perfect host, putting The Who on the stereo and the Charlie on the table as I explained a bit about myself (an edited version), the music-business people that I sold drugs to, the concept of Limousine, how I'd been looking for someone with their sound for ages and then told them that I could get us in the studio next week to try to record something. I would be paying, of course. The fact I couldn't afford anything of the sort was a problem I thought I'd deal with closer to the time, my thinking being that I came as a package – voice/words and connections all combining to make me somebody they wanted/needed in their band. How they valued this package and in what order of importance they viewed the components was not something I cared to consider. If they needed me more than they wanted me, I was happy with that. Surely they'd warm to me sooner or later, eh?

Even the dangerous-looking very tall person seemed vaguely excited at the prospect of some 'free' studio time and by the end of the evening, as I saw them out, I knew I was in with a shout.

Things moved fast; cocaine has a habit of making that happen. Someone I knew fronted the recording money after hearing us rehearse, and we went into a studio where the big fella and his undeniable talent took over. Getting whatever was going on inside his head onto tape was not something I was really qualified to assist with; besides, I don't think the rest of us knew what really went on in his head until it was manifest as some glorious noise screaming out of the amplifier. Anyway, I was just there to sing over the top and supply the cocaine to expedite the creative process.

We recorded two songs. One worked; the other didn't. I thought we'd had a result – a view not shared by everyone.

'Look, it's just not right. I don't know if this is going to work out, man,' said our clearly very frustrated, very tall genius as he paced up and down in the mixing room listening to the results of our endeavours.

I got that oh so familiar sinking feeling, so I quickly scuttled into the nearest toilet, snorted a massive line of cocaine, then returned to the conversation.

I glanced at the bass player and drummer, my eyes begging for support. Skinny bleeder spoke up for me. I can't recall what he said; I was staring up at my future right in the face, desperate to hear his response.

'All right, all right, it's not that bad, but he's going to have to have some singing lessons to get his voice stronger.'

I would have taken hot-poker-up-the-arse lessons at that point.

'Yes, boss. Whatever you say. I know I've got to work on my voice but I'm up for it, man, really, big time. I'll book lessons, whatever it costs.'

It costs dedication, hard work and vision; I only dealt in shortcuts, drugs, cash and delusion.

'Listen, I reckon I can get us some good gigs, too. You know my friend Hugh that I told you about?'

'What, cokehead nightmare Hugh?'

'Yeah, that's him. Well, anyway, he's managing a signed band that is going on tour to promote their album and I reckon I can get us support on some gigs, maybe them all.'

I brought more hope and cocaine to the table to get away from the subject of my vocal issues. I was an arch-manipulator; I was desperate.

Snnniffffffffffffffffffffffffffffffffffffffffffffffffff.

'OK, make sure you call a singing coach first thing tomorrow.'

'Sure, sure, sure, I'll get the best available, no problem. First thing I'll do tomorrow, promise.'

Obviously I didn't call a singing coach until after I'd spoken to Hugh and attempted to sell him the concept of my band and convince him to get us on the tour in a few months' time.

'H, look, I'll give you half an ounce now, the rest midway through the dates. C'mon, mate, what's the problem?'

Which summed up my concept of reality perfectly.

'I don't know, Simon. I'll really have to come and see you play first. Are you lot any good? What do you sound like?'

What kind of question is that?

One that needed an answer.

'Yeah, we're fucking brilliant, H, even though we've only been together a few weeks. We're still at the writing stage but we'll have a set together in a month. Come down to the rehearsal room and have a listen, please.'

'Got any racket?'

'Yes, H, of course I have. We'll be down at Backstreet Studios all day tomorrow.'

'See you there, don't forget the . . .'

'Racket, yeah, I know.'

Ironically, H's new 'code' word for cocaine pretty much described the issue I was supposed to be trying to address with the help of the singing coach I'd completely forgotten to call, distracted as I was by my attempts to bribe my way onto the upcoming tour.

Back on the Road

Limousine got the tour support slot, the headline act's manager got paid half the 'buy-on' fee as promised (before no doubt promptly proceeding to bung it up his beak) and I ticked another box in my misinformed mental equation for personal happiness. To be more precise, Limousine got a mention in the weekly music press after a similar 'gesture' to a coke-loving journalist gave us a reasonable live review prior to our imminent jaunt up and down the country. The tour was confirmed, the ad went in the press and I was by now possibly in the running for most annoying/arrogant dickhead in the world!

Christmas 1974 – my mum, dad, auntie, grandparents and sister. Within six years only my mum, my sister and I were left.

Smiths fanatic, 1987.

This Charming Man – prior to discovering the joys of
crack in LA, 1988.

Malaysia, 1996 – the day before I returned home
and started using again.

Turning yellow in 1997.

On Holloway Road, London, 1998.

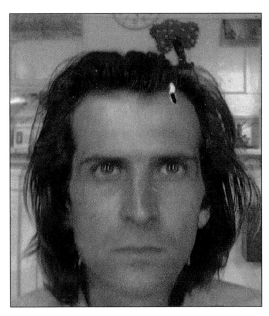

A mugshot from rehab, 2001.

Coming out of rehab yet again in 2002. I think I thought I was Sick Boy from *Trainspotting*.

Monkeyman, 2004 – trying and failing to stay clean.

2005 – the night
Monkeyman finally ended.

2006 – me and my mum. I was ten days clean, and this time, so far, I have stayed so. Note the state of my forearm.

Clean living under difficult circumstances – on my 1963
Lambretta in Southend, 2009.

The most precious gift in my life – Tabitha and me, June 2012.

There were some further details to be discussed, of course, and during a meeting of respective managers, some conditions were put in place. More singing lessons for yours truly seemed a reasonable request, particularly when the idea was sugar-coated by all concerned by suggesting that they would perhaps teach me some valuable techniques used by all 'famous' singers prior to a tour and therefore also help prevent me losing my voice during the rigours of the nightly performances that lay ahead. As I had already decided I was about to become famous, I agreed.

The only way anyone could generally make me listen to anything by now was to appeal to my ego or ask me if I had any drugs for sale, which leads to another of the issues discussed. This concerned the possibility of what both groups' respective management thought likely to inform the nightly post-gig revelry that lay ahead. Considering the narcotic preferences of the assembled cast and crew, the fact that a couple of individuals were already teetering on the brink of 'nervous exhaustion' and the fact that the support band's singer and mates, or 'entourage' as he now preferred to call them, were currently supplying almost everybody involved, the potential for things getting too messy needed to be addressed.

An executive decision was made and a cunning plan proposed, which decreed that I had to stop selling drugs and possibly not continue to take so many either – not that I ever told anyone what or how much I was using. I was given my own personalised tour T-shirt with 'Limousine' on the front and 'No, I haven't got anything' on the back. Rehab is obviously for weak-willed idiots. Why spend thousands when you can just get a T-shirt made for a few quid?

The party line now being touted, as opposed to being snorted, was clearly written on the back of my T-shirt, worn with some pride but zero conviction. I believed in the band on the front because I had to. As for what was written on the back? I went along with that because I thought that I was about to swap my status as 'supplier to the stars' to 'star being supplied'. I did however argue the point that if I was to display this stunning revelation and avoid the incessant attention of people on the hunt for drugs I would need a fresh T-shirt every night of the tour, which would cost money. The notion that this ludicrous idea, mine in case you hadn't already guessed, might in any way actually be effective did not seem to be of any real concern, conjured up as it was while coked out of my mind one night, while drinking with 'our' management. It was, after all, an insignificant fiscal issue compared to the other steadily rising costs being accrued by our management. A significant outlay had already been made on new equipment, rehearsal time, singing lessons and this would be added to very shortly by keeping us on the road and in hotels, so, being the forward-thinking, selfless, industrious type I am, I came up with another inspired solution.

Would I help to try to offset the outlay already provided by my manager to help propel me towards impending rock 'n' roll superstardom? No! But I would buy my own T-shirts, the money for which would be made by selling more drugs to purchase them and the statement on my back proclaiming I didn't sell drugs any more! This, I considered to be a touch of pure genius as I sat at home smoking heroin, hoovering up coke and plotting my upcoming fundraising campaign at the Phoenix Festival.

Phone calls were made, guest lists sorted out, tents purchased, supplies obtained and a few days later I was busy oiling the 'wheels' of industry, or at the very least chipping away at the nation's supply of small plastic zip baggies and going for first prize in the coked-up cunt of the year competition while in pursuit of whatever it was I thought I was pursuing. I was having 'fun'.

I'd been backstage for a few days, hopped on and off most of the assembled tour buses, sold a lot of drugs, taken a lot of drugs and given away a lot more drugs. I'd spent a night in a tent smoking crack with and fending off the sweaty advances of a drummer, and been taken 'hostage' for an afternoon by a band considered to be a mid-'90s human narcotic landfill site as they tried to figure out if I had any smack to sell.

My main partner in crime that weekend was the keyboard player from a band who were still just about popular enough at that point to afford him a credit card of the 'right' variety and with which we would make regular 'withdrawals' from the bag of coke I had stashed under my real tent – as opposed to the decoy tent I'd set up.

This was where we now found ourselves as we sat, sweated, talked bollocks and hoovered up two half-gram lines each in the mid-morning sunshine. As we were about to stagger back out into the fray we both suddenly realised we needed to find somewhere to have a coke-induced shit.

'Where's the nearest bog, Si?'

'Fuck knows, mate. Here, have a line of smack. That'll keep you from shitting yourself for a bit. Works for me every time.'

I racked out two more lines and within seconds the need to pebbledash the nearest plastic toilet had vanished.

'That's better, Si. Nice one, mate. Shall we do an E?'

As the smack kicked in and kissed the cocaine already massaging my brain cells I pulled out a couple of pills from my stash, chucked one in my friend's mouth, swallowed one myself, licked my finger and cleaned up the remaining combination of brown and white powder from the CD case, rubbed the powder over my gums, lit a joint, then retrieved my work bag from the corner of the tent. A quick check confirmed I had enough product for my morning rounds of the backstage area. The bag was loaded, as were we, but just to be on the safe side we also popped a couple of blue Valium each before heading out to work.

'Right, mate, you fit? I fancy a drink.'

Keyboard man nodded his approval and we clambered out of the tent to greet the day.

As we emerged into the sunlight we heard the unmistakable sound of a couple having 'in-tent' sex with each other a few feet away. The tent in which they were obviously engaged in their own sweaty pleasure was no more than ten feet from mine and surrounded by about twenty others, from which various low-level indie band musicians were now crawling out, I assume also inquisitive as to who exactly it was that could be grunting and 'Ohhh, ohhhhh, ohhhhh, ohhhhh, ohhhhhhhhhhhhhhhhhhhing, yeah, fuck me like that, fuck me, fuck me' at such volume.

The temperature outside was by now rapidly approaching what might be considered a heatwave in England in mid-summer, so you can imagine the kind of sweaty inferno that must have been raging inside a plastic two-man tent pitched in a field bathed in sunlight, devoid of any sort of shade. Our two mystery lovers were by now, judging by the increasing noise levels, going at it hammer and tongs.

'Argh, argh, argh, argh. Yeah, fuck me, baby. Yeah, yeah, that's it!'

And the number of people now sprawled out on the grass or standing around staring at the tent, smoking joints and giggling uncontrollably had risen to about 30.

The temperature continued to rise, the crowd of onlookers continued to grow and the two, I assume, blissfully unaware lovers continued to make the beast with two backs. The tent pegs were coming out of the ground as one or other of them adjusted their position inside and still they went at it.

'Oooooggghhhhhhhhhhhhhhhhhhhh, oh god, oh god, oh god . . . arghhhhhhhhhhhhhh, oh yes, oh yes, oh yes, oh yes.'

My friend and I were by now standing slack-jawed, completely out of our brains as the pills we'd swallowed started to kick in.

'Arghhhhhhhhhhhhhhhhhhhhhhh, oooooooohhhhhhhhhhhhhhhhh, arggghhhhhhhhhhhhhhhhhh, oooooohhhhhhhhhhhhhhhhh . . . oh my god, oh god, ooooohhhhh, aaarhhhhh . . . .'

This continued for a further 20 minutes at least until some bloke who by now had collapsed onto the grass – without spilling his pint, I hasten to add – crying with laughter, pointed at the source of his and everybody else's merriment.

'I'm going to fucking piss myself in a minute. FOR GOD'S SAKE, MAN, FINISH HER OFF!'

That was it. Everyone was instantly on the floor, tears streaming down their faces just at the moment our two lovers reached their point of no return and collectively issued an 'Arghhhhhhhhhhhhhhhhhhhhhhhhhhhhhhhhh . . . .'

The sound of over thirty people beside themselves with laughter must have finally disturbed whatever post-coital moment was occurring in the tent because a hand appeared and fumbled with the zip, soon to be followed by two of the sweatiest people I've ever seen in all my life, as they fell out onto the grass, steam actually rising from their bodies, to be met by the sight of the assembled crowd rising collectively to its feet, applauding madly.

'Go on, my son,' said the 'For god's sake' bloke.

'Good work, fella . . .' said the editor of *Loaded* magazine, who had also been present for the previous half-hour.

'Good on ya, girl,' said one of the girls from Elastica.

'Fucking hell, that's worn me out. Fancy some more smack?' I said to my pal.

'Why not?' said he.

We went back to my tent to chill out for a bit after all the excitement.

Be Here Now?

The music business is forever disposing of people who peak too early in their creative lives. It has no use for the useless and waves them away with a swift, pathetically unsentimental goodbye. They soon disappear, their early success eclipsed by the eventual day-to-day normality that not being able to maintain it brings. For many, the well-travelled route of 'better to burn out than fade away' provides another exit, as they are ignored by the music-buying public prior to being ignored by the rest of the music business. Whether this is done as a matter of choice or not is a moot point – is addiction really a choice?

Success is, of course, relative and it's possible to question whether the trappings are a suitable reward for the pitfalls of fame and adulation it also brings. It can be dangerous to be surrounded by sycophants and freeloaders providing counterfeit opinions that help maintain illusions but they are often as difficult to avoid as a guitar-shaped swimming pool. I was very much looking forward to diving head/nose first into the fray, because, if I was honest with myself, I just wanted to be famous. I had, however, persuaded myself otherwise, utterly convinced that I was about to create something wonderful that would help me achieve my dream and then stay there.

I was going to make people UNDERSTAND.

But what hope was there when I didn't really understand anything myself, couldn't really sing in tune or play a musical instrument?

It's fair to say that lack of talent or ability has never and will never stop those desperate enough to sell their very soul in pursuit of adulation. People like me who don't recognise themselves as being cut from a particularly shabby, talentless cloth. In my case, a patchwork of hope, fantasy, good drugs, bad drugs and the fear and confusion that hemmed the whole sorry mess together.

I needed something to believe in, in the ever-diminishing moments when I wasn't out of my tiny mind, trying to avoid the acknowledgement of my own shortcomings. I needed someone, something, anything other than what remained of me when not fucked to bits on booze and drugs. So I chose to believe that fame and success would take me to a place where I could happily live with myself and maybe a porn star for a girlfriend and a pile of drugs that would never disappear.

I thought lots of stupid shit, the vapour trail from which followed me at all times until I'd managed to take enough of something to ignore the smell of my own stinking thinking.

I thought I had some good lyrics: 'Nothing's more beautiful than being understood,' I'd written in my lyric book. At rehearsal I showed it to the tall guy and just got a request for more coke in return.

He understood I was a chancer who just might get him a chance to shine. I knew the right people, I was in amongst the animals and I fed them whatever they asked for. He needed me to get him closer to the people he would then need more than me. He believed I could help take him inside the machine and in return he would accommodate me in his plans – for how long, I'm not sure he or anybody else knew.

As the tour approached I somehow suddenly almost understood this and agreed to give up selling drugs, thinking I could possibly live without the money/parties/drugged-up nonsense, etc. if he would try to understand something other than what he saw on the surface. Surely I was not a lost cause? I believed in me – at least I thought I did when I was whacked off my tits on coke and smack, whereas the people I was trying to convince managed that trick without drugs.

You can't buy, sniff, swallow or inject talent and self-belief; you've got to work at it. Of course I made all the right noises suggesting I got that, but my actions were of a man still intent on buying shortcuts while protesting his desire to walk the mile with his 'friends'.

Shout loud enough, Simon, and they'll get it. The drugs told me everybody else needed to get their shit together. I guessed I could stop the dealing, possibly take less drugs and make the band work. After all, I believed in it and continued to try to make my bandmates believe in me. I didn't think I was asking too much of them or myself.

What I couldn't see or understand, of course, was that the rest of the band did work and there is a difference between believing and needing to believe.

On Tour

So, this is it! I'm about to put in place one of the final elusive pieces of the fantasy/reality mental jigsaw I have spent my entire life trying to assemble. The piece that will now allow me to stand back and show the world the bigger picture, worth all the exasperation and annoyance over the years because now you will all fucking see that I was right!

I am about to become a very famous rock 'n' roll star, adored by the masses as I prance and preen, shake my skinny arse and sing my songs to my adoring audience. This is the start of what will surely be an ongoing communal acceptance ceremony welcoming me into their lives as I rescue them from their mundane existences with words they cannot write themselves and a lifestyle they can only dream about. I carry the hopes and frustrations of a generation that without me will surely be lost forever.

Or maybe I was doing too much coke?

The tour was under way and as I took my seat on the bus I knew without any doubt that soon enough the rest of the world would be paraded before me. I raised my fingers to all my previous detractors while inviting my fans and admirers to stand beside me and bask in my reflected glory.

Or maybe I was doing too much coke?

The pasty I was struggling to entice into my mouth at the motorway service station near Luton was rapidly deposited onto the floor beneath me shortly after I'd covertly snorted a line to alleviate the monotony of tour-bus existence that had set in a mere ninety minutes into day one.

The solids were rapidly replaced by a can of Stella and another cigarette as we resumed our journey north towards Manchester for the first night of our three-week crusade.

The guitarist was quite possibly wondering if I could be so easily replaced and had more or less stopped talking to me. The Judge, our tour manager, was already trying to figure out a way of hiding from me the cash he had been entrusted with to cover our expenses for the next 21 days, while the drummer and bass player sat gazing silently out of the window. The rhythm section were certainly doing a convincing job of sounding/looking excited, despite possibly wondering what the fuck they had let themselves in for when they'd agreed with me, rather than the tall guy, that my voice was a unique component of our 'sound' rather than a cause for concern and quite possibly going to be the reason his songs would be ridiculed rather than embraced by those about to witness the Limousine live experience.

The headline act were travelling in their own bus just ahead of us and by the time we made our next scheduled stop to empty bladders, purchase more culinary delights and in my case quickly sneak into the toilets to snort some coke alone, I had decided to take a seat on theirs for the rest of the journey to our Manchester hotel. My thinking was that I would then be able to avail myself of the first wave of any waiting groupies rather than being left with what remained, who perhaps lowered their sights and knickers further down the pecking scale and settled for fucking support acts and roadies. It goes without saying that in reality I would have happily entertained anyone for as long as they were willing to tolerate me and my ego while getting naked and behaving badly with me. Over the ensuing three weeks, which covered most points of the country, there was only one girl willing to subject herself to this ordeal. She was from Middlesbrough – make of that what you will.

What can I tell you about the first night of the tour? Not too much really. All I can remember is being chased through the corridors of our hotel by the Judge as he brandished a Maglite torch while attempting to smash my head to bits at some ungodly hour of the morning. I'm therefore assuming it could have gone better and perhaps I'd not really contributed much to Limousine's plans for world domination or the slim chance that our management might get a return on the money they had invested. Not that I ever gave that a minute's thought, of course – you pays your money, you take your chance.

Further highlights over the next few weeks included my random 'acquisition' of a lunatic who'd apparently only been released that morning from a lengthy prison sentence for some hideous act of violence. This occurred while I was endeavouring to score some heroin in Glasgow and on discovery of his crime I quickly entrusted him to the 'care' of one of the guitarists from the headline act. On reflection this did little to help the guitarist's already obvious signs of 'tour fatigue', the onset of which was a direct result of spending too much time with me and being caught up in an incident when armed police were called to my room one night. This somewhat distressing episode began shortly after I'd used my 'on-tour' cigarette lighter to wave away yet another polite request from the hotel's management to discontinue the after-show party that was still going on in my room at 4 a.m. My 'on-tour' cigarette lighter came in the shape of a fake gun, which when waved in the face of some unfortunate hotel employee at some ungodly hour by 'the fucking singer in Limousine, you cunt' wearing only his pants possibly looked more like a real gun than something you'd spark up a fag with or indeed use to smoke heroin in a hotel room toilet when no one else was about.

As for the rest of our jaunt through the lower end of the music venues of the country I not surprisingly have little recollection. Obviously people took too many drugs, drank too much, slept with a heavily overweight, tattooed girl from Middlesbrough and stole things from motorway service stations – in between playing some music each night, of course! Some of the shows were, so I was told, not actually too bad, a few even engendered some strong suggestions from various industry types that Limousine were actually being considered for a record deal, the providers of which would possibly reveal themselves at our homecoming show in London. Whether this was an indication of the musical climate at the time and a sense of desperation to sign anything with a decent haircut, or maybe a direct result of pretty much everyone concerned in that particular pursuit being off their fucking head on drugs, or maybe, just maybe, the songs I was attempting to do justice to being actually quite good, we will never know.

I suspect it was actually a combination of all three and perhaps if people had listened to our guitarist rather than entertain my nonsense, albeit while snorting and swallowing my drugs, things could have worked out for the tall guy and his talented accomplices. His collection of songs were, for the most part, a wonderful creation; unfortunately for him and everyone else involved, the singer of those songs was, for the most part, not.

Another incident that has survived my memory loss occurred after the penultimate show in Brighton. Back at our hotel after by far the worst gig we'd done, for the entire duration of which the guitarist had stood with his back to the audience while simultaneously refusing to acknowledge that the rest of the band were even on the same stage, then walking off the second he played the last note of our set closer, I got a very late/very early phone call from our tall and clearly misunderstood genius. He'd necked two Es I'd previously sold him and had after much thought decided I had destroyed his life by singing his songs so badly. I had ruined his big chance for superstardom and he wanted me to know that he was now contemplating killing himself and hoped I felt guilty.

I was totally unmoved on hearing his news, as by this point, in true rock 'n' roll tradition, we hated each other. I quickly informed him I had no idea why he'd bothered to call me prior to killing himself. He'd paid me for the pills, so as far as I was concerned we were quits and could he please fuck off and bother someone else?

The lines of cocaine I was frantically trying to persuade my decrepit nostrils to hoover up eventually began their journey into my bloodstream, rapidly dissolving the fleeting notion that he'd not actually done anything wrong other than doubt my capabilities to deliver his wonderful songs. Without doubt we'd both given ourselves a chance to shine but on a platform built from my drug-dealing connections and paid for by the people who inhabited my world. Surely the cocaine that cemented the whole sorry mess together had not 'lied' to us all? It cost a lot of money, had opened doors and given me lots of friends. It was fucking rock 'n' roll, man!

He should have been grateful that he'd met me and, besides, it's not as if the entire tour had been a disaster. We'd sold a few T-shirts and I'd shagged a girl in Middlesbrough who thought we were great. Were we about to split up before we'd even signed a deal?

As I licked the remnants of the wrap and smoked a few lines of heroin to keep it company, I concluded not. He was just an arrogant, ungrateful prick and if he didn't actually kill himself in his room tonight I was sure we'd sort things out soon enough. Surely it was only a matter of time before our moment arrived? Snnniffffffffffffffffffffffffffffffffffffffffffffffffffffff.

The previous night's gig at Shepherd's Bush Empire had been our chance to prove something in front of nearly every record company that was ever likely to sign us.

None had.

It was not entirely my fault that it wasn't one of our best shows. We didn't get a soundcheck and at the last minute we were told that another band who were on before us needed to borrow some of our equipment. Not the end of the world, really, and as far as I was concerned we went on and played the greatest gig ever – or maybe it was the speedball I'd hit up before we went onstage that gave my performance that little something special.

On finishing the gig I sat backstage waiting for my five-album deal to be offered. I waited. No one that mattered spoke to me. They ignored me apart from telling me what time we were leaving for Brighton in the morning. I was so off my tits on heroin and coke I could quite happily have just chatted to myself, which was just as well because no one else seemed inclined to listen to me talk about myself all night. Those who felt the need to excuse themselves did so under the guise of having to get an early night prior to the shortest drive between shows on the entire tour.

Seeing as we were in London I went back to my flat to see if the pre-planned homecoming celebration party was in full swing only to find Pete and Ronnie gouged out on the sofa, a crack pipe lying on top of the backstage passes I'd given them earlier that day. They hadn't even turned up for the gig but then again neither had I.

We managed to get from Brighton to Stoke-on-Trent for the final gig without anyone committing suicide or killing anyone else, although the trip from the coast to Stoke was possibly the longest silence I've ever experienced between people sitting next to each other in my entire life. The tour finished, I was dropped off outside the flat and a few days later I was officially sacked from the band.

I cried like a baby as I walked out of the pub we'd met in just ten minutes previously. I knew the second I'd walked in, as the big fella refused to even look at me, leaving the drummer to let me down gently, which considering he was a drummer was always going to be a big ask.

The same week I was asked to leave the flat and there was an article written in a popular monthly magazine detailing the fall from grace of a guy who sounded very similar to me. Once seemingly 'going places', well connected, always out and about in the right bars and clubs, he was now reduced to stealing from his friends to support his heroin habit. Word spread quickly that it was me. It wasn't. I still had about six months to go before I started stealing from the few friends I had left.

I might have self-indulgently and arrogantly chosen to use smack before this point but from now on I began to feel like it was choosing me.

I was 26 years old, homeless, totally broke, angry, resentful, jealous, confused, paranoid and still unable to figure out the difference between reality, fantasy, good drugs and bad drugs. As far as I could see, there was only one thing that would make this situation bearable – some very good bad drugs, so I made my way to see Ronnie.

So I've scored, had a hit at his place before making my excuses and heading towards the door.

'Where you off to, Mr Rock Star?'

It then dawned on me all of a sudden; everything that had

occurred over the past few years suddenly caught up with me and asked some serious questions.

I didn't have anywhere to go any more, nowhere that I wanted to go anyway. The reality that I'd just wasted my best chance to achieve what I'd believed for so long would make me happy could not be avoided by any amount of heroin. I knew I'd fucked it up good and proper as I stumbled out of Ronnie's flat onto the busy streets of Camden Town. I was finally alone with reality, bad drugs and myself, and therefore in very bad company as I began to plot my revenge.

First on the list?

Probably me!

What kind of stupid fucking idiot would agree to put his name on the lease of a property, the sole purpose of which was to allow other people to sell drugs from inside without them paying him a single penny from the subsequent profits?

Did I mention that the property I had put my name to was quite possibly the worst flat in the world from which to conduct illegal activities?

Sighs

Up the Beach

I am sitting on a beach, feeling sick and tired. Jet lag doesn't even come into it; this is heroin sick. Sick because I do not have any smack, sick because I cannot get off this fucking island – sick, sick, sick.

A late monsoon storm has whipped up the sea that separates me from the Malaysian mainland and the bus that would carry my rattling bones to the opiate paradise of Thailand.

'No boats today, no problem, no problem, mister.'

No? It's a big fucking problem if, like me, you're a heroin addict stuck on an island in the South China Sea, having just run out of heroin and the willpower to go cold turkey.

How did I get here? Somebody else had paid.

I'd flown out fully intending to clean up, having robbed my landlords of a couple of thousand quid which I'd convinced myself was rightfully mine due to all the business I'd put their way over the years – that and the fact they were greedy cunts of the highest order who deserved it anyway.

My plans for revenge, such as they were, had thus far involved little more than a sharp increase in my heroin habit and putting myself at risk of a decent stint in jail when the concierge of the apartment building eventually concluded that turning a blind eye to what was taking place on the 12th floor was not worth the occasional bottle of cheap whisky he got from the 'web-designers' who occupied the flat.

He didn't even receive his 'Christmas bonus' – a very expensive bottle of malt offered as a bung to offset the seasonally increased traffic coming in and out of the lifts. I'd given it to my heroin dealer in exchange for some gear within seconds of being entrusted with it by my 'employers'.

His comment to me one morning shortly after our new year's party of, 'You must think I'm fucking stupid, sunshine. You're taking me for a cunt, eh? Web-designer? You'll be getting a new arsehole designed in the Scrubs sooner or later,' was enough to convince me it was time to review my current living arrangements.

When some money came my way a few days later I had a ticket to the Far East in my grubby hands within a few hours.

Obviously I'd concealed some gear upon my person for the flight and the ensuing period of time it would take to get to my tropical detox island of choice, but it wasn't until I was walking towards the customs officers at Kuala Lumpur airport, past a big fuck-off sign that basically said: 'We hang drug users for fun here' that I started to realise I had quite possibly made another in a long line of seriously bad decisions.

The gram of smack in my ass suddenly felt like a kilo, a kilo of heroin that could actually talk and was now screaming, *'I'm stuck up this silly bastard's bumhole, you stupid slanty-eyed, dog-eating twats. Let me out . . . let me out, hang the cunt, hang the cunt . . . Put him out of his misery.'*

174

The customs men at the desk looked me up and down, and asked me the purpose of my visit to their country, to which the heroin in my ass replied, '*To deal smack to your kids, get your daughters hooked and turn them into prostitutes, and fuck your mothers up the ass while smoking crack and shouting Allah is a lady boy.*'

My own response was slightly more considered.

'I'm here to enjoy the natural beauty of the Perhentian Islands for a few weeks; I've heard they are the most beautiful islands in the Far East.'

I was offered a smile and my passport was stamped as they wished me a good vacation and waved me through.

'*He's a paedophile junkie devil-worshipping faggot,*' screamed the heroin in my tightly clenched ass. '*Stop him, search him . . . hang him, hang him . . .*'

I was 30 feet away from the desk when, 'Excuse me, sir . . . stop, please. Could you come here for a minute . . .'

'*Hurrah!*' said the heroin, '*that'll learn you, won't it?*'

I turned back towards the customs desk to see a group of about five officers chattering excitedly as I tried to not shit the contents of my ass all over the floor.

'Me?' I queried, pointing at myself.

'Yes, sir, please come, come.'

As I walked the ten million miles towards the desk the customs men seemed to be laughing and joking amongst themselves, no doubt overjoyed at the prospect of capturing a '*smackhead, a dirty English smackhead scumbag,*' as the contents of my ass were calling me, even louder than before. '*Hang him, hang the cunt . . . hang him, string him up and let the flies eat him. Smackhead, smackhead . . . dirty junkie smackhead.*'

'Yes, officer, is everything OK?'

He was looking right into my soul. Well, he was certainly staring at my body, obviously looking for telltale signs of nerves that might indicate the concealment of the talking heroin.

He smiled. 'Sir, sorry to trouble you, sir, but is that Liverpool Football Club shirt you're wearing? My friends and I think Liverpool is number-one team. Can we have photograph with you, please, sir, if no trouble?'

'He's a Man United fan in disguise, a smack-dealing Man United fan.'

But they couldn't hear the voice due to the sound of my own laughter as I smiled and draped my arms over two Malaysian fans of the greatest football team on earth.

'Thank you, sir. Liverpool, number one . . . number one.'

Ten minutes later I was in an airport toilet doing a much-needed shit before smoking some heroin, not in the least bit bothered by its now rather pungent aroma. Ten hours after my photocall I got to my tropical paradise. A day later I'd 'killed' the rest of the talking heroin, a few hours after which I started to feel like death myself.

The handful of cohabitants on that small piece of paradise snoozed in hammocks or played backgammon and smoked too many cigarettes, if that was indeed possible when there was actually fuck all else to do. The guidebook had said as much: *'Beautiful, but not much to do except watch coconuts fall out of the trees.'*

Well, when you've seen one . . .

I threw up onto the white sand and watched my European junkie bile disappear into the sand. I cried as I went through withdrawal and visualised how much smack I could have brought with the contents of the money bag that lay covered in sick by my side.

'No boats today, mister. No worries, no boats until storm goes.'

Fuck off, you useless cheerful cunt.

Useless like me on this fucking beautiful nightmare of an island with nothing to do but watch fucking coconuts fall out of the trees while I shook and shivered and thought too much – about myself, of course.

I threw up again, whether due to the physical upheaval now firmly under way or just at the thought of myself, I wasn't sure. Either way I was sure that I was about to die as I crawled towards the beach hut I'd rented.

A few days, three bottles of whisky and two hundred duty-free fags later, I re-emerged into the sunlight having convinced myself beyond all doubt that I would never use heroin again.

The monsoon didn't shift for another few weeks, by which time I'd got over my 'food poisoning' and begun to enjoy the company of my fellow island-dwellers, regaling them with tales of the Manchester (City) Frisbee team and my other famous chums back home. Whether or not they were enjoying my company became irrelevant shortly after I managed to hire a boat back to the mainland and returned with some essentials, namely a huge bag of weed, some locally produced whisky and a crate of Special Brew I'd discovered while schlepping through the back streets of Kota Bharu. I'd also managed to procure some incredibly strong purple tablets of possibly a much higher opiate content than the heroin I was trying to escape from back home.

I flew back to face the music a few days later, having survived my paradise-island cold-turkey detox and not used any heroin for six weeks. I remedied that situation within six hours of touching down at Heathrow airport, my excuse being it was currently too cold in the UK for someone like me.

In the City

Never again . . . I swear to fucking god . . . never doing smack again. I can't handle another cluck, man . . . and I can't handle those fucking stairs . . . the stairs that torment the bones and muscles inside my skin . . . the stairs that lead to the bed I lie in at night, thrashing around, muttering my never-again mantra. The bed that I'd prayed to be offered, when was it – five, six days ago?

'Hello, City Roads, can I help you?'

'Please . . . oh, please god, I hope you can.'

The end-of-the-line bed, the bed that has become my enemy, the bed that countless others have sweated and cried in like I do as the clocks seem to have stopped and I shiver and tremble while my head inhabits a landscape so bleak yet so full of noises.

Never again, never again!

My bones no longer wish to be contained by the battered skin that holds me together. Those fucking stairs, man . . . Why do the fucking staff here expect me to go up and down them every morning to sit and stare at the ceiling in a different room? Just let me lie here and die.

They're not giving me enough methadone, cunts. Never again . . . never again!

I hate heroin, hate it . . . hate it. I hate that fucking crackhead in this room who seems to do nothing but fucking sleep, cunt. I remember sleep, vaguely . . . Get a proper habit, you fucking crackhead prick, snoring all fucking night . . . What is he trying to do to ME?

ME, ME, ME, ME, ME, ME.

Never again, never again, fucking crackhead . . . He sleeps, eats, showers, sleeps some more.

I sweat, shake, blame, cry . . . Never again . . . never again . . . How much methadone am I going to get this morning?

Not fucking enough, cunts . . . cunts . . . Why don't they give me something to help me sleep?

Detox fucking tea?

Sleep tea?

A teabag of dried fuck knows what that tastes disgusting and has no proper drugs in it!

My legs, my back . . . Fuck, I stink . . . cunts!!

'Have a shower and a shave, Simon, you'll feel better.'

Fuckofffuckofffuckofff. Water? On my skin? . . . No, no, no, no, that would be too much to bear . . . Never again . . . never again! NEVER AGAIN.

The clock on the wall goes into reverse. If only I had a bit of gear to take the edge off. If only I had just a few cans of Brew and some Valium, and then I could make it through this rattle. I could maybe get home and do the rest of this indoors . . . get a ten bag, some Special Brew, some Valium . . . What day is it today?

Day six, seven? . . . At least I'd be able to get some sleep. They don't understand what I'm going through here, putting me in a room with a fucking crackhead who sleeps all fucking night . . . cunts.

Maybe just get some money? It's Thursday, giro day . . . I could cash my benefit book . . . go see Ace. . . get a ten bag . . . go back to the hostel . . . No . . . go and stay with . . . Fuck it . . . she won't let me in . . . cunt . . . OK, think, Simon . . . think . . . yes, get some lovely beautiful heroin . . . just a ten bag and some Brew . . . some Valium . . . I can do the rest of this rattle . . . somewhere . . . Go and see Jack . . . He'll let me stay . . . We can come off together . . . I can help him get clean . . . He's got a Valium script . . . He fucking owes me a favour . . . I could do it there . . . Just smoke a bit of gear . . . not needles . . . What day is it? . . . just have a smoke . . . take the edge off . . . Maybe buy some methadone off Terry in Camden, Yes! That's it . . . Go and see little Terry . . . score . . . give him something for his troubles . . . have a smoke at his . . . just to stop my legs from . . . get a good night's sleep . . . Sleep? . . . Fucking crackhead over there in the other bed . . . probably sells smack himself . . . cunt . . . That's it, I'm not sharing a room with a fucking smack-dealing crackhead . . . cunts . . . Now where are my trainers? . . . OK . . . think . . . Terry's number is . . . 079 . . . 9 . . . 8 . . . Fuck, what's that little cunt's fucking number? . . . He's only in Camden . . . 20 minutes if I get a move on . . . 20 minutes until I can have a smoke . . . beautiful . . . heroin . . . stop all these voices in my head for a while . . . Maybe I'll . . . Nah . . . what if the gear is no good? . . . Nah . . . been a lot of that stuff that doesn't run on the foil lately . . . What if I score and I can't smoke it? Fuck it . . . I'll get a couple of pins from the Cross on the way to Terry's . . . just in case . . . What's that cunt's fucking number . . .?

0794 . . . yesssssssssssssssssssssssssssssssssssssssssss.

Brit(popped)

Terry was in.

I'd jumped the gates on the Tube, staggered up Camden Road to Agar Grove and knocked on his window.

'All right, Simon? You look well.'

Terry looked like he'd just escaped from a concentration camp, so compared to him anyone would look well.

'What's happening?'

'Got any gear, Tel?'

'Just a bit on the foil, mate, and a few blues. But I can score for ya if you sort me out.'

'Yeah, course. Can I get a boot on your foil before, though? I'm about to shit myself . . . Just got out of detox, mate, know what I mean?'

He looked at me and shrugged what was left of his shoulders. He didn't really know what I meant because he'd never been to a detox, nor was he ever really 'sick' for any length of time, due to the fact he was one of the only junkies I'd ever met who wouldn't rip you off blind if he went to score for you. As a result of this, lots of other people were also happy to let him do the running about in return for a few crumbs of whatever he came back with. He did a lot of running about and the crumbs added up to a tidy habit.

A tidy habit? That sounds like an oxymoron if ever I've heard one.

Thirty minutes later and two of Camden Town's most pathetic morons (of the smackhead variety) were sitting down in his bedroom, cooking up a hit and trying not to make too much noise in case his mum came barging in and made a scene. What currently separated us from her – aside from an entirely different world view and two raging drug habits – was Terry's bedroom door and the paper-thin walls that currently contained us. This was the demarcation line between us and 'normality' – the seemingly meaningless, mundane existence of a life involving daytime television, cheap cigarettes, long-term unemployment and a son slowly killing himself by injecting drugs in his bedroom. Our side of the divide often didn't seem that bad, certainly not after being safely plotted up behind his bedroom door with some crack and smack. Everything prior to that point was, of course, the nightmare, the daily escape from which was by now the blood-splattered canvas illustrating the sole purpose and at the same time utter lack of meaning to my life.

Terry has just inhaled a huge hit from the empty Coke can that serves as his crack pipe and is trying to not make too much noise as he throws up in the bin in his wardrobe. I am trying to decide whether to inject or smoke my rock, opting for the latter option as he wipes the puke from his mouth and the sound of him gagging breaks the pathetic silence we are trying to maintain.

'Terry . . . you got someone in there with you? One of those fackin' drug-addict friends of yours?'

'No, Mum, nobody here. You'd have seen 'em walk in, wouldn't ya?'

Access to his bedroom usually involves climbing in through his bedroom window so as to avoid parental contact.

Silence . . . I feel the rush of the gear into my appreciative veins and signal to my associate to pass me the pipe can so I can decorate my heroin pie with a lick on the 'cherry'.

'I'm off up the shops, son . . . You want anything?'

'A Kit-Kat, please, Mum, and a nourishment drink, vanilla.'

'OK, son, don't let any fackin' druggies in the house while I'm out, will ya?'

'No, Mum, don't worry about that, I won't.'

He passes me the can, I wipe off the dribble and with trembling hands place a big rock upon the ash on top.

'Got a light, Tel?'

He retches again then passes me a lighter.

'Nice bit of white that, Simon . . . strong.'

He's right: it is strong. I also projectile vomit into the bin as I hold the still-smouldering can aloft to ensure I avoid contaminating the remainder of my rock of crack with the remnants of my breakfast.

'Yeah . . . nice.'

The crack is rapidly demolished – there is no other way I know to behave with it – but I manage to save some heroin for later as I leave Terry to empty the bin and do whatever else his day will involve, which in reality means waiting for someone else like me to knock on his bedroom window. Thankfully I am allowed to exit via the front door, as his mum has yet to return with the shopping. Still a little unsure on my feet, I stumble out into the 'real' world and begin to consider my next move.

The next move?

Find some more money from somewhere is always the next move, as the other next move might be to consider the fact that there isn't another next move. I have nowhere to move to, either physically or mentally, and nothing left, possession-wise, to take with me even if there was.

I feel for the tiny bag of smack in my penny pocket and shrug to myself. I can't feel anything other than the effects of the drugs I have just taken, which means that for now they are still working. I am numb and that is really all I need or generally expect from them. Always hoping for more than that, of course, but rarely getting it. The expectation prior to ingestion is often the best bit, maybe the first few minutes after they hit the bloodstream can feel like a bit of a roller-coaster ride, but the reality is that, occasional decent hit aside, this is it – nothing more than self-medicating against the prospect of having to deal with anything at all. Homelessness, hopelessness, people, places, things . . . stuff, you know?

Life.

My life.

Doesn't bear thinking about, does it? So consuming my time by thinking about how to get the money together for the next shot of disappointment is in itself an adequate way of passing the time.

I want to see heaven and feel the earth move, yet routinely settle for hiding away in a bedroom, throwing up into a bin in a council flat in Camden Town.

When you are as fucked up on drugs as this, puking into a bin hidden in someone's wardrobe after a crack pipe is one of the few times when you are 'almost' not thinking about yourself and that in itself is 'almost' a relief. Obviously not sustainable relief, as things are always going to get worse again, aren't they?

Yeah, they are.

Yes, they did.

How quickly?

As soon as the drugs began to wear off, of course, which for me at that particular time was in no time at all. In fact, I was looking for a pub toilet in which to do the rest of my gear within a couple of hours of leaving Terry and his bucket full of vomit. A few hours after that I was already wondering how I could get back into detox again.

Cunts.

Knebworth

It's a big step up from a mid-afternoon gig, slaying Scotland's mashed-up indie boys and girls, travelling the country in a white transit van and tolerating the presence of a two-bob, drug-addled 'personal chemist', to arriving by helicopter, being greeted by supermodels, low-level celebrities, paparazzi and 150,000 'fans' at Knebworth.

As 'the Chief' walked out and informed those gathered in front of his band that 'This is history, right here, right now, this is history,' the Cat in the Hat was writing the next chapter of his own sorry tale, with a needle hanging out of his arm in a disgusting bedsit in Kentish Town.

While the biggest band in the country celebrated with the masses on that Hertfordshire estate, I was sucked further into my opiate black hole in a bedsit on a council estate in north London. Twelve hours earlier, I'd been hoping to be part of the day's history making as I'd bagged up my supply of baby's teething powder, slightly cut with some already cut-to-fuck cocaine and headed out to catch a train to Knebworth. The smack already massaging me as the train left London assured me I'd have no bother convincing whoever was in charge of handing out the AAA passes that day to admit me into the fray. It was also my birthday and I had no one to celebrate it with aside from the uncaring, unwashed, unconscious heroin dealer upon whose sofa I'd passed out the night before.

From the point at which I'd initially tried to wake him up, Ronnie had taken nearly two hours to sort me out with some gear, eventually dropping into my trembling, sweaty hands three tiny bags of what my terrified mind and body was by then screaming out for. The opiate alarm clock does not have a snooze button!

I'd spent the previous 90 minutes/hours/days/months/years killing time, chain-smoking and supping on a warm can of Special Brew, while trying not to puke, pacing up and down his flat, which, as it was a tiny cockroach-infested shithole, didn't take up too much time at all. I'd been through the bin in the vain hope of finding some discarded tinfoil with some unnoticed surplus gear stuck to it. There was none. Ronnie was not the sort of heroin addict who would commit such an error.

I had no money to score from anyone else. I had just enough to get me to Knebworth, where I intended to rip people off with my pretend cocaine. It had actually been cocaine the previous day but Ronnie and I had washed most of it up into crack and smoked it during the course of what had turned out to be a long night attempting to be nice to each other. This was partially the reason he was clearly unhappy about being woken up early by me as I continued my efforts to get him out of bed. I even made him a cup of tea – lots of milk, five sugars – all the while muttering under my breath, calling him a cunt of the highest order as I struggled to raise him from his stupor and sort me out.

'Cunt, cunt, cunt, fucking dirty junkie cunt.'

'You made that fucking cup of tea yet, you prick?'

'Just coming, mate. Cunt, cunt, cunt, cunt, cunt.'

Prior to him disdainfully tossing those three bags of instant salvation in my direction I would have let him fuck me in the ass or sucked his filthy cock, or would at least have considered it an option if I'd thought it might have expedited that event slightly. The second the contents of the first bag were dissolving onto the spoon and the syringe was sucking up the resulting filthy brown fluid, I wouldn't have pissed on him if he was on fire.

'Sorry, your name's not on the list, mate.'

'It must be. Are you sure? Look again. I spoke to him an hour ago. He said he'd sorted it. Simon Mason – it should be on the Creation Records list.'

'Listen, mate, there's about 2,000 fucking people on that list, OK, and you aren't one of them! Now, please, do me a favour and fuck off, eh?'

Where once I'd, albeit briefly, been deemed necessary enough to warrant being rescued from the side of a motorway ahead of most of the rest of the band while en route to Glasgow, now I couldn't even scrape my way onto a guest list populated by has-been '80s pop stars, 'it' girls and people who were probably there because, 'Everyone's going, darling.'

Lighting up a fag, I slithered into the shade to consider my options.

'Hey, Simon! You got anything?'

The cavalry arrived in the shape of one of the few remaining music journalists who still thought purchasing drugs from me was a good idea. He made me his plus one and we sauntered towards the backstage area. As far as I was concerned he must have been as desperate to buy some shit drugs as I was to get in and sell some.

He got a gram of baby's teething powder cut with a few grains of shit cocaine. I got his money, the opportunity to make more money and maybe now actually enjoy my birthday in the company of the Manchester (City) Frisbee team, various support acts, 150,000 paying punters and the remaining 1,998 wonderful people on the guest list.

Before that, however, it was time for some of my personal real drugs prior to descending upon the assembled throng to try to sell some pretend ones.

'Fuck, fuck, fuck, fucking fuck, no, surely not, where's that fucking bag of gear?'

While the vast majority of people now gathering to enjoy their day in the sunshine were gradually, or not in some cases, working their way into whatever state they felt the need to get into to maximise the experience, I was in a portable toilet backstage, frantically searching through my pockets, desperately trying to locate the heroin I'd scored from Ronnie earlier that day.

My habit was such by now that the contents of the needle I'd poked into my arm five hours ago were not sufficient to carry me through the rest of the afternoon's events and I was already starting to feel 'sick'.

The huge rock of crack I'd just smoked in the toilet had not really helped matters much, so thank god for the remaining bags of heroin I'd brought with me, eh?

There is, of course, no such thing as god and now apparently also no such thing as the two bags of heroin I'd concealed about my person, the crushing certainty of which was clear to me in the toilet inside which I was rapidly disintegrating.

As I realised that I'd left my own drugs back at Ronnie's flat and that the likelihood of them still being there was about as high as its occupier having a bath any time soon, the contents of my stomach emptied themselves all over the toilet floor as the contents of the crack pipe hit my bloodstream. I spent the next two hours stumbling about the backstage area searching for the couple of individuals I knew to be similarly afflicted and therefore maybe in possession of some drugs that might stop me rapidly progressing further into heroin withdrawal. I didn't find them.

There were 1,998 utterly useless cunts all having a good time, and, OK, I sold a bit more teething powder and collected more money, but as any self-respecting junkie will tell you, having cash without also having someone present to exchange it for heroin is possibly the most horrifically frustrating situation you can find yourself in.

As the backstage toilet cubicles filled up with the great and the good powdering their noses with my teething powder, I was staggering back through the oncoming sea of people as I sweated, cursed and stumbled towards the station and the first train back to Kentish Town and my best mate Ronnie.

I did hand my AAA pass to some bewildered kid as I went and told him to enjoy himself with the 'famous cunts' backstage, though. I'm good like that.

Ronnie obviously denied I'd left anything at his earlier but was pleased to see my money; whether or not he was pleased to see me was completely irrelevant. I cooked up a big hit, melted into the sofa and then scowled at the TV as it showed the news and a story about some fucking band paying a gig somewhere in the English countryside.

Happy birthday, smackhead!

Desolation Row

There are a few certainties that accompany the daily grind of attempting to support a heroin habit in Britain, particularly when the individual concerned in this process of ever-diminishing returns is attempting to stay in the game minus a regular source of income. One is that for an individual like me there will never be enough drugs to satisfy my greed; another, directly related, is that you will rarely wake up with any drugs left over to allow at least some respite before having to get up and try to get some money to score some more.

It's a fucking nightmare, other than the glorious day that occurs every two weeks when the involuntary contributions of the taxpayers of our country afford the dole-scrounging junkie wastrel the luxury of a morning off.

Giro day, happy days, the 'got-no-chance-in-hell-of-quitting-today-even-if-I-wanted-to' day. When the memories of the preceding 13 days of waking up sick as a fucking dog, wishing you'd saved something for the morning are gone the instant you realise you've been 'paid'. The morning when the only barrier between the absolute belief, both physical and psychological, that you need to ingest some nasty drugs and the moment when the needle hits the groove is having to locate an industrious teenager on a BMX who is already 'working' and to whom you don't already owe your entire fortnight's benefit money.

The powers that be do of course have a solution for us poor heroin-dependent scumbags – hello, methadone, pleased to meet you! This is the highly addictive, government-sponsored liquid 'solution' to opiate dependence doled out to dole-queue junkies and high-rolling, low-life rock 'n' roll casualties alike. Those with no money become addicted to it for free; those with money pay for the privilege! I was a dole-queue smackhead who thought himself destined for rock 'n' roll superstardom at any minute and therefore an ideal candidate for the script provided by the well-meaning but clearly fucking clueless drugs worker I was now seeing in my attempts to try to control my habit.

My 'efforts' in pursuit of this (for me, at least) utterly nonsensical ideal now revolved around bi-weekly meetings with my key worker to talk about my 'feelings' and daily trips to a chemist to collect and ingest my 'juice' and the magical cure it alluded to. It quickly became apparent that I still desperately wanted to score some smack regardless of how much fucking methadone I was getting. Figure that out if you will?

So it didn't stop me using gear and, not surprisingly, nor did it stop me from getting arrested as I pursued the funds to score. A jail sentence was on the cards, and soon, as a magistrate was quick to inform me after yet another failed leg-of-lamb heist had resulted in me being presented before him once again. He gave me one more chance to stay out of trouble and my key worker gave me an increased dose of methadone, which was very kind of her as I now had an excess to sell each day and thus didn't have to run in and out of Sainsbury's stealing bottles of vodka, razor blades and cuts of meat to get £10. A pyrrhic victory indeed.

The methadone did help to keep me from doing heroin as regularly but the truth is that the overriding fear of getting arrested again and going to jail provided a far greater deterrent to an utter coward such as myself.

The months passed and I swallowed my methadone each morning as prescribed, rapidly followed by some heroin that obviously wasn't. As far as I was concerned, topping up on the juice with some gear was fine as long as nobody noticed or I didn't inject. Considering the amount of other drugs most people I knew at that time were on, I think I could have strolled about Camden Town naked with a bazooka full of smack aimed at my own head and nobody would have paid much attention. Nobody seemed to give much of a fuck really, least of all me of course.

With a head so full of nonsense that it had struggled at the best of times to make much sense of the world and how to survive within it, there came something akin to relief when life was reduced to a few simple daily tasks.

No more wasted hours worrying about the future. There is no real future any more and what little remains of it has been boiled down to its bones. The skeletal remains have only basic requirements – heroin and the money needed to get it.

Apparently he who lies down cannot be knocked over but I think I'm correct in thinking that gouging out on a rotten sofa belonging to a fellow junkie in Camden Town falls somewhat outside of that suggested survival mechanism. I had a battle on my hands with an enemy whose opening salvo every morning suggested that scoring more smack was a daily victory of sorts and thus the only requirement to maintain our uneasy truce, providing as it did a drugged-up smokescreen preventing me from seeing the horizon and therefore the only chance of real victory, which was to escape and get the fuck off the battlefield.

Did I have even the slightest idea at the time of what exactly I was up against?

Of course not! What was I, stupid?

Ronnie resembled a troll, a grumpy, unwashed, angry, arrogant and controlling troll, who remarkably, despite all that, was also sometimes capable of being an incredibly insightful and funny, almost compassionate, human being, who looked like a troll.

He also did possibly the worst £10 deals of heroin in Camden but offset that fact by always having some to sell and tolerating your company while you ingested your drugs on the relative comfort of his sofa.

Ronnie's bedsit (I think it was a bedsit but I never ventured past the sofa and god forbid going anywhere near the toilet) offered a more anonymous space to conduct one's affairs for the pathetic two-bob smackhead I had rapidly become within a few short months of walking offstage for the last time with my band.

Supersonic to super-stupid and super-sad in super-fast time, refreshments provided by Special Brew, Tennent's Extra and Skol Super, the main course being shit deals of heroin from Ronnie the Troll while gouging out on the world's smelliest sofa.

It wasn't supposed to have turned out like this. When I'd been planning my life journey I'd always assumed my surroundings were going to be much nicer once I'd entered the decadent phase of my rock 'n' roll life, but that was back when such things seemed possible.

It was supposed to be like Keith Richards' stay in the south of France while cooking up *Exile on Main Street* as well as his smack, surrounded by the beautiful people paying homage to the work of genius that the band were creating in his basement.

I just had Ronnie the Troll calling me a cunt and making me go out to get Pot Noodles from the corner shop in return for a crumb on his crack pipe, on receipt of which I would always say a heartfelt thank you. This might well have done nothing to ease my sense of worthlessness but by now I felt nothing but pain so it didn't matter what I said to the troll; thank you or fuck you, it made no difference at all. It all added up to nothing more than a big FUCK ME.

No Problems

If you need a useful solution to a problem, it's helpful to be able to understand the exact nature of the predicament you face so you can at least ask the appropriate questions before deciding if the answers you get are of any value. Heroin has an uncanny knack of being the provider of the problem while also retaining the ability to cunningly disguise itself as the solution. When I say cunningly I mean it's only as smart as it needs to be, which in the case of any junkie is just that little bit smarter than the individual concerned.

You could have the IQ of a large puddle, heroin will have that of a small pond; you might have a first-class degree in astrophysics, smack will explain the formation of the universe perfectly beyond refute; it's a fucker like that.

There is elasticity to this battle of wits, stemming from the fact that heroin addiction is not exactly renowned for its track record of delivering a regular stream of good choices by those it romances, yet at the same time is utterly convincing in enthusing users with the belief that they will be able to sort *everything* out just as soon as it is familiarising itself with your bloodstream again.

If you don't care to think too much about anything it will facilitate a state of mental and emotional flat-lining so utterly enveloping that the idea of having to ever deal with anything ever again, other than getting more heroin, seems as about as desirable as being asked to carry the rotting corpse of a child to the top of a mountain then flinging yourself off its summit before making the same climb again to retrieve it and throwing it to a waiting pack of starving vultures to feast upon. Heroin withdrawals kindly place this mental image firmly at the forefront of your mind but make the body involved that of your own child, just to add more mental torture to the deal. It's nice like that.

If you are a more involved and cultivated kind of thinker, enthralled by tales of opiate excess providing the fertile ground from which great music/literature/tabloid headlines have flourished, it will convince you that you too are going to join the pantheon of junkie superstars who have without doubt given the world some of its greatest works of art. Of course the real truth is that for every Keith Richards *insert name of favourite famous junkie musician/ celebrity* there are thousands of dead/as good as dead individuals who had similar aspirations but never got the chance to throw televisions out of expensive hotel windows while having their daily narcotic requirements met by the CIA in order to avoid potential arrest and further political embarrassment. These junkies with serious amounts of money as well as serious habits provide serious tax revenue while touring and get treated differently from some poor bastard with exactly the same problem and no fancy expensive lawyer on hand 24/7.

Basically smack tells you you're going to be OK no matter what, as you slide into a state of not giving a flying fuck what happens as long as you can get some fucking smack, regardless of what you gotta do to get it.

Now, when you look at this in print my guess is that, just like I did when I read similar opinions and personal statements, most far more literate than this often cack-handed account, you might well conclude that the idea of getting involved with heroin is about as bad a plan as it is possible to have. But one day, who knows exactly how these situations arise, you may well find yourself presented with an opportunity to have a dabble, you know, see what all the bloody fuss is about, eh?

Go ahead, do it, what can I tell you? Nothing I ever read – and trust me I read a lot on the subject prior to getting involved – ever stopped someone like me from doing something that some ageing ex-junkie told me not to do.

I just hope that you're nothing like me, because then in all likelihood you'll be fine. You'll puke your guts up, nod out, disappear into whatever comfy seat you are hopefully reclining in and possibly talk total nonsense all day/night before probably never touching the shit again.

If, however, you sadly recognise something of yourself in what you've read so far and decide to have a go anyway . . . well, good luck, you're going to need it! You're going to have problems and, like myself, Pete and Matty as we all sat on the sofa one morning at Ronnie's, pretending we were all there for the first time in ages, you may well also be unable to get anywhere near a solution. This is because of the remarkable ability of the reason we were all sitting there, clucking our tits off, to make us believe we didn't really have a problem at all. We could, of course, all stop any time we wanted, but unbeknown to us none of us were anywhere near ready for that mental walk up the fucking mountain carrying dead children, whether ours or anybody else's, even if we wanted to.

'Fuck sake, Ronnie, call the cunt again. How long is he going to be? I'm fucking dying here.'

'Chill out, Pete, OK? I've phoned him four times already. He says he's on his fucking way and his gear's good, so I'm gonna wait for him. Besides, I can't be feckin' arsed to go out to the phone box again. It's pissing down outside.'

It's safe to assume that, unlike the three amigos all currently struggling to sit still while we waited for whomever it was we were waiting for as we collectively rattled away on the couch that currently stank more than I certainly had ever noticed before, Ronnie had already done some gear that morning.

Sitting waiting in silence, chain-smoking butt roll-ups while waiting for a runner to turn up was not an unusual situation for any of us any more; it's all part of the deal when waiting for a dealer who gives less of a fuck about you than you do yourself, which is really not much of a fuck at all. When one of the assembled losers has for whatever reason managed to hold on to some gear from the previous day so as to avoid the rapidly progressing stomach spasms and dry retching, it only serves to make the situation seem even more unbearable. I could at least focus some of my own self-hatred towards the Troll as he casually flicked some ash from his fag onto his floor and tried to prevent himself from nodding out, while his guests stared at him for any unlikely sign he was about to put us out of our misery by dipping into his personal stash.

Did he even have a bit of personal on him? I chose to believe he did, as it just added to the seething resentment I needed to feel towards him and whoever it was that was keeping us all waiting on a day when there seemed to be a shortage of heroin in the area.

This was evidently the reason the three of us had ended up on that fucking sofa, all arriving separately before going through the pathetic masquerade of pretending to be surprised to see each other as we settled in to wait for our relief.

We had money – not much, but enough, which in itself is frustrating beyond belief when you cannot exchange it for gear by your own endeavours. Multiply that frustration by three then add a stinking troll-like dealer with no drugs to sell but clearly off his cake with what the rest of you are in ever-increasing desperation to ingest and you ain't exactly gonna have a party on your hands.

'Call the cunt again. What's his fucking number? I'll go to the fucking phone box.'

'Sorry, Matty, you don't know him. There's fuck all else about today, mate.'

'Tell me something I don't know,' the three of us retorted in unison.

The clock on top of the telly had seemingly lost the ability to count minutes in sixty-second episodes, instead now taking about ten minutes to incrementally move time forward at the usual rate, or at least the rate that you don't notice after you've scored as opposed to the one that torments you before you do. The smell from the couch was added to by the odour of three desperate smackheads engaging in a clucky-fart symphony while they stared with even more toxicity at their heavily sedated host as he attempted to tell jokes about the situation from the comfort of his own stinking armchair.

'Hee, hee, hee, that was a feckin' ripe one, Si . . . feckin' smelly bastard, you, eh?'

I couldn't talk. My mouth was salivating heavily and I was convinced if I were to open it I'd go into a spasm of dry retching. Instead I chose to concentrate on fostering my silent belief that after today I would never score from the Troll again. Utter nonsense, of course, but it seemed to help.

The doorbell rang.

'About fucking time!' came the chorus from the couch as Ronnie began to ease himself out of his chair while being serenaded by three more expectant farts from the occupants of his sofa.

'Feckin' hell, you boys feckin' stink, eh?'

'Answer the fucking door, you cunt.'

There then followed the longest 15 seconds known to man as the Troll went to the door. Matty, Pete and I destroyed a roll of tinfoil as we prepared our 'equipment' in expectation of what was by now the most valuable £10 of heroin in the world.

(For some bizarre reason, we were all pretending to prefer smoking smack to injecting it at this point, certainly in front of each other anyway.)

Tubes were rolled, squares of foil flattened and burnt with a lighter in order to avoid 'lung damage', cigarettes lit and as the front door shut we waited for the messiah to come back into the room.

'Sorry, boys, he's got fuck all, still . . .'

The world stopped, my stomach informed me I might need to actually visit the Troll's toilet to deposit its contents somewhere other than over my own lap and tears suddenly streamed from my eyes.

'What?'

'He came over to tell you he ain't got anything – you lying cunt.'

'Hee, hee, hee, I'm just having a laugh, boys, calm the fuck down. I've got an eighth, OK?'

Fifteen minutes later we were all laughing at Ronnie's jokes; he was suddenly more amiable than Terry Wogan. Matty had popped out to get some beers, the clock had returned to normal, the sofa didn't stink and none of us had a problem any more.

Glastonbury, 1998

I arrive on site a week prior to the punters. There's no one to collect me in a jeep with flashing lights this time, no pills to sell, no weed, acid or speed. I'm carrying two ounces of cocaine and an ounce of smack, which I've managed to obtain by borrowing the money from someone clearly more stupid than myself and more importantly someone not likely to send anyone to kill me when I fuck things up and use more than I sell over the next few weeks.

They have known me long enough to trust me to smuggle the drugs on site to sell but not long enough to realise that once I'm safely inside it's highly unlikely I'll be sending anyone out to get them in as well. My intentions are almost honourable but my habit is not.

It's raining. I have no backstage passes, only the knowledge that there are people I can possibly do business with who, like me, do not feel the need to see any bands, visit the circus tent or pretend to be a hippy for a few hours in the stone circle.

I need to find my old traveller acquaintance, Steve, and his blue Bella Vega bus, complete with gas stove and a telly, because the World Cup is on and watching football on heroin while at the greatest festival in the world now seems like the best idea I've ever had.

I find him.

Two ounces of cocaine, an ounce of smack, a bus, a telly, some bicarbonate of soda, citric, needles and a spoon.

'Got any good drugs, Simon?'

'Yeah, Steve, mind if I hang out here for a bit?'

'Be my guest, man, shall I put the kettle on?'

'I guess so, man, I guess so.'

Who won the World Cup that year?

Two ounces of cocaine, an ounce of smack, a bus, a telly, some bicarbonate of soda, citric, needles and a spoon.

I did?

About three weeks after getting on Steve's bus and winning the World Cup, I stole his car and fucked off back to London. It was clearly time to leave. Steve had invited me in for a cup of tea 21 days ago and I was still there but my drugs were not. Clearly tolerating me without the cushioning affect of some heroin was not something my host wanted to endure. I was not only incredibly annoying but by then I probably smelt pretty bad too. The fact that he'd 'suggested' it was time for me to move on made me resentful enough to feel entirely vindicated as I picked up the keys to his car and crept off the bus at some ungodly hour.

Apparently it had been a mudbath that year. Can't say that I'd noticed really; never got off the bus all the time I was there. Why would I? The World Cup was on, wasn't it?

True to form I'd used more than I'd sold and the money I had left was now, as far as I was concerned, all mine. The idiot who'd fronted me the money to buy the drugs in the first place obviously wasn't going to come and find me, because having now vacated my previous address on site at Glastonbury I actually had nowhere to live other than the back seat of 'my' car.

I drove off site while my host was nodding out and made my way to Weston to see someone who would have what I needed to get me back to London.

Gus was in, but seeing as he had a visitor decided to quickly go out to the local shops and get some bits and pieces, namely a few litres of white cider and some crisps, before returning twenty minutes later with one of the dodgiest blokes I'd ever seen in my life in tow.

'Be with you in a minute, Si. Got someone here who needs . . .'

I was nodding out in the front room, having availed myself of the 'house specialty' already, but just as I was reaching yet another

196

planet, somewhere in my stupefied solar system it kicked off, big time.

'Give me the fucking gear, you cunt. Give me the fucking gear now.'

Out in the hall, it suddenly sounded like Gus and his new best mate were having a bit of a row. I sloped over to investigate, opened the door and had a gun pointed in my face by our guest while he was simultaneously stamping on Gus's head and screaming at him to hand over the parcel of smack stuffed into the pocket of his jeans.

I resisted the temptation to turn into James Bond, disarm him and save my mate's facial features. My mouth was refusing to do anything other than hang open and stutter some nonsensical gibberish, like 'But, yeah, fuck, Gus, OK, fuck, shit, fucking hell,' and so on.

'Give me the fuckin' gear, mate, or I'll fuckin' kill you . . . Where's the fuckin' gear?'

Gus, bleeding from his mouth, nose and ears, screamed, 'Fuck off. Fuck off, fuck off . . . it's all gone, all right? Just fuck off, will ya?'

Psychopath person then smashed the butt of his gun into Gus's head a few more times.

'Where's the fuckin' gear, you dirty smackhead cunt? I'll fuckin' kill yer. I fuckin' mean it . . . and your mate too.'

I suddenly regained the power of speech.

'Give him the fucking gear, Gus! Give him the . . .'

The front door suddenly came off its hinges as a new arrival gatecrashed our little domestic tiff. The cavalry appeared in the shape of Gus's flatmate/business partner, who in one seamless motion disconnected the door from where doors like to hang out, then managed to crowbar our unwanted psycho over the head, forcing him to abandon his gun and the desire to rob us at the same time. Several more swift blows to the head saw our unwanted guest staggering off down the front path, blood spurting from various wounds, get into a car and drive off.

Silence.

'It's a fake, the fucking gun's a fake!'

Gus was holding his head with one hand and the replica pistol in the other. He started to laugh as a police car sped by, obviously not intent on joining our little soiree, which was a good thing, considering the circumstances.

We all looked at each other. Gus dropped the gun, then put his hand into his pocket, retrieved his bag of smack and headed off towards the kitchen.

'Light the fuckin' gas ring, someone. I think I need a hit, a big one.'

Is there any other kind?

As I rolled up my sleeve it suddenly occurred to me that I had just come close to dying a rather unglamorous and untimely death at the hands of some random West-Country psychopath who would probably have beaten Gus to death had the junkie-cavalry not arrived when they did and then had to ensure my silence in a similarly unpleasant manner. I mean, who wants to go out like that? And in Weston-super-Mare to boot? Doesn't bear thinking about, does it?

Sleeve up, needle and the damage done, I watched as my hosts both unfastened their belts and dropped their trousers and pants before injecting into their respective groins.

Silence.

One . . . two . . . three . . . four . . . five . . . Altogether now: 'That's better.'

'Yeah, lovely.'

'That's disgusting,' I thought to myself as I licked the blood off my own arm and lit a fag.

'That's really disgusting.'

A short while later I bade the chaps goodbye and drove back to London in the stolen car, only remembering as I passed Membury Services that I had nowhere to live when I got there. I decided to live in the car, so all that was left to determine was north, east, south or west London? It's all about location, location, location, you know!

Southern Man

I found somewhere to live in south London. The car park on the St Martin's Estate offered the basics for survival insomuch as a large percentage of the residents were drug addicts, there was a chemist nearby that offered a needle-exchange scheme and the local dealers offered a 24-hour home-delivery service.

Location, location, location.

I also found a new 'career' to keep me in gainful employment; I decided to become a minicab driver in the West End. Obviously not the kind of cabbie that worked out of an office, held a licence, worked a shift system and had an ornately decorated box of tissues on the back shelf of the car. I was more of the '£20 wherever it is you need to go' type of cab driver.

A £20 minimum fare meant I had enough to score afterwards and I charged more if it meant going somewhere weird, like north London, away from my 'base' in Tulse Hill and the next £20 rock or bag of gear.

I worked hard and 'played' hard for a few weeks, usually returning to the car park in the early hours of the morning, when I would drape a couple of dubiously stained sheets around the inside of the car, have a little after-work drink, crack pipe and hit of smack, then pass out until whatever time my habit started screaming in my head that I had to get up and do it all over again.

Some new 'friends' of mine from the estate would occasionally allow me to have a cup of tea, maybe a wash, or if feeling particularly generous let me spend the night on their sofa. It goes without saying that these acts of kindness always came with an entry fee. If I could spare some heroin and/or crack, they could spare a bit of soap and a teabag – just like people did during the Blitz, eh?

The gods, however, obviously had better things in store for me than the life of a drug-addled minicab driver, either that or they were just concerned for the safety of the people mental enough to actually get inside my car.

One morning I was trying to have a shit in the garages containing the estate's communal rubbish bins – a process that could either take a few seconds or considerably longer, depending on whether or not I was withdrawing. By some minor miracle I'd managed to keep my wake-up hit intact, so this was proving to be a long-haul session as I squatted, grunting, in the bin sheds. After what seemed like a lifetime I returned to where I'd parked the car, only to discover my livelihood and home had been towed away.

How many people can say that in the time it took them to complete their morning's ablutions they lost their home and career along with their crack pipe, needles and entire stash of highly addictive, will-be-feeling-very-fucking-sick-in-a-few-hours-unless-I-get-some-more-drugs?

I started crying.

Taxi driver? I needed a fucking ambulance but instead I called my sister, one of the few people who still cared about me, to tell her I needed help and fast.

Going up the Country

I'm half-asleep, half-dead in the back seat of my sister's car as she's driving us back to 'Punch-up-on-Sea'. Just when I thought things couldn't get any worse, I'm now heading towards possibly my biggest fear: the distinct prospect that someone, or some institution, was about to make me stop taking the extremely powerful, wonderful/ horrible, dangerous drugs I'd adopted as a way of trying to avoid dealing with the utter mess that was my life.

My family rarely saw me. Or, to be more accurate, I rarely went to visit them. My 'life' in London and all that entailed was usually badly reported via occasional phone calls generally containing my deluded notions that they'd soon be seeing me on *Top of the Pops*. I didn't ever consider they might actually have a firmer grip on reality than anything I could muster, let alone the notion they might be worried about me.

By the time we were approaching the 'Mare I'd managed to convince my sister that, 'Going to see Mum right now isn't a good idea, you know. I don't want to upset her. Maybe if I go round to Paul's flat and chill for a while until you get me into that rehab place . . . I mean, you know, I'm not exactly looking my best, am I?'

Perhaps the thought of me puking, crying and probably lying through my back teeth all day at either her or my mum's house, for however long it was before I escaped and scored anyway, resulted in her pulling the car over in the centre of town and watching me stumble off, sweating and retching, to see my friend Paul before she then headed off to see her mate at the local drug-dependency unit who'd promised to get me a bed in a neighbouring rehab – at a price, of course.

'Listen, you selfish twat,' she shouted loudly and accurately after me. 'Meet me at the DDU tomorrow at 10 a.m. If you're not there I'll go and get Mum and come and find you. Believe me it won't be hard . . .'

I went to say something but gagged viciously as she drove away crying and quite possibly absolutely terrified that I wouldn't be there the next day.

Meanwhile, as far as I could see, visiting Paul was the next best thing for me to do to try to resolve my current crisis, whereas my big sister realised I needed something with possibly a higher rate of success in getting people clean. Paul was my friend; he was also similarly afflicted and thus unlikely to assist in the task ahead. Getting me into treatment was, if left to my own devices, about as likely to happen as getting Ian Paisley to kiss the fucking Pope – a nice thought but not going to happen.

I wasn't thinking about any of that at the moment, though. I had more important things on my mind as I shuffled away.

Five minutes later I was banging on Paul's door, reciting the junkie prayer: 'Please, god, let him be home. Please, god, let him have gear . . . Please, god, let him be home. Please, god . . .'

The door opened.

'All right, Simon?'

We looked into each other's eyes. His pupils were tiny, which made me 'happy'.

'Got anything, mate? I'm clucking my bollocks off here, man.'

He looked into my massive pleading and scared eyes and nodded his head.

'Come in, mate. Just scored myself.'

The god of the sad, fucked-up and desperate had obviously heard my pleas.

Ten minutes later and I was telling my mate that life was OK, really, all things considered, but I had to meet my sister the next morning to see about getting myself on another methadone prescription, maybe some Valium and whatever else I could cunningly convince the doctor to dole out to me.

'Yeah, man, life's all right.' I mumbled as the smack wrapped me up and I instantly cared about nothing, least of all those running about in tears outside trying to help save me from myself.

The portable telly flickered away in the corner as we stared blankly at the news. The story being relayed was about the singer from the Manchester (City) Frisbee team getting arrested again.

'Silly cunt,' we mumbled in unison.

I had a hit left for the morning and therefore made it to meet my sister, when of course I then insisted that I would have been there regardless. She looked at me and ignored this obvious lie, given that the fact I was there and one more lie from me wasn't either surprising or indeed likely to make any difference to the outcome of our meeting with my key worker. I was going to rehab, that afternoon, end of.

'So Simon, you think you're ready for treatment then, do you? Ready to quit using?'

I did the decent thing and raised my opiate-saturated head as I replied, 'Ready to give up heroin, yeah . . .'

I tried to sound convincing, partly because somewhere in my stupefied mind I maybe thought I should . . . for a while at least.

'No, ready to give up all drugs, Simon . . .'

He had my full attention all of a sudden.

'What do you mean "all" drugs?'

'I mean all drugs, Simon.'

'Even smoking puff . . . and having an E every now and then?'

'I think you'll find that you might have to, Simon.'

'Well, good job I've never had a problem with drinking, then, eh? Imagine if I had to give up that as well, I'd really be fucked, eh?'

'You are fucked, Simon, haven't you noticed?'

As you've probably noticed, I only really noticed anything when I ran out of smack.

'Your mum has paid for you to go to into a detox this afternoon. We rang round a few places and got you a bed. They're expecting you this afternoon. You're very lucky to have a family who care about you and want to help. Your mother has used some of her savings to get you a place quickly; it normally takes months on the NHS. We can't all be Tara fucking Palmer posh bird, can we, eh?'

I didn't feel like being her to be honest. I didn't feel lucky or cared about; I was so fucking terrified it was all I could do to not throw up on the guy's lap.

'Any questions, Simon?'

My sister and the do-gooder both looked at me intently.

'Er . . . no . . . I've just got to go and collect my things from my mate's place . . . I . . .'

My stomach turned over. A feeling, the thing I tried really hard to avoid, was suddenly simultaneously slapping me in the face, kicking me in the nuts and punching a massive hole in my stomach.

What could I do?

Crying my fucking eyes out and feeling sorry for myself, I could always manage, often without hesitation and with a certain well-rehearsed conviction if it meant I could manipulate a situation. But this was different. These people were professionals. They'd suss me out in no time. What had I agreed to put myself through?

Poor me, poor fucking me, me, me, me, me, me, me, me, me, me . . . . ME.

If the path of excess was going to lead me to the palace of wisdom, I'd currently lost the map and was about to be marched into the large country pile looming in front of me that, in my opinion, contained the weak-willed, selfish, desperate, sad, lonely and scared. If there's anything someone like me is more terrified of than being alone, it's being confronted by lots of other people with a similar fear, minus the self-medicating properties of the drugs we use to escape ourselves.

We parked out front and I stumbled into the hall of mirrors to meet the gang.

Country House

On arrival we were greeted by a minor celebrity – and when I say minor I mean less significant than anyone who would probably appear on *Celebrity Big Brother*, not that we'd yet been 'blessed' with that particular stain on popular culture at that point in televised human evolution.

It's hard to decipher the depth of people's compassion when someone is standing next to you, writing out a cheque to pay for the care you are about to receive, or maybe that was just my junkie cynicism hard at work trying already to devalue the opportunity in front of me?

You get nothing for nothing on planet smackhead, a fact that does little to allow the process of trusting people much of a chance to develop. Yeah, I was of course well used to giving people money to make me feel better, but that daily transaction produced almost instant results, the instant nothingness I desired. This scenario was already looking like it might involve some honesty and serious physical discomfort, and the chances of me producing the first in order to endure the latter were as paper-thin as the cheque being handed over by my sister.

I was given a good staring at as I sat and chain-smoked while trying not to make eye contact with anyone. A few people asked me where I was from and I came up against my first problem: I kept lying.

'All right, mate? Where are you from?'

'London . . . I'm from London.'

'You don't sound like you're from London, mate.'

'I am. Tulse Hill, St Martin's Estate, actually.'

I clearly had a problem that was nothing to do with drugs, although the two issues happily co-exist in many junkies. I couldn't tell the truth even when it concerned something as relatively unimportant as where I was from, which begs the question of why I was so concerned with what anyone might think regarding my place of birth. We were all in rehab and therefore surely had more important things to think about?

Apparently, it was now time to 'get real'. Oh dear, oh dear, oh dear, oh dear, this situation was clearly going to require something I was not exactly very good at – being honest and facing my fears. Honesty and bravery – I must have been standing at the back of the queue when these qualities were being handed out and then told they were out of stock. As compensation I got some low self-esteem, the ability to lie pathologically, a premium-grade ego, a tanker full of self-pity and a bullshit generator instead.

The doctor wrote me up for a two-week reduction on methadone, the last dose to be administered the day before I left. My mum couldn't afford any more money for a longer stay and I didn't exactly try to convince her to find it from somewhere. I did, however, shortly question the doctor's medication regime, my thinking being that I'd be more or less OK while I was on the methadone but likely to start feeling really sick when I finished taking it – the day I was due to leave. Still, I guess these people were experts in getting people off drugs, while I was an expert in staying on them.

I went to my room, had my possessions searched and was then asked to join a group already in progress where a girl was talking about being raped by her uncle. It clearly was time to get real. I chose to keep my mouth shut.

I attended the groups, heard a great deal of sadness and some brutal honesty, which eventually inspired me to speak up. It seemed to be the correct thing to do to divulge some details about my own issues and pretend I was ready to stop taking heroin, so I did. The days passed quickly, the nights not so, but I took my medication, possibly set a new world record for furtive late-night wanking as the meds wore off, maybe convinced a few people I was going to be OK then left after my two weeks' treatment was up.

It had been agreed that, amongst other things, I needed to break away from my old 'friends' in London but the suggestion of moving back to Weston was, I informed my counsellor, tantamount to giving me a bag of gear and set of works as they waved me off down the drive. It was therefore suggested I consider somewhere else that could provide a support network to assist me in my attempt at starting a new, drug-free life.

Why the fuck they kept banging on about a 'drug-free' life I had no idea. I mean nobody fucking does that, do they? An hour after leaving treatment I was weighing up the options regarding what drugs I might need to avoid while on a train necking a large brandy and ginger en route to Brighton. It was very much out of season and cheap hotel rooms were not hard to come by, even ones that came with a residents' bar and offered reduced weekly rates for people on benefits, so I quickly found somewhere with the money my mum had given me.

Checking in to my 'new life' should, in theory at least, have been a positive experience had I not been suddenly, seriously withdrawing from the methadone, the last dose of which was now obviously vacating my system and skipping off into the Brighton sunset, holding hands with the brandy and ginger I'd been drinking throughout my journey.

The notion of seeking out a support network such as Narcotics Anonymous, as suggested by the people at the treatment centre, flashed through my mind but actually seemed like far too much hassle; besides, I wasn't really in the mood to join a cult so soon after leaving one of their recruitment centres – sorry, I mean rehabs!

I went out to score some smack instead – just a one-off to celebrate my success in getting off it and help alleviate the last of the withdrawals, something which in Brighton took approximately five minutes to do.

As I scurried back into the guest house after my excursion (find *Big Issue* seller, offer to sort them out if they introduce me to a dealer, score, go home) the landlady cornered me as I trotted past reception.

'Give me ten minutes please, love. I've just got to go up to my room, slight case of food poisoning, need the loo, won't be long.'

When I returned one miracle-cure later, I found my hostess helping herself to a large gin and tonic from the residents' bar and it felt like the right thing to do to join her.

'Mr Mason, how long do you think you'll be needing the room for? We offer weekly rates that work out much cheaper, you know.'

'Well, let me see.'

I leaned towards her in a conspiratorial manner, as if what I was about to tell her was a secret of great importance.

'You see, Mrs . . . er . . .'

'Smith, Doreen Smith.'

'Well, Doreen – can I call you Doreen?'

She returned my smile.

'Yes, of course, Mr . . .'

'Simon, call me Simon, Doreen.'

'OK, Simon, thank you.'

My hostess was now blushing slightly as I held my lighter up to the Silk Cut hanging unlit from her overly made-up lips.

'You see, Doreen, I'm a journalist working undercover to get a story about drug addicts here in Brighton. You know, heroin addicts, junkies, those dirty dole-scrounging beggars that make the place look so unattractive – scumbags, Doreen, the lot of 'em.'

I smiled.

She blushed again.

'Did anyone ever tell you, you have beautiful eyes, Doreen?'

'Oh . . . no, I mean . . . thank you, Simon . . . thank you. Which paper do you work for?'

'I can't tell you, Doreen. I wish I could but like I said I'm undercover so to speak . . . very undercover.'

I leant in to mutter in her ear.

'They're dangerous criminals, some of them, Doreen . . . into all sorts.'

She looked worried.

'But you can rest assured I'll not mention the wonderful establishment you keep here in my article, Doreen. Nothing bad will happen, I promise. I may be here a while but I'd prefer it if you ignored me as I come and go. You see, I don't want to let anyone know what I'm up to. You can't trust people these days, Doreen, you just can't trust people.'

'Oh, no, of course . . . you're right, Simon. You just don't know what people are up to half the time, do you?'

I gave her my best smile and accepted the large brandy and Coke she offered as she refreshed her own glass. We chatted about the hordes of filthy, unwashed drug addicts contaminating the streets outside for a while before I went back upstairs and had another hit.

You couldn't make it up, could you?

I could – anything was preferable to the truth.

My 'research' continued and after three weeks during which I'd run up a drinks bill that I obviously had no means or intention of paying I ended up 'borrowing' £20 from Doreen, which she offered while pissed out of her head one night after I'd told her I was waiting for my paper to send me more money. I continually refused the daily offer of the in-house linen service due to the fact my bed sheets were splattered with blood, telling my host that doing my own laundry was just my way of not adding to her own workload and it also allowed me to get on with mine.

'You see, Doreen, a lot of the junkies hang out and buy their filthy drugs in the launderette. I think I've got a few leads. I may even have found "Mr Big", you know. He's Albanian, proper scumbag, probably into the white-slave trade as well. Scum of the earth, Doreen, scum of the earth.'

'Oh, you are brave, Simon. Aren't you scared you'll get found out?'

'It's a risk I'm prepared to take, Doreen; I know God is looking after me.'

'Well, I think you're very brave, Simon. I can see how hard you must be working. You're always running in and out of here and you look so thin. You're not looking after yourself, are you? You hardly ever eat a thing; I hope you're getting well paid for this.'

(Coincidentally, by now I'd managed to start selling a bit of gear to some other 'junkie scumbags' at the launderette to maintain my own habit and actually pocket a few quid myself.)

'I'm not doing it for the money, Doreen; I'm just trying to expose the truth.'

I woke up one afternoon and decided my time as an investigative journalist was over. Doreen was going away and leaving her ex-husband to look after the hotel for the weekend. Her ex-husband was also an ex-policeman.

I therefore became an ex-journalist and an ex-resident of both the hotel and Brighton, and in true undercover style left through the back door, leaving no forwarding address. It's not as if I had a forwarding address anyway.

Simon Mason Esq.
Somewhere surrounded by junkies and crack whores
London

That would have been a big ask for even the most determined of postmen.

Police and Thieves

A few days later and it was back to the streets of London, sleeping in hostels, crackhouses and squats, wallowing in self-pity and denial. I didn't have a problem with alcohol or weed but sometimes reluctantly considered the notion that I might, just might, want to stop using heroin. Perhaps it's closer to the truth to say I was toying with the idea that I might need to stop. But these were fleeting thoughts that were submerged by the more seductive, albeit ridiculous, desire to have enough smack to ensure I'd never run out and therefore not have to exist with the daily consequences that being skint and in love with heroin bring.

I say 'in love' but what I really mean is 'scared to let go of', 'co-dependent with', 'obsessed by', which isn't really the same, is it?

It had become apparent in a very short space of time that I wasn't going to win any prizes for shoplifting, unless eating the slop masquerading as food in London's police stations could be considered recognition for my daily endeavours, of course.

Running about in the West End getting arrested on a fairly regular basis while committing petty crime was something that not only was I really rubbish at but I was also not particularly fond of. (The fact that I was even worse at not looking like a desperate junkie willing to nick anything in order to get his next hit didn't help further my cause much either.) It was, however, a necessity if I was to keep myself safe from the mental tsunami of my past, which rolled towards me every morning within seconds of waking up in need of heroin.

As for considering another jaunt through rehab, it sometimes crossed my mind but after asking various other street junkies their thoughts it became obvious that rehab didn't work.

'What's such-and-such treatment centre like?'

'Yeah, it's great. I've been there three times. Food's great, counsellors are OK, you can get a bit of gear in from time to time, too.'

This was a eulogy given by a 'friend' of mine as we were both poking about in our battered arms trying desperately to find a vein that hadn't gone on strike, citing unfair working conditions.

The other somewhat off-putting issue about rehab was that, as far as I could make out, none of them let you have a drink or a puff while you were there, which to my mind seemed a little draconian considering it was heroin and crack causing all the problems. It was a no-brainer that I'd have to have a drink and a smoke after being in rehab and 'getting real' for a few months. Fuck me! That sounded like a real pain in the arse – talk about stressful! I mean, nobody lives life without something in their system to take the edge off, do they? No one that I knew anyway.

One afternoon, while attending a homeless persons' drop-in centre in Soho, the latest do-gooder/key worker assigned the unenviable task of trying to stop someone like me from hurting themselves managed to get me a room in a hostel in Covent Garden. I was as delighted as was possible considering my opinion that a room somewhere in the West End meant easy access to an unlimited supply of drugs 24/7 and the availability of all those stores that had stuff I could steal in order to fund my habit. I might not have enjoyed being a crap criminal but it was slightly less soul destroying than male prostitution, though you'll have to take my word for it on that matter, I'm afraid. Put it this way, if you can imagine that at this point I resembled a malnourished, foul-smelling scarecrow, you'll perhaps get some idea of the personal hygiene of the kind of bummer who'd consider paying me for sex.

Thanks, but no thanks. I'm off to rob some books from Foyles.

As I was shown up to my room it was explained to me that I'd be sharing it with another 'client' and in the same breath was also informed, 'We're obviously not responsible for anything that gets "lost" while you're here.'

Furthermore: 'You may want to keep your trainers on while you sleep at night. They often have a habit of disappearing if you don't,' which considering the state of my trainers might not have been a bad thing but it wasn't exactly a comforting statement.

And finally: 'The use of illegal drugs on the premises is strictly forbidden. Please dispose of all sharps in the bins provided.'

Oh well, it's good to be given a few pointers when moving home and meeting one's new 'flatmate' for the first time, eh?

As I entered my room there was a bloke with a striking resemblance to Gollum sitting on his bed, rolling up his trouser leg. He looked up at me as the porter departed after wishing me luck.

'All right, mate?' says I.

He looked down at his leg, then back up at me, then pointed to a golf-ball-sized lump of green and grey rotting flesh where part of his calf should have been.

'Do you think this abscess has gone septic, mate?'

Nice!

The next morning, after a sleepless night mainly spent trying not to vomit because of the smell coming from my roommate's bed/leg, I squelched into my trainers and went down to reception to ask if I could make one phone call.

'Hello, City Roads Crisis Intervention, can I help you?'

'I hope so, I really hope so.'

They agreed to give me another chance. I'd have to wait a short while, maybe a week, but to them it sounded like I was in a worse state than when I'd called them before.

I took my chances out on the street again. I couldn't stand another night in that room for obvious reasons. Did I mention the bloke was wearing a Man United shirt? Can you imagine?

City Roads accepted me a few days, a lot of phone calls and no little desperation later. When I say desperation I actually mean self-piteous pleading coupled with thinly veiled threats about ending my life if someone didn't help me.

My best efforts to back up my pleas of, 'I swear to god, I'm going to put myself out of this miserable existence soon,' were as follows.

I got nicked one day for another crap attempt at pretending to not look like a crap junkie trying to steal some crap from a crap shop in order to put some more crap drugs into my body. The crap security guard had been just a little less crap than he normally was and therefore managed to stop me from walking/jogging out of the crap shop with whatever it was I'd managed to conceal upon my crap body underneath my crap clothes.

I'd intended to take my booty up to the crap/crack/smack cash-converters shop in Camden but it obviously was not meant to be that particular day. (A crappy, cold and wet-weather kind of day, of course.) Two crap coppers arrived, who talked a lot of crap in between my speaking a lot of crap as they marched me up to the crap copshop.

Enough crap – you get the picture, I'm sure.

So I was slouched in the corner of the cell as time slowed down in direct relation to the speed at which I started to go into withdrawal, the first major sign of this inevitable torment being the re-arrival into the world of the can of nourishment drink I'd had for breakfast earlier, which I managed to projectile vomit into my lap just after the copper had given me a friendly punch in the stomach as he'd thrown . . . sorry, I mean helped me into the cell.

Time slowed down some more as the retching, coughing and crying began in earnest, some time after which the custody sergeant banged on the door and threw my 'lunch' through the hatch.

Seeing as I wasn't feeling exactly peckish, I wasn't too bothered that the culinary equivalent of a club 18–30 resort for food-borne viral infections, served on a paper plate, was 'accidentally' spilt on the floor. No doubt the various forms of bacteria contained in the food were suddenly having a merry old time mingling with their floor-inhabiting cousins.

Anyway, what I did see that might come in useful in my dazzling idea to kill myself right now and show these cunts whatever it was they needed to be shown was the plastic knife and fork that were delivered with my food.

I'm fairly sure that by now, if you've been following this tale of woe I sometimes chose to call my life, it will have come to your attention that I'm not exactly the sharpest knife in the drawer; well, certainly not the plastic knives they give you in the nick, anyway. If I'd really wanted to have a good go at topping myself I should have simply eaten the food that had been airmailed to me through the hatch in the cell door. If I hadn't popped my clogs immediately it's possible that I would have rapidly fallen into some sort of semi-comatose state of chronic food poisoning, which, coupled with the smack withdrawals, might have been enough to convince the duty sergeant I was in immediate need of a doctor and possible hospitalisation.

Hospitalisation was, to my deluded mind, the surest chance of getting to the head of the queue for City Roads but also the fastest route to some Valium and methadone, neither of which seemed to be on offer at this particular copshop.

It's possible I might then have spared the duty sergeant the pathetic sight of me trying to self-harm with a plastic knife and fork the next time he answered my thumb, which was stuck on the cell 'room-service' bell while I just about squeezed a few drops of blood onto the floor to mingle with what remained of my food.

He came in and had a word.

'Listen, you pathetic junkie scumbag, it's turned into a nice sunny afternoon out there and the two officers who arrested you want to go out and look at birds' tits for a while. They're almost done with the paperwork now cos they'd much rather be outside doing that than sitting in the station listening to you rattle your nuts off, OK? They get bored with that game very quickly. So we'll be charging and releasing you in the next 20 minutes or so. Until then, shut the fuck up and keep your fuckin' finger off that fuckin' bell. If I hear one more fuckin' noise from you, we'll keep you in till fuckin' Monday with all the old bedwetters that shit themselves every few hours. Okey fuckin' dokey, sunshine?'

Okey fuckin' dokey it was.

I was admitted to City Roads that night.

Another 21 days were spent mainly climbing the walls, where I declined the offer of a place in residential rehab immediately afterwards, choosing instead to take another room in a different hostel and attend a day programme.

Within ten minutes of arriving there I was given £20 to go and get a weekly travel card, the procurement of which I decided could wait until after I'd had a swift half in the nearest pub. A further ten minutes after which I decided I needed to go and see how my old mate Terry was doing in Camden Town, so I could tell him what it was like being clean.

I'd intended to pop in for a few minutes, just for old times' sake. Within a few hours it *was* old times and over the next few days I quickly got reacquainted with Terry's bedroom, the bin in his wardrobe, numerous phone boxes and street corners in Camden town, waiting . . . always fucking waiting, of course. Waiting for 'X', 'Swan', 'Ninja', 'Bogey', 'Ronnie', 'D', whoever.

A . . . B . . . fucking . . . C. Whoever 'had' or said they 'had' or said they knew who 'had'.

'Yeah, yeah . . . meet me in ten at the phone box in Queen's Crescent.'

'Ten minutes? You sure?'

'Yeah, yeah . . . ten.'

Queen's Crescent? That's a good 15-minute walk and I'm sick as a dog . . . but I must get there.

You get there in ten.

Then wait twenty or thirty.

You phone back two or three times.

'Yeah, yeah, just round the corner.' Click.

You call again, more coins in the phone box and the £15 you need to score is now £14.

'Yeah, yeah, I'll be there in five. What you need?'

I need help but heroin and crack sounds better right now.

'What you need? I've got both.'

That's when the stomach really starts churning and you have to clench your arse.

Click.

Five minutes, then ten, maybe less and back to Terry's. Reckon I'll be opening the bag and sorting myself out within . . . five minutes?

How long ago did he say that?

Five million years?

Maybe it was?

'Who's got change for the phone?'

He doesn't answer this time.

You stagger to another phone box, call from a different number so he doesn't know it's you bugging him again.

'I'm there . . . where are you?'

Fuck.

'I'm there, mate . . . wait . . .'

'Fuck shit . . . cunt, cunt, cunt, cunt, fucking cunt . . .'

You drop the receiver and make it back to the Crescent in two minutes, lungs exploding, sweat pouring, legs almost giving up on you. 'Cunt . . . cunt, fucking . . .'

But as you turn the corner and see the messiah, you know you're saved.

'One of each, mate, please.'

One of each, heroin and crack, one of each on a 'good' day.

Ten minutes later you're waiting for Terry to open his bedroom window, ten seconds after that you go to work.

Terry looks at you.

'Sorry, Tel . . . here . . . take a bit out of the bag, mate.'

Your eyes zero in on his hands as he takes his 'tip'.

'Don't take fucking liberties, you cunt.'

You can say that now, because right at this precise moment you don't need him, you don't need a dealer, you don't need anything other than the brown powder and the rock that you are clutching in your sweaty, shaking hand.

Thirty seconds later everything is OK again.

You don't need anything.

You certainly don't need to hear the sound of his mum's voice demanding to know if he had any 'of your fackin' junkie friends in there with you, son?'

'No, Mum. I'm on me own, just having a kip.'

There were four of us there at that particular time. Four men aged between twenty-five and forty-five cowering behind a cheap door and paper-thin, nicotine-stained wall from the sound of our 'mate's' mother's voice while wishing she would just fuck off so we could take our drugs in her house in peace.

Nice.

Any wonder I hated myself?

But without the drugs I also felt empty, scared and lonely whenever the self-medicating properties of whatever was on my daily menu began to wear off. Underneath all that there now also seemed to be something altogether more frightening trying to crawl out of the dark recesses of my mind.

What was so wrong?

Everything.

Absolutely everything was wrong, or so it seemed to me.

Me, me, me, me, me, me, me, fucking well me!

Wrong past.

Wrong present.

Wrong future – should I stay alive to inhabit it.

Wrong feelings.

Wrong dreams.

Wrong nightmares.

Wrong 'friends'.

Wrong drugs?

Surely not the heroin and crack that spoke to me when they were eventually placed in my yellowing clammy hands in return for money, stolen goods or promises of such? They told me that as soon as I found somewhere to ingest them everything would be OK. They told me that I could stop if I really wanted to, just not today, of course. They told me it was pointless stopping, though, because sooner or later I would have to start again. They told me no one ever really stops anyway. They told me there is only one way out but that wasn't going to happen to me. I wasn't going to die; 'we' were all going to live forever, remember? They only ever told me that immediately after I used, though. They told me I was born alone and would always feel alone except when 'we' were together, preferably alone behind closed shutters to keep others out.

We often peered through the shutters to make sure no one was coming, of course; we often thought we heard them. They told me lots of things I seemed to have no choice but to believe in because my doubting of what they told me always came in tandem with the feelings of 'wrongness' and there was no way I could deal with that, was there?

Years passed, dissipated and dissolved into burnt spoons, crack pipes and broken promises.

More people died.

I went in and out of treatment centres and heard you could stop using drugs, all drugs and alcohol too, a solution I privately maintained was not something that would work for me but I learnt to make people think I was convinced. I also learnt to keep people away by pretending to get close. I heard often that people like me could stop destroying themselves but as far as I was concerned there was no one like me. Not really.

I met many wonderful people over the years, both on the street and in detox/treatment, plenty of people I condescendingly thought to be not as off-key as me who I liked, and plenty of others that my arrogance told me were much more fucked up than me who I liked even more. I latched onto them because they were good people and also because they allowed me to stay 'wrong' simply because, as far as I was concerned, I was not as 'wrong' as them and therefore must be doing something right. Amazing! I could sit in a fucking rehab, half-dead, family distraught, teeth falling out with holes in my arms and make decisions about who was or wasn't as messed up as me!

That's as good as an example of my best thinking as you'll find. You gotta laugh in a sad and deluded kind of way.

Eventually, though, I became the most 'wrong' person I knew and that took some doing, I can tell you.

I went into one particular rehab because they promised me a flat of my own on completion of their programme and a stint in a 'dry house' for a few months afterwards, rather than anything they claimed to be able to do to address my seeming inability to stay off drugs.

The treatment was a drug-free experience, the dry house afterwards not so, but my ability to avoid detection only served to convince me that I was some sort of recovery enigma who could find his own way out of trouble while also still being able to find his way to the bar.

End of a Century

I closed the door to the hostel, put on my headphones, pressed play on the Walkman and started walking. In the time it took to listen to The Stone Roses' first album I got to where I was required to be.

As I made my way to Islington, I found myself hoping that it wasn't going to take me the five years it took them to record and release their next album to get where I needed to be, a place that would find me content and no longer making such a mess of my life, wherever that was. It was one of the many things I didn't know but sometimes thought I did.

I stood still and lit a cigarette, feeling alone as ever while surrounded by millions of others who were to my eyes already lost, or in the process of losing 'it' while trying to . . .

This was another thing I didn't know . . . what was everyone else trying to do? I was too busy thinking about myself to consider it.

Me, me, me, me, me, me, ME.

'Spare any change, mate?'

Looking into the beaten face of the beggar sitting alone in the doorway, I saw a reflection of my previous life.

I was over five months clean(ish) and waiting to be given a flat of my own. This time I was sure my days of addiction were over. They must be – I hadn't used any smack for ages, so surely I was cured?

I handed him all but two of the packet, not to help him out so much as to make *me* feel better, then walked away with my feelings and the Stone Roses for company.

'Nice one, man, god bless . . .'

Apparently it's not where you're from, it's where you're at, or so their singer once said. Perhaps it's not where you're at or from but where you've been and where you're heading?

Me, me, me, me, me.

I'd received a letter, and aside from worried ones from my mum from time to time I hadn't got a letter for a long time, not a real letter.

This was no different. It wasn't a real letter either; it had arrived in a brown envelope with one of those transparent windows, beneath which was me and where I was at.

Mr Simon Mason
Horseferry Road Project
London SW

I was in a hostel for former drug addicts who were trying to stay clean, in my case by pretending I no longer adored drugs.

Drugs no longer adored me. Judging by what they did to me I guess they fucking hated me, truth be told, but, again, this was another thing I didn't know. Besides, I'd often liked people who hated me, so why should drugs be any different?

Indeed.

I got to where the letter had sincerely asked me to be, on time but half a song too early and, refusing to interrupt the final coda of 'I am the Resurrection', I smoked another fag as I shuffled from foot to foot almost in time to the music, almost.

That's how I feel most of the time . . . almost, not quite . . . enough.

Song over, feeling a bit inspired and a bit jealous (see?) I entered the building on St Johns Street to meet Natalie, who was trying to help me.

My probation officer looked up over her morning's work consisting of an ever-increasing paper heap of damaged, fucked-up lives and enquired, 'How's it going, Simon? Did it take long to get here?'

'Yeah, pretty good, no, not really . . . it's better to travel than to arrive, you know.'

I don't think she did know much about my travels but then again neither did I and I had been there, had the photographs, T-shirts and backstage passes to prove it. I used to anyway.

I just can't remember much about anything really, which is strange considering how much time I spend thinking about me, me, me, me, me, ME. Until now.

We talked at each other and agreed that I was doing well: I'd avoided jail (so far), was off drugs and had a roof over my head.

'Do you need anything in particular, Simon?'

'Yeah, I need to remember, so I can eventually forget.'

'Forget what, Simon?'

She looked at me, unsure if I was taking the piss.

'I'm not sure, yet. I'll let you know when I remember. See you in two weeks, Natalie.'

She gave me a very professional smile and my travel expenses.

'Take care of yourself, Simon.'

How do you do that?

Really. How do you?

This was another thing I didn't know but didn't know I didn't know.

After ten more or less drug/alcohol free months I was given a flat of my own in Hackney, the new millennium was a matter of weeks away and surely no one expected me to not celebrate that without at least a drink?

You and Me

Stoke Newington became my new stomping ground, with my own flat and very shortly the drinkers in The Yucatan pub being the foundations upon which I would construct my own brand of rehabilitation. This was a process I rapidly discovered to be thirsty work; fortunately the local off-licence sold cans of Special Brew for less than a quid and would give me credit at 3 a.m.

For the record, I spent the Millennium evening alone, unconscious on the floor of my flat after six cans of Special Brew and a cheeky £10 bag of heroin. I began the new millennium resolved to not ever find myself in the same state and for a while at least there was progress. I had a flat, some new friends and had also fallen in love!

My girlfriend, whom I'd initially first briefly met and dated while in my mid '90s 'pomp' when stomping about one Friday night at Smashing on Regent Street, had no idea as to why I'd kept fucking up in the past but was soon to find out.

Within two years of her moving in with me she'd been to visit me numerous times while I sat talking bollocks in detox/rehab, pumped full of methadone and ignoring the hard-earned experiences of my peers and counsellors.

She had been invited to a family group on the day of one visit, during which, I'd learned, she would also be given the same pamphlets and advice I would eventually throw in the bin on the train as I came home. I'd have had no problem with her going to the group if it was to hear how well I'd done but there was an issue I didn't want her to hear about: drinking, or to be more precise the suggestion that I probably needed to stop drinking for good. This was the one idea that I considered utter lunacy and as such used it to underpin my complete disregard for almost every other piece of advice offered to me.

We'd been apart for nearly six weeks and I therefore convinced my dearest that rather than attend the family group we should instead avail ourselves of the privacy of the beautiful grounds surrounding the centre so we could get my 'needs' met, rather than listen to anything said by the people who'd been trying to save my life.

Simon Mason 1, Reality 0.

I completed the six-week stint in treatment and returned to Hackney making all the usual noises about what was going to be different this time and, for a while at least, it started to look like I might just be serious.

Back at home it appeared as if my recovery was going well. I'd entered another day programme after the six weeks away and within a few months I'd secured a mentoring position at that project, a post I thought I was well suited to considering my numerous spells in such establishments over the years.

I was actually pretty good at supporting other people and suggesting what they might need to do to stay on the right track, facilitating groups where clients could discuss any issues they had as they acclimatised to living back in the community, hopefully free from problematic drug or alcohol use and in some sort of process where they could become empowered to stay so.

Yeah, I was great at making positive suggestions to others; in fact, trotting out tried and tested 'recovery-speak' soon got me the offer of an interview for a paid job at the same project, something I celebrated that evening with a few pints followed by a few more, followed by some heroin and a bit of crack.

The next morning I went into work still somewhat spannered but full of enthusiasm for proclaiming the theory of unlearning learnt behaviour and quite possibly also in line for first prize in 'do as I say, not what I do' hypocritical dickhead of the year.

Unlearning learnt behaviour?

What exactly did that mean? It sounded achievable as the general gist, at least as far as I could understand it, was that perhaps going to college or doing some sort of voluntary work would help develop a sense of self-esteem and the stringing together of some positive choices. This in turn would then help unlearn the learnt behaviour of what was for most of the group many years of making bad choices

222

due to hardcore active drug addiction and the inherent lack of purpose and self-worth that accompanies this ongoing nightmare.

Sounds pretty straightforward, doesn't it?

Unlearn what you've learnt, don't avoid your feelings with nasty substances, just bloody well DON'T, OK?

It sounded a lot better than not being able to drink or smoke the odd joint as far as I was concerned, anyway.

This theory does in fact work for many people; I cannot pretend otherwise. Perhaps it worked for some of my clients in the long term. I don't really know because it soon became apparent that my appointment was about as beneficial to all concerned as Margaret Thatcher's premiership was to Britain's coal miners.

I got the job and my girlfriend became my wife at a civil ceremony in Bournemouth, a remarkable testament to her love for me and her belief that I would remain on the straight and narrow to become the man she somehow saw I was possibly capable of being.

I'd managed to stay in reasonable shape, as far as she or anybody else knew anyway, for quite some time and on the few occasions when I'd slipped up and either been caught out or 'fessed up I had tried hard to get back on track quickly. God may indeed love a 'trier' but I don't think he'd like to actually marry one.

We went to Mexico for our honeymoon, which for the most part was great and involved seeing the sights, soaking up the sun and, wherever I got the chance, drinking as much mescal as I could and at some point procuring a golf-ball-sized lump of Mexican tar heroin, most of which I gave away to some Italian junkies I chanced upon the day before we flew home to begin our married life in our little home in Hackney, complete with my new career, secret trips to the pub and the stuff that usually happened to me after I went there.

A few months into married life and I was frequenting The Yucatan most evenings on my way home from work, having by now also made the acquaintance of Vic the Beggar, who swiftly introduced me to my local heroin and crack dealers, after which my visits to them also became a regular, if not daily, occurrence.

As I sat locked inside the staff toilet one day, smoking heroin on some tinfoil I'd pinched from the canteen, I began to think I perhaps wasn't the right man for the job of aftercare worker in a rehab, a hypothesis that was confirmed while scoring from a crack house in Hackney one lunch break and bumping into one of my clients.

After what must have been one of the most awkward silences in the history of awkward silences, he broke the ice with an invitation to smoke some rocks. We chipped in together to buy a couple of stones, our thinking being that if we smoked them just before we went back to work/aftercare, our eyes wouldn't look so pinned from the smack we'd smoked and maybe no one would notice that we were in a slightly different state of being from the rest of the staff/clients respectively. Now that's what I call working closely with your clients!

We both somehow managed to escape detection but I have to say I found facilitating that afternoon's relapse-prevention group a bit of a challenge. I think I actually nodded out once. On my way home from work I stopped to finish smoking my gear and began to ponder how I was going to hide my eyes from my wife. She was by now more than capable of telling if I'd used anything. In fact she could tell from about half a mile away but of course my smack-addled brain came up with a cunning plan to avoid detection.

I say cunning but what I really mean is . . . well, read on and you decide.

I parked my scooter in the garages on the other side of the street from our flat, took out the heavy-duty bike chain I used to lock the scooter up and proceeded to bash myself around the face with it for a minute or so, concluding with a couple of self-inflicted punches in the mouth before running over to the flat, bursting through the door and yelling, 'Babe . . . babe . . . you'll never believe this but . . . [this was a regular sentence opener for me and most junkies I knew] I've just been attacked . . . I mean mugged . . . right by the garage as I was putting the scooter away . . . fucking hell, I can't believe it. Look at the state of me . . . fucking hell . . .'

She stood in the doorway of the kitchen, took one look at me and started crying. 'You cunt . . . you sick fucking bastard. Get out and leave me alone . . . you've done it again, haven't you? . . . Oh, Jesus fucking Christ . . . I'm going to have to leave . . .'

'But . . . babe . . . I . . . I . . .'

'Just fuck off, Simon . . . I hate you.'

End of job?

Definitely.

End of marriage?

What would you have done if you were her?

This wasn't the first time she'd been confronted by me and my madness demanding her acceptance of what was clearly the most ridiculous bullshit while I became even more indignant.

'I haven't used any gear, for fuck sake. I've just had a few pints. What are you, mental?'

'You're driving me insane, Simon. Please stop, please.'

Not much of a choice really? Stay and go insane or leave and wait for a phone call to say your husband is dead. The Manic Street Preachers song 'La Tristesse Durera' was playing in the background and it serenaded our stand-off as I patronised her misery.

She moved out and waited for the call; I stayed and asked Vic the Beggar if he wanted to move in. He did for a few days then left, probably because by the time a week had passed there was nothing left in my flat worth selling.

Junkies usually only hang out with other junkies if there's something in it for them, and having to listen to my self-piteous shit day after day without the promise of a bit of gear for breakfast was, as far as Vic was concerned, a bad deal.

He went back to sleeping behind the bins just off Church Street; I, eventually, went back into detox.

Maybe this time?

Maybe all these feelings won't overwhelm me.

Maybe I can cope?

Blood on the Tracks

The notion that true love conquers all was probably as seductive to my wife as drugs were to me, as I tried to cope with being me and my apparent inability to continue to accept and reciprocate her feelings despite the fact that I was deeply in love with her.

I'd written in my diary, the very first night I'd seen her grooving away on the under-lit dance floor at Smashing years earlier: 'Just got the phone number of the most beautiful creature I've ever seen. I'm going to marry her one day.'

I'm no psychiatrist but it's not hard to accept the notion that if individuals are barely capable of liking themselves for any given period of time it's going to be a big ask for them to accept and return the love of another human being. Truth is, the more she, or indeed anyone else, demonstrated any love and affection for me, the more I ran away from it.

A short while after I'd left the club that night, clutching her number even tighter than the wad of cash I had stuffed in my pocket at the end of my night's work, we found ourselves in the same vicinity again.

A very messy, very rock 'n' roll weekend at the Reading festival was more or less the starting point of her first brief foray into my world. Despite already being in the company of some very famous and successful rock stars, she accepted my invitation to come and hang out with my 'almost' famous musician friends. To my mind, if you could call it that, this clearly meant she was going to let me have sex with her. The fact that she didn't let me get anywhere near her bra, let alone anything else, served only to re-invigorate my determination to seduce her in perhaps a less-crowded situation. She was clearly not the type of girl who was going to let me shag her while I was dribbling pure Ecstasy from the corner of my mouth in a cheap hotel room in Reading, in the company of a has-been keyboard player and the drummer from a crusty indie band from the West Midlands.

How could I not love her for that?

A few weeks later, after much harassing from me, we went on a date. Me, the most beautiful creature I'd ever seen and some heroin she didn't know about, went on a date.

She'd just got rid of one errant boyfriend who'd had a secret lover; she now had me and my soon-to-be not-so-secret one. It was never going to work, was it?

A few weeks after she'd moved out and Vic had gone to live in the bin sheds I managed to get myself into yet another detox, on completion of which, along with my usual statement of intent to stay off the drugs, I decided I was going to win her back and make our marriage work.

Somewhat remarkably, over the years I'd managed to learn a few chords on the guitar and as I was once again settling into another attempt at a drug-free life in Stoke Newington I began writing songs, mainly about her and how much I loved her, or was trying to love her.

My pursuit of the woman I adored coincided with the calmest period of drug use I'd ever experienced. There was almost none. This fact, along with the dreams we shared and the love we made, was thus the sweetener that apparently made good the desire to believe our love for each other was enough to save me from myself.

I wrote her songs, serenaded her with heartfelt words and promised her the earth, all the while hoping I could drown out the sound of a voice inside me saying, *'C'mon, don't forget me. It'll be different this time, you're happy now, we won't make it a regular thing.'*

I ignored it, because love conquers all, right?

A Year Later

My wife and I were driving through the countryside and as the hire car turned a bend in the road I saw a sight I had not witnessed in nearly 20 years. The feelings that suddenly consumed me were the same as they were when I was a boy: fear, guilt, shame and a sense of remoteness and detachment from anyone who tries to get close to me.

The sight of the school and all it represented to me now suddenly released the floodgates to memories of my time there.

School days the happiest of your life?

Not mine.

I pulled over as my grip on the steering wheel suddenly tightened and I began to sweat.

'You OK?'

I paused and took a deep breath as an avalanche of feelings froze my body and my grip on the wheel tightened even more.

'Yeah,' I lied.

Staring at the imposing building less than a mile away I am suddenly 12 years old again, sitting next to my mum as she drives me back to school for yet more weeks of dark secrets, fear, shame, loneliness and rugby!

She thought I was getting an education. I was in all of the above, apart from the rugby, that was the easy bit.

'You sure you're OK, honey?'

'Yeah . . . just . . . yeah . . . I was just . . .'

My grip loosened just enough for me to put the car back in gear and continue.

As we approached the entrance to the school I found myself holding back tears I should have cried a lifetime ago. I couldn't then because I was too scared to cry. I couldn't now for exactly the same reason. If I started I might not be able to stop. If I showed vulnerability I would get hurt. Like I was hurt back then. Another, somehow different, lifetime ago, except it wasn't; it was mine.

So much of my life had been contaminated by that man's sickness. The man I had shown my pain to. The man I trusted. The man who'd said, 'I know I can never replace your father . . . but if you ever need to talk.' The man who came into the dormitory late at night as I lay there paralysed with fear, consumed with pain, bringing me shame and dark secrets as he fed his sickness. A man of 'God'. The man who'd made the almost unbearable pain of losing my dad when I was 11 even more painful. What he did in itself was appalling, the long-term effect even more so. The fact that the people running the school knew what was happening and did nothing was quite possibly the most horrific aspect of it all.

He was long gone but that school had never let go of me and nor had the ultimately most damaging consequence of what he'd done. He'd virtually destroyed my ability to trust another human being.

The car came to a halt; I rolled up a fag, smoked it like my life depended on it, then looked at my wife and smiled.

'Let's go, eh? Don't want to keep them waiting, do we?'

We rang the bell and as we waited she held my hand tightly and told me she loved me.

'I know you do, babe. I know you do.'

She wouldn't let go as we walked towards the main entrance, my stomach knotted, but yet again I felt utterly alone in the world. That was the most pronounced consequence of my education at that place. Three O-levels, a hatred of authority and the ever-present, all-consuming sense of distance between me and the entire planet.

Things had to change; I needed to find a way to make them.

How do you do that?

The passing of time?

That hadn't worked.

Pretending 'it' hadn't happened?

That hadn't worked.

Blaming?

That hadn't worked.

Hating him?

That hadn't worked.

Hating myself?

Nope.

Girls?

No.

Boys?

No.

Heroin, crack, speed, cocaine, LSD, magic mushrooms, weed, brandy, Valium, Ecstasy, Ketamine, Peyote Cactus, hashish, Special Brew and cider?

No.

That hadn't worked either – and it wasn't for the lack of trying.

I guess I was running out of ideas.

The door was opened by a thin-lipped, overly made-up woman who introduced herself as the current headmaster's secretary and ushered us inside. It smelt exactly the same as the day I'd walked out 18 years previously.

Of course it did.

How did this meeting come about?

Obviously I didn't just decide to drive the wife and me up to my old school and all the things it represented for a laugh on a whim or because I was bored one day. I'm not altogether insane, you know. The Internet is a powerful tool for retrieving and reviewing our memories and a few months prior to finding myself waiting outside the head's office (again) I'd found myself sitting at home waiting for my wife to get back from work, surfing the net and typing the name of my old school into a search engine.

Vroom, vroom, up came a photograph and back came my past, as instantly as the webpage that appeared on my screen.

The school had its own site and a section where ex-pupils could post messages recalling their time as pupils there. A few clicks of the mouse and I was reading post after post of people's thoughts on:

'The happiest days of my life.'

'I wish I was still a pupil . . . I learnt so much.'

'I remember Mr —, he really helped me discover my passion for history, today I am a teacher myself . . .'

'I remember Fr —, he really took time to help me through my religious studies.'

THAT MAN.

Him.

I'd not had his name consciously on my mind for many years; it was buried under gallons of alcohol and mountains of powders and pills. As I sat staring at the screen, however, reading message after message of people's fond memories, I started to feel something I had never felt whenever I would wake up from a dream about school and what had happened there. Dreams I'd been having regularly since I'd left, dreams that always left me confused and often tearful. I can't call them nightmares because they weren't and that's what made them so distressing, if you know what I mean? His face and the smell of stale whisky returned. The anger finally came.

The final post I read, the one which unleashed the rage and tears that followed, simply said: 'My time at — set me up for the rest of my life. I cannot thank the staff who were there at the time enough.'

That fucking killed me.

I'd sobbed uncontrollably for a few minutes then went out to find Vic the Beggar. As I stumbled up Amhurst Road and turned into the high street I bumped into Colin, a recent acquaintance of mine that I'd met at the occasional Narcotics Anonymous meeting I'd been attending in my attempts to stay off the smack.

'All right, Si? You look terrible, mate, you OK?'

'No, not really, Colin.'

'Fancy a cup of tea at mine?'

Colin was clean – had been for a couple of years. He instinctively understood where I was at just by looking at me and was offering to help, having already figured out where I was probably going.

The anger, hurt and fear started talking to me.

'Fuck Colin . . . go and find Vic . . . You know you want to . . . You can't deal with all this without something to take the edge off . . . Come on . . . you know you will sooner or later anyway . . .'

Colin looked at me, softly.

'Well?'

'OK, yeah . . . let's go have a cuppa, eh? Got any HobNobs?'

'Chocolate digestives?'

'I'll get some HobNobs.'

We talked. We talked through several cups of tea and two packets of chocolate HobNobs. We talked until the voice that had told me to not talk to Colin had been silenced. Maybe it had been drowned in sugary tea or crushed under all those HobNobs?

Maybe the value of two (ex?) drug addicts talking together but not taking drugs together had more power than I'd previously thought? Nobody has ever overdosed on chocolate HobNobs as far as I'm aware, so, whatever the reason, I was grateful to Colin for that afternoon and the respite it gave me.

I say respite because although I now understand what transpired between us during our tears, tea and chocolate tête-à-tête, I didn't get it then.

Colin knew what had occurred, he understood the value of two human beings of similar disposition supporting each other and he practised it pretty much on a daily basis back then until, like so many, he stopped and returned to active addiction himself. So I had a respite from my addiction; Colin was eventually killed by his.

Yep. No more tea and chocolate for me and Colin, although

before he died we did sit and talk a great deal more, mainly about where we could score more crack and heroin. I saw him last in the toilet of my flat, injecting himself in his groin with a crack/smack speedball while I was doing the same in my leg in the front room. Shortly after that I went away for a while. A few months after I'd gone Colin checked out permanently.

So my wife and I sat down to lunch with the current headmaster and a senior teacher from the school I'd stumbled out of years before. As they rapidly devoured their food and made their apologies, my past resurfaced and began to devour me once again.

I'm not allowed to write about the sequence of events that occurred as a result of that meeting in the headmaster's office, so to cut a very long story short: lawyers got involved, a legal process involving doctors, psychotherapists, senior members of the Catholic Church, myself, my wife, my family and other 'interested' parties all got dragged through months of questioning, examination, theorising and conjecture before eventually I signed something that prohibits me from saying any more.

For my wife, family and friends, who had all supported me through the process of having my childhood trauma cross-examined, I guess it felt time we all moved on. The man at the centre of this 'sorry'-sodden situation now had his apology and whatever it is I'm not allowed to write about to complement the profound love of his beautiful wife, wonderful friends and some sort of 'recovery'.

On top of all that, I was managing through all this to stay off 'hard' drugs, which was clearly an encouraging space to be in and certainly somewhere from which I could attempt to sling a few more positive choices together.

On the outside it all looked rosy; surely all I now had to do was continue to avoid using heroin? Considering how marvellous everything looked to the people who loved me, the general consensus was I'd have to be some sort of fucking idiot to want to get involved with that shit again. What on earth did it have to offer me now?

They'd obviously never injected heroin.

Monkeyman

The songs I'd been writing, inspired by the two major 'loves' of my life, needed to be heard. Both parties, however, initially had differing views on this.

My wife enthused about my songwriting and completely supported the idea of me getting together with some friends to form another band and have some fun, although that was about as far as it was likely to go, given I was 'getting on a bit'. If I wanted to self-finance the recording of my songs that was just fine and dandy as well, which was sort of what I wanted to hear.

The other 'love' of my life constantly 'suggested' that without its input I'd be unable to continue writing such 'amazing' songs, but perhaps an occasional secret rendezvous was probably all that was required to keep my creative juices flowing, give me that little bit of angst and edginess that was the hallmark of all my heroes. The fact that I was not really in need of any more angst kind of passed me by. Moreover and usually shortly after we'd had a little bit of each other, it also suggested that my band would, without doubt, achieve great things and I, after all this time, would finally make the world understand me. Which was exactly what I wanted to hear.

I needed a band; I got one. A very good one, comprising some old friends who had also been through the madness of addiction themselves but were now making much better use of their time, particularly when they plugged in their guitars when we got together to rehearse, and a rhythm section that arrived together as a unit and soon not only added serious talent to our/my merry band of brothers but also became good friends.

I had some money to spend on rehearsals and equipment, and I was surrounded by and making the best music of my life with good friends. I decided we were to be called Monkeyman after the Stones song of the same name.

We became very brilliant surprisingly quickly and when I say 'brilliant', I mean the music they helped create made sense to me in a way no other band I had previously been involved with ever had. I had the entwined drama of the love for my wife and my confused relationship with drugs to inspire my songwriting and a band of musical brothers who could turn my words and basic chord structures into a noise that made me cry with joy.

Surely I just had to stay off the smack and all the madness that it brought with it every bloody time. How hard could that be?

Regardless of the fact I could now claim to have all the things in my life I'd ever dreamed of, it proved impossible.

Why?

I still couldn't tell the difference between reality and fantasy, good drugs and bad drugs, that's why!

It only took a few isolated incidents where I'd used some smack but then not used again for a while to convince me I could change the parameters of that particular relationship. Two or three enjoyable bouts of secretive dabbling using tiny amounts of gear while my wife went to visit her folks for a weekend was all I needed to simultaneously obliterate me and the years of evidence that suggested it wouldn't ever stop at that, just like the song says:

> Because the needle is really a chain,
> it sets you free then it makes you a slave
> and all the while that you're banging that drum,
> you fight a war that'll never be won.

Whose song? My song, so I won't need to seek permission to include those lyrics in this book, cos I bloody wrote 'em shortly after also penning:

> If we feel, it matters,
> if we don't we'll lose,
> extinguish the flame,
> that shines on our truth,

I know that I love you,
the air that I breathe,
you don't ever hurt me,
when I need blood,
you bleed.

Which I thought was about my wife but on reflection might not have been. Either way, the subjects of both songs were providing me with musical inspiration even if I often couldn't seem to distinguish between the two.

The rehearsals were getting better, the band becoming exactly what I wanted it to be and therefore further evidence that I was Stoke Newington's answer to Keith Richards and Mick Jagger rolled into one.

How deluded can any one man be?

Depends how much heroin he's using, I guess.

The dabbling was informed by and contributed to the ongoing delusion about how I perceived myself and the situation that was evolving regarding my drug use again.

In simple terms, I only had to use once without returning to full-blown addiction to happily convince myself I could continue to do so.

Hurrah?

Monkeyman, the band, was something else entirely. It wasn't a fantasy; it was real, very real and very, very good.

Willpower, Simon. Just say no, eh?

How much willpower does it take to stay off heroin when you're that fucking mental, consumed by ego, arrogance and self-centredness, yet somehow writing the best songs of your life? Willpower doesn't come into it unless you really want to stay off it, in which case it's definitely required but probably in conjunction with some other stuff too. So did I want to stay off the brown? Or did I still actually think I could control my relationship with it?

In the cold light of day it was clear that could never happen but I wasn't existing in that most revealing of climates. I was constantly wrapped up in the dimly lit, fuzzy, warm, psychological blanket of opiate saturation.

Ego? Delusional thinking? Greed? Lust? Fear? Arrogance?

All were driving me on, all disguised by the myopia of addiction, the self-centred nonsense that told me I was in charge, not only of the songwriting but also of the personnel involved.

The band got better and better, the gigs a sweaty, loud, beautiful, live manifestation of our 'chemistry' and the simmering tensions between me and 'my band'. As the pressure rose, somehow, or certainly as far as I could tell through my increasingly drugged-up haze, the songs and the gigs became even more wonderful.

Chemistry is a word often used to describe the feeling between people who seem able to inhabit each other's thoughts, fulfil each other's desires without having to think about it too much and connect and spark off each other. As a band we had that in spades. My own personal chemical intake was, however, proving to be yet another ill-thought-out experiment that was going badly wrong, again.

Monkeyman and the cast and crew therein collectively threw up their hands in exasperation each time I arrived at the studio or a gig with my shades clamped firmly over my face to disguise the pin-pricks where my eyes should have been and through which I saw nothing but imminent glory. Above anything else they were my friends but I couldn't see this any more, or if I did I certainly didn't treat them as such as I continued to throw money at something I believed in almost as much as I still believed the lie that I could carrying on using and expect them to hang about forever.

Me, me, me, me, me, me, ME.

Monkeyman?

Junkieman.

Willpower?

I seemingly had no solution to my problem, none whatsoever, as my wife left me again to protect her own sanity and I decided to go to Morocco to try to clean up yet again before I lost everything that I tried to believe I held dear to me.

Marrakech Express

Marrakech gets on average 14 days of precipitation a year; they don't even call it rain. So not surprisingly the sun shone relentlessly as I scuttled through the medina, showering anyone who came within a few feet of my wretched body with an obnoxious smack-saturated sweat that probably contained more moisture than the two weeks of rainfall the city annually experiences. Unlike the rain, it probably didn't do much for the plants and flowers that I'm sure wilted and died as I stumbled past, trying to do the impossible.

The impossible?

Score heroin in Marrakech?

More of that later!

Go cold turkey in Marrakech?

Stranger things have happened!

Just as had happened when I arrived in Malaysia a few years earlier on a similar mission, the assortment of drugs I had stashed where the sun don't shine found a voice and began screaming at the Moroccan immigration officer who stood before me and the opportunity to remove them from my arse and get them into my bloodstream.

This time they spoke in Arabic, so I have no idea what they were saying but my guess was that it wasn't anything a drug-addled junkie desperate for a fix would want screamed at a heavily bearded Moroccan immigration official.

I have no idea what, *'This man is a dirty smackhead who's come to forcibly inject King Mohammad and all his family with heroin, crack cocaine and a couple of pork chops, while defecating on a copy of the Holy Quran'* sounds like in Arabic but by the grace of merciful Allah it fell on deaf ears. I glided away from passport control and into the nearest toilet cubicle, promising myself I would never put my sorry arse through that experience again.

The next couple of days were spent ensconced in a rented riad deep in the heart of the medina in Marrakech, sending local boys out on errands to get booze and high-quality hashish while I pretended to be the thing I always thought I wanted to be: 'Cool like Keef.'

Yep, Mr Rock 'n' Roll himself, plotted up in Morocco with a big pile of drugs, some cash, a guitar and the 'problem'.

The problem?

Me.

Mr Rock 'n' Roll.

Famous 'actor'?

Limousine?

Monkeyman?

Drug dealer to the stars.

ME.

Exactly.

Did I say 'big pile of drugs'?

Not big enough.

Same as ever.

Day four found me unable to drink my usual bucket of Jack Daniel's for breakfast due to the onset of a heavy dose of cold turkey in a hot climate. Very hot, very cold, very hot, very cold and very lonely too.

I managed the first mouthful then found my stomach emptying itself all over my lap as I lay in bed, the regurgitated bourbon I was now lying in rapidly mixing with my foul-smelling sweat, more vomit, then topped off with tears and snot.

'Cool like Keef'?

Possibly not, Simon.

I crawled across the floor towards the bathroom, dragging the sheets with me as the half-empty bottle smashed on the tiled floor and I almost shat myself before I could make it to the toilet, which all of a sudden might as well have been in another continent, the contents of the medicine cabinet within it on top of Everest.

Steadying myself, I managed to reach for the bottle of methadone tablets within and with my hands shaking like an epileptic in an electric chair I threw four of the chalky white pills in the general direction of my mouth. But despite the fact my jaw was hanging open like a snake about to devour a small mammal I only ended up throwing the tablets into the puddle of puke and second-hand whisky surrounding my ankles, where they began to dissolve rapidly. Mr Rock 'n' Roll scooped them up and managed to hit the target this time, swallowing heavily as I turned on the tap and drank the water that spluttered from within. The tap water you are strongly advised to not drink.

Not that I recalled this well-intentioned advice at that precise moment as I guzzled mouthfuls of the warm water to wash down my little tablets of relief. Thirty minutes later I was sedated and drifting off to sleep again in the sweat-soaked, nailed-on certainty for the smelliest bed in North Africa.

A few hours later and my malodorous slumbering was disturbed by what appeared to be an evil, reptilian, heavily clawed creature that had climbed inside my stomach and begun to dig out a nest amongst the alcohol, methadone and the small loaf of bread that had constituted my breakfast shortly after I'd swallowed my pills, washed down with more tap water.

I began to cry again as the midday sun tore through the open windows, found me in its beam and began to suck out what life was left in me. Me and my inner reptile did what many creatures that crawl do in the heat: we curled up in whatever shade we could find, which in this case was the floor in the corner of the bedroom next to that morning's puddle of vomit and tears. And there we lay for almost two days with a bottle of pills and some fags for company. The reptile left about the same time the methadone ran out and within a few hours, as chronic cold turkey replaced whatever had poisoned me after drinking the tap water, I was missing it already.

The acoustic guitar that had been untouched in its case since my arrival could have turned into a violin and played something as sad as you could imagine and still it would not have sounded melancholy enough, not that I stuck about long enough to have heard it.

I had to score some drugs, strong ones, opiates . . . Hmmmmmmmm, isn't opium an opiate? I'm sure one of 'my boys' had said his uncle had a carpet shop but also sold a bit of opium on the side the other day, so I'll just have to find him. Now what was his name?

Oh yeah, Mohammed. I'll ask about.

Ever been to Marrakech? Every bastard's called fucking Mohammed and has an uncle with a carpet shop. It wasn't so much like looking for a needle in a haystack, more like looking for a particular needle in a pile of fucking needles the size of a haystack. This you may well assume was to be the 'impossible' I mentioned earlier; not at all. You'd be amazed how fast news travels when a member of a 'very famous rock and roll band called Monkeyman' from England decamps amongst the hustlers of Marrakech.

My boys were all waiting outside the house as I opened the door for the first time in nearly three days.

'Ah, Mr Monkeyman from England, how are you today, my friend?'

'Not feeling too clever, boys . . . not feeling too clever at all.'

We headed off for a stumble about in the pursuit of a carpet/ opiate dealer or whatever strong drugs we could find. As you do.

We walked. I say we, what I mean is my three companions walked while I shuffled along behind them, trying to explain as best I could to three teenage Moroccan boys who only spoke enough English to avail them of the opportunity when it arose to sell a bit of hash or lure people into carpet shops, that what I needed at this point was not 'Some good shit hashish . . . best in Marrakech, my friend,' nor indeed, 'You want to see my uncle's shop now, Mr Monkeyman, maybe buy beautiful carpet to have back in England . . . you like football? . . . Manchester United . . .'

As I'm sure most of you will be aware, as a Liverpool fan, albeit of the armchair variety (spending money to watch football had obviously not been high up on my agenda for years), I'd rather have watched my bollocks catch fire than in any way support Man United and as for buying a 'beautiful carpet', at that particular point in my life the only use for one would have been to wrap me up inside it and throw me into a shallow grave.

One of my new friends seemed to have a slightly more advanced understanding of the English language and as I did my best to swallow mouthful after mouthful of bile that kept demanding to become acquainted with the streets we were plodding through, I pulled him to one side and said, 'Opium . . . you know where I can get some opium?'

He looked at me with an expression that hinted at some kind of disapproval.

'Opium? Very bad thing, Mr Monkeyman. Very bad. Make for big problem, you understand?'

No shit, really?

'Yes, I understand, my friend, but I am very sick . . . Can you take me somewhere I can buy some, please . . . please?'

As the pitying gaze of a teenage street hustler from Marrakech met the sad lonely eyes, yellowing skin and green teeth of a 34-year-old waste of space from Weston-super-Mare there was a pause that seemed so long you could have made a film about it, a very long and boring film laced with desperation, hopelessness and pain that no one would want to sit through.

Apart from me.

'OK, we go see my uncle.'

Showtime.

The recuperative powers provided by the possibility of procuring what my body so badly craved never ceased to amaze me. One minute I could barely walk, the next I was doing a pretty good impression of an Olympic sprinter. OK, maybe that's a slight exaggeration but let's just say I would have won any audition if the part of Lazarus was up for grabs. So miraculous was my apparent sudden transformation that my new 'Messiah' looked at me and asked, 'Are you sure you need opium? You look better. Maybe we just go to steam room in Hammam. My uncle has best Hammam in Marrakech, not far from here . . .'

I needed a sauna and massage like the Queen needs more bling at that point.

'No, no, no, my friend . . . Maybe later we go there . . . first we get opium . . . make Monkeyman better . . . please.'

I stood shuffling from toe to toe, eyes pleading for some sign we were going to get what had been established I needed more than anything else Marrakech had to offer.

'OK, let's go. Come, come.'

*

Two hours later I am reclining on the terrace of my riad, drinking my third cup of opium tea, smoking a joint of double-zero hashish and washing it all down with a bowl of Jack Daniel's with chilled beer chasers. If I am not yet king of the bloody world, I'm certainly king of Marrakech, and that'll do me for starters. My three 'friends' are getting drunk on the case of Moroccan beer I'd brought them as a thank you and I am considering the possibility that perhaps I should just stay out here for the rest of my life.

The devious mind of the drug addict has already contrived a way of possibly securing a source of income from the multitude of backpackers who roam the city pretty much year round, my thinking being that if they are going to get ripped off by someone in their pursuit of the Moroccan experience it may as well be me, with a little help from my three friends, of course, and with whom I will obviously share the proceeds. Yes! I will be a sort of dodgy North-African Fagin, with suntan, guitar and an opium habit.

I have almost convinced myself that this scheme is possibly man's greatest idea since Liverpool signed Kenny Dalglish or a teenage Paul McCartney agreed to go for a jam with some fella called Lennon when one of the boys asked the kind of question I could really have done without.

'Monkeyman, when you going to stop with opium?'

Nosy fucking bastard. But a good question nonetheless and one for which I had no honest answer seeing as I was seemingly as incapable of being honest as I was of finishing with the opium.

'Soon, my friend, soon.'

'How soon, Monkeyman?'

Pass.

A few days and several gallons of opium tea later I decide to venture out of my lair and mingle with the locals again, having been inspired by the memory of a previous visit with my wife, made during the early days of our romance, during which we'd shared a real moment of beauty. As we'd stood wrapped around each other on a rooftop cafe, the sun descending and the call to prayer serenading the city from the minarets surrounding us, I had felt as in love as I think is possible to be for someone like me. Something buried deep beneath the years of chemical abuse and fear flickered into life, forcing a smile and a tear to simultaneously appear on my face.

Giving my little crew the day off, I wandered out to see if I could find that cafe again and maybe re-ignite my love for myself and other human beings, rather than the drugs that hated and dehumanised me so much. Or maybe that was just a load of fanciful bollocks brought on by all the opium I was taking?

We Are Family

My cup of coffee remains untouched as I light another cigarette that I don't really want, but it serves to occupy me for a few minutes as I stare blankly at the crowds of Moroccans scuttling past me. The backpackers and tourists that populate the cafe with me compare notes from various translations of *The Rough Guide to Morocco* or other travellers' 'bibles', which for some reason fills me with contempt as I chain-smoke in the shade and contemplate my answer to the question my young friend had asked me a few days previously.

'Monkeyman, when are you going to stop with opium?'

The bag of dried poppy heads provided by his uncle was almost gone but seemingly had served its purpose as I'd not felt even slightly ill for a week, despite having finished the methadone I'd brought with me within a day of arriving.

The band were waiting on a progress report from our 'manager' Gully, whom I'd already been in touch with, and much as I was beginning to warm to the insane idea of trying to convince them all to relocate to Marrakech with me permanently, even I could see that this scenario was about as likely to occur as was the possibility of finding myself wearing a Man United shirt instead of the Liverpool one currently drawing condescending looks from the identikit hippy travellers sitting next to me.

'Nice shirt that, mate!'

My train of opiate-informed, self-obsessed nonsense was interrupted by a northern accent, which on investigation as I raised my head from yet another brief 'nod' belonged to a wiry, silver-haired gentleman standing a few feet in front of me and pointing at my footie shirt. He continued, 'Where you from, mate? You a Scouser?'

I couldn't be bothered to attempt my fake Liverpool accent and yet again pretend to be something I was not. I had enough on my plate as it was as I attempted to decide if I was going to try to pretend to be a grown-up and sort myself out any time soon.

'No, mate, I'm not. I live in London.'

Fuck me! I had just answered a question honestly, which allowed me to continue to do so rather than having to keep making things up in a desperate attempt to impress someone. Wow! This might seem incredibly insignificant to most people, insomuch as it is what 'normal' people do all the time. For someone like me, however, it was a massive change, indicating that there was a part of me that, subconsciously or not, believed that actually just being me was good enough.

My new friend sat down, refusing my offer of a coffee as I continued with my new-found approach to making friends. Within an hour I'd told Colin pretty much everything that had led to me sitting there in my dubiously stained football shirt, pondering the next move in the ongoing catalogue of errors I called a life.

At over 20 years my senior Colin had seen and heard much of it before. He felt like a friend, like someone I could actually trust, as he sat and showed me what that word meant by inviting me to come and spend the remainder of my time in Marrakech living in his house with his Moroccan wife and young kids.

He accepted me for who I tried to explain I was over the next few weeks, until we both decided it was time for me to go back to London and continue that process with the rest of the people who deserved to hear it and, more importantly, see it, too.

Colin and his wonderful family took me to their hearts and it was an emotional farewell indeed as he waved me off on the morning of my departure, both of us seemingly convinced that all I had to do was stay off the smack and, 'Give yerself and every other fucker a chance, eh, mate?'

Simple, straightforward advice that in the early-morning sunshine that caressed my pre-flight sobriety seemed to make perfect sense. I went into the airport bar to celebrate the dawning of a new era.

A Million Reasons

Gully drove out to pick me up at the airport and quizzed me as to 'What happens next then, Simon?'

'I need a drink, mate. Here, pull over at that off-licence, please. You want anything?'

'Bottle of Coke, please. It's a Sunday night.'

I handed the bloke in the shop money for the Coke and four cans of Special Brew for me; it was a Sunday night after all. I'd almost finished the first before I'd got back into the car and necked another two as I waffled on about my ideas concerning what to try next as far as my bid for world superstardom went. The basic gist was that if I could somehow get the band into the studio with a half-decent producer to record everything I'd (we'd?) written, I was absolutely convinced a record company would find the material irresistible and promptly agree to sign us up.

Gully agreed to talk to the others and as I fell out of his car he suggested I might consider having an early night.

'You might want to stop drinking that stuff too, Simon. It turns you into a bit of a cock, mate.'

More simple, straightforward advice. I was really getting spoiled that day!

As I proceeded to unpack (throw everything all over the bedroom floor), I suddenly realised that I hadn't had any 'tea' for nearly three days but was apparently, physically at least, not feeling too bad, which confirmed that I didn't have a habit any more.

OK, I was paralytic as I staggered around my flat trying to find a lighter, but, hey, one thing at a time, man. How hard can it be to stop boozing when you've managed to get off heroin?

I was off heroin until I found a tiny blue bag of gear next to the lighter I'd placed in my 'emergency' hiding place the day before I'd jetted off to Morocco, just in case.

In case of what?

It wasn't a question I pondered for long as I reached for the roll of tinfoil in the kitchen while a Monkeyman song played at full volume on the stereo.

So here we are again,

Staring at the end

And as this day begins, our songbirds do not sing,

Can you and I be saved?

If every day we're scared?

Maybe we'll make it in the end.

The script was you and me, joy and tragedy,

Guess I need to say,

Never dreamt about today,

I asked so much of you

But I could not let you through

So now we stand apart,

With broken dreams and hearts

Our kingdom has been sacked

And I can't win it back.

And there's a million different reasons for this final act of

treason,

that one day I might discover

But there'll never be another me and you,

Who loves me like you do?

The way that I love you

The way that I love you.

I smoked the heroin then started to cry as I nodded out on the carpet and said goodbye to my band as my own voice continued to haunt me from the stereo.

The script was you and me,

In search of remedy,

For something with no cure,
All the things I saw before,
All the words I said to you,
On the day we said 'I do'
I wish that I could be,
Half the man you saw in me,
The kingdoms laid to waste
But I hope you can escape
Yes I do,
But there's a million different reasons
For this final act of treason
That one day I might discover
'cos I'll never love another, like I love you.
Who loves me like you do?
The way that I love you.

At some point during the night I must have crawled into my bed, still clutching the smoke-blackened tinfoil in my hands before passing out again, only to wake mid-afternoon the following day, still dressed but now finally stripped of my dreams.

It later transpired that the guitarist and drummer had both called me the previous night to welcome me home but instead had to listen to my comatose voice mumbling vague instructions for our next rehearsal down the phone. That was that: they'd had enough of me and yet another broken promise, which was pretty much exactly the way I felt about the situation as well.

Standing in front of the bathroom mirror, I see my face covered with black fingerprints from the burnt foil I'd used to send my musical dreams up in smoke the previous evening.

There is a half-empty (well it certainly ain't half fucking full) can of Brew on the table and my guitar case is still lying unopened in the hallway. There is no gas or electricity left on the meters and when I eventually stagger up to the cashpoint at the top of Amhurst Road no money left in my account either.

An hour later I am queuing up at the Cash Converters on Holloway Road with my guitar, shortly after which I put some money in the gas and electric and some heroin and crack into a syringe, then into my left arm.

Do I care if the first 'proper' hit I've had in over a month is going to kill me?

Truth is, within seconds I'm planning on living forever again. At least it certainly feels that way as the contents of the 1ml syringe hit the mark and I am instantly removed from me and my real feelings to be replaced by somebody I immediately much prefer and their perception of things.

Going Solo

Scouse Paul was gouging out in his front room, an experience he was visibly thoroughly enjoying but a situation I was not best pleased about as I needed him to get his fucking shit together and score for me.

Sunday mornings in Stoke Newington had become something of a nightmare, not that the other days of the week ever saw me leap joyfully out of bed whistling to myself while throwing open the curtains and greeting the day. A trip to the cashpoint one day had finally revealed there was no more money available to me to pursue my rock 'n' roll dream turned nightmare, or indeed anything else. Up until that point I'd managed to convince myself I had a grip on things solely due to the fact I could always get my hands on some cash. But the halcyon days of ignoring the deteriorating harsh reality of my situation by throwing money at it were over.

I now had to commit various acts of usually very pathetic petty crime each day because I had no possessions of any value left to sell before I could visit any of the multitude of local dealers who supplied me and those with a similar affliction. 'Tommy', 'Bishop', 'Tony', 'Wayne', a couple of 'ninjas', 'Fatboy' and 'Sharon' would all have been on speed dial if I still possessed a mobile phone and a regular source of income, neither of which seemed likely at any point in the near future.

By some minor miracle I had passed out the previous night while I still had some money in my pocket, a scenario that occurred with less frequency than the appearance of Halley's Comet but was greeted that morning, at least by my good/bad self, with more enthusiasm than a field of amateur star-gazers pointing at the night sky every 75 years or so.

It continued to baffle my chemically abused, fragmented mind as to why certain junkies I knew could always manage to keep something for the morning and therefore avoid the tidal wave of despair that washed over me within seconds of my eyes opening each day. There were countless times I'd be left twitching, post crack pipe, in the flat at lonely o'clock, staring at what remained of my stash of gear, trying to accomplish that. Each time knowing full well that I could take the edge off the coke prang with a can of Brew and maybe the opiate-sodden filter sitting in the spoon and leave myself with a hit for the morning that would get me out of trouble when I came to.

I couldn't do it. I simply could not do it. You put me in a room with some drugs and I would not stop until they had all gone. As for the consequences? Fuck the consequences. The very fact that I had just thought about tomorrow made me so depressed I needed to self-medicate NOW!

Did I say self-medicate?

Good, cos that's what I meant to write. I certainly wasn't getting high any more; I was just caught up in an ever-decreasing circle of one, trying to escape myself but regardless of how many times I tried, no matter how insane the size of the hits got, the problem would not go away.

'Fuck sake, Paul, you gonna call him or not, mate? No one else has got their fucking phone on yet and my arse is hanging out, mate.'

'Yeah, nice one, Si. Yeahhhhhhhhhhhhhhh, his gear's fuckin' boss, mate, I'm tellin' ya. Proper boss, la. How much do yers want, mate?'

'A score's worth; does he do one of each for that?'

But my Liverpudlian friend had goofed out again and was currently licking up some of the Skol Super he had just spilt all over the floor.

'Paul, just give me his fucking number, mate, please. I'm dying here. Either give me that wanker's number or let me have the filter from your last hit, eh?'

Paul decided to stop slurping the Skol off the floor and staggered to his feet before kicking the remainder of the lager all over the cheap carpet then walking straight into the door, bouncing off and collapsing back into the puddle of beer and dribble he'd just created.

He tried again.

'Fuckin' hell, Si mate. This gear's fuckin' boss, mate. Let's go, eh? You got money for the phone? I'll throw in a ten-spot so we can get some white as well; £30 quid will sort us out nicely, I reckon.'

We called Wayne. You never met Wayne, you just called him and he sent a runner. Rumour had it he'd been serving up gear unhindered in Stokey for many years, primarily due to the fact nobody knew who he was and none of his various runners would dare grass him up for fear of an extremely violent reprisal. I didn't want to meet the cunt anyway; I just wanted to see a kid on a BMX pedalling towards me very fucking soon.

After the first call it took us nearly 30 minutes to walk the few streets to another phone box and call again to say we were there, mainly due to Paul struggling to remain on two feet because he was so off his tits and me having to stop and heave every minute because I wasn't.

A boy no older than 12 eventually pedalled into view. He was obviously of school age but perhaps he preferred being one of Wayne's runners. I had no idea which would benefit him more in the long term, nor did I really care. There was a very fleeting moment when what remained of my morality felt somewhat perturbed to be handing over money to a kid in exchange for heroin and crack but it was quickly dispelled by another bout of dry retching and the sight of my Scouse pal trotting off home with 'our' drugs.

Thirty minutes, two bags of smack, two rocks of crack, a can of Skol and a can of Brew later we were discussing the possibility of us both getting to Istanbul to watch Liverpool in the upcoming Champions League final.

*

I have no idea where Paul watched the match but it wasn't with me. He went into hiding a few days later after the girlfriend of a local dealer allegedly overdosed and died in his flat. I never saw him again.

As Steven Gerrard lifted the trophy on behalf of the greatest football club in the world for the fifth time a few weeks later I was slumped in the toilet of The Yucatan pub, having decided the half-time score was enough to justify risking another massive hit despite me already being so drunk I could not actually stand up.

The second half of that match became known as 'the Miracle of Istanbul', as the mighty Reds came back from a 3–0 deficit to eventually win the match on penalties and carry the cup back to Anfield. I missed the entire second half, so as far as I'm concerned the miracle that night was that I didn't die in that fucking pub in Stoke Newington as I drifted in and out of consciousness in a cubicle in the women's toilets.

No Future

Something's on fire. The putrid smell of burning man-made fibres has disturbed me from my post-hit gouge and it soon becomes apparent that whatever it is, it's not far away from the corner of Wes's caravan, where I'm currently slumped.

Rubbing my face while at the same time pulling the skin from under my eyes downward to hopefully persuade them not to instantly close again, it soon becomes obvious what is causing the sudden stench and accompanying black smoke.

Me.

I am on fire, or at least the sleeve and hood of the dark blue parka I'm wearing most certainly are.

Wes's minuscule pupils appear from beneath his heavily sedated eyelids as he also detects that something is not right inside his home.

'Si, you're a fire, mate,' he says, before closing his eyes again and returning to wherever he'd drifted off to prior to being disturbed by the smell of someone on fire in his caravan.

The complete lack of urgency in his voice does little to placate my suddenly somewhat freaked-out self. I have been called many things over the years, most fully deserved, but never 'a fire'.

Whether I'm 'on fire' or 'a fire' is not something I have the luxury of debating as the fake fur on my parka hood rapidly disappears in a cloud of noxious smoke while my eyes scour the candlelit surroundings for something with which to douse the flames.

There is a large bottle that once contained mineral water a few feet away. What it currently contains is the former contents of Wes's bladder. Despite his caravan being of the small variety he has obviously found walking to the door to piss outside too much hassle.

His caravan is parked up on a bit of wasteland a few minutes' walk from what has become known as 'murder-mile', or Upper Clapton Road if you're a postman. There is no other immediate source of liquid to hand with which I could fight the flames now starting to melt what remains of the right arm and hood of my coat. What follows is probably as good a reason as I'd ever have to stop wasting my fucking life, treat myself and others with some respect and leave drug-taking to people clearly better equipped to deal with the day-to-day trials and tribulations inherent to this particular career choice.

I have no idea how other more famous junkies than I have managed to create mindblowing music and poetry while entertaining their own heroin addictions. I am clearly not cut from the same cloth as I now seem to be reduced to little more than hurting people's feelings, crying, making promises to myself and others I cannot keep and pouring bottles of my mate's stale piss over my head while attempting to stop myself from being 'a fire'.

Yeah.

As I stumbled through the caravan door, emptying the bottle of second-hand Skol Super over myself, it didn't occur to me that I could just as easily have removed the coat prior to dousing it with the rank-smelling piss that formerly belonged to my still comatose mate inside.

'Shut the fucking door, Simon, you're letting the cold in and what's that fucking smell, mate? Jesus, you pissed yourself or what?'

After discarding the still-smouldering coat I returned to the caravan and attempted to dry my hair with an old cloth I found stuffed into the corner I'd recently evacuated while putting myself out.

'Don't use my fucking pants to do that, man. I've only got two pairs for fuck sake. They've gotta be washed, so you might wanna use something else, eh?'

It is roughly 2 a.m., I am penniless and sitting covered in stale urine, wiping my head with my mate's unwashed pants, wondering what the fuck I had ever done to deserve this and also if things could really get any worse. I decide to have another hit to calm myself down and instantly things do get worse.

Outside the caravan what remains of my parka is still smouldering away. There is nothing left of the right arm, inside the pocket of which were my drugs. 'Were' being the operative word here.

I cry. And smell of stale piss. Someone else's stale piss at that – rotten junkie, alcoholic, stale piss that possibly didn't smell or even taste much different from when it was in the can prior to Wes drinking it. I was, as you'd expect, disgusted. He didn't even drink Special Brew; Wes was a proper tramp and drank Skol Super. Not like me, I was different; I'd never lower myself to drinking that shit.

I Wanna Be Your Dog

Vic the Beggar and his brother John existed together in a tiny one-bedroom flat just off Manor Road. I say existed because injecting drugs into your neck, not washing for weeks and spending all your time sitting outside the cashpoint on Stokey High Street, poncing money off people to purchase the drugs you then stick into your neck can hardly be called living, can it?

The front-door key to the flat had long since vanished and the probability of either of them ever wasting precious drug money to get a new set cut was about as likely as Vic coming back with your drugs should you ever be stupid enough to front him money to score for you. The regular appearance of a couple of black eyes on his drug-ravaged face was testament to the fact that some people, clearly stupider than myself, would entrust him with their cash, only to be left waiting for however long it took them to accept he'd fucked off with it and was now back in his flat or more likely the nearest bin shed.

Vic would sooner or later casually take the beating he had coming to him but saw this as an occupational hazard rather than anything he might be able to prevent. I had more sympathy for Vic than I did the posh narco-tourists he regularly ripped off, who would drive over to our neighbourhood to try to score. In fact, if I wasn't so vain and such a coward I'd probably have done the same thing, so in some respects you might even say I admired him. He'd had me over for money plenty of times and it's not as if I'd never ripped anyone off either, so who am I to judge?

Anyway, back to the missing door key!

You could only gain entry to their festering bolthole via the broken window adjacent to the door. Should you be a more corpulent variety of human being you had no chance of squeezing inside to witness the blood- and shit-stained walls and floors, nor indeed the bizarre organisms growing in the bath and toilet. Most of the visitors to Methadone Mansions resembled emaciated famine victims, so this rarely proved to be an issue. It did keep Big Damo out, though, and he was a fucking nightmare to be around if you had drugs, so it did have its uses.

I was attempting to score two bags of brown and something bordering on actually being crack from Bishop, who was on his way to smash a brick into Vic's face for non-payment of something he'd been persuaded to lay on the previous week. (You had to hand it to Vic, he could convince even the most ruthless of Yardie dealers there really was a giro in the post!), and so found myself trotting up the stairwell behind him as he went about his business, promising me he'd sort me out just as soon as he'd sorted Vic out.

By some remarkable quirk of fate Bishop actually owed me money and I was therefore going to have to witness him removing the few teeth remaining in Vic's mouth before he provided me with my morning's entertainment, the source of which was secreted about his person and required somewhere private in order for him to retrieve it.

'Bishop, man, c'mon, this is none of my fucking business, mate. Just sort me out then you can deal with that cunt, eh?'

He was a man of few words. He didn't have to say much, he'd just look at me a certain way and my sphincter would start twitching. He'd been a bus driver back home in Jamaica, but a cousin of his had been serving up in Hackney for a few years by the time he'd been persuaded to give up his steady but very badly paid job and come over to join in the fun here.

'Simon man, I make more dollar in an hour doing this than I did in a month back home, get me? Besides, I like dem English bitches 'ere, dem proper nasty bitches love the black man, love me, seen?'

Can't really argue with that, can you?

As we approached the flat I suddenly decided that witnessing someone getting assaulted with the house brick my dealer had in his hand was not really something I wished to experience. Much as I really couldn't give a flying fuck about the individual about to be on the receiving end of it, the almost overwhelming sense of fear that now gripped me was doing a pretty good fucking job of persuading me to walk away immediately before the scene got nasty. If Bishop killed him, and there was every chance of that, I would be a witness, and if I was a witness I was in trouble, big fucking trouble.

The trouble that my opiate-starved stomach was having in retaining the can of Brew I'd had for breakfast that day paled into insignificance at the thought of either owing Bishop my silence or him accurately assessing me as the kind of spineless junkie who'd spill his guts the minute the Old Bill got heavy with him and was therefore a liability that needed to be silenced.

Bishop looked at me, then the window/front door.

'I owe you, right?'

'Yeah, B, you do – £30, mate, from that intro I sorted for you the other day. C'mon, man, I'm ill. Sort me out first, eh?'

Bishop's shoulders were probably wider than I am long. There was no way he was going to fit through the window to get at Vic, who, at only 9.30 in the morning, was most likely still passed out inside.

'I'll double it – four brown, two white. Go in and wake 'im up, tell him you got dollar and need to score. Him wake up and come out to the phone, then me sort everybody out, seen?'

Fuck me! That was quite an offer – four bags of smack and two stones for climbing through a window and waking someone up! OK, I was more or less guaranteeing him permanent disfigurement at the very least, but hey fucking ho, four brown and two white and I was rattling my fucking nuts off.

This was obviously a real 'damned if I do, damned if I don't' situation and, much like the recent scenario that left me pouring stale piss over myself, one that would have been avoided had I acted on the advice of Colin and everyone else who cared about me.

My inner self-hate generator went into overdrive but I shut my eyes as I tried to picture my wise friend and his parting advice.

'*Give yerself and every other fucker a chance, eh?*'

His words flashed through my mind but were silenced by the sight of Bishop holding a brick in one hand and a bag containing about fifty smaller blue baggies of the drugs I was so enslaved to in the other.

Window it is then. Sorry, Colin, sorry, sorry, sorry, fuck it.

Just as I was about to clamber through the porthole of desolation, a dog came bounding out of the front room of the flat, barking viciously and snapping its salivating jaws in my/our direction. It was a big dog, not the size a dog should be; it was almost bigger than Big Damo and clearly more dangerous, although probably not as annoying if you were smoking crack together.

The Great Dane was also obviously hungry and clearly not enjoying its stay at Vic's residence either, although how the fuck it was ever able to get inside is not something Bishop or I cared to contemplate as we decided to leave the dog and its current master exactly where they were and retreated back down the stairs and into the car park for a rethink.

Bishop was obviously not a dog lover and the incessant ringing on his mobile phone seemed to convince him that attending to his other customers was likely to be his most profitable course of action for the time being. He stashed the house brick in the bin shed for next time and I began to argue my case for what exactly he now owed me in drugs. We agreed that although I had not actually got Vic out of the flat, I had tried my best and under the circumstances was deserving of three brown and two white, all of which I had dispatched a few hours later as I sat in my own flat trying to figure out how that fucking dog had ever got inside Vic and John's.

Maybe they'd found the front-door key?

A rumour soon had it that a short while after our visit an unknown assailant shot the dog through the open window, a few weeks after which John, who was actually the tenancy holder of the flat, died from an overdose and the council boarded the place up.

Such is life amongst the junkies of London N16. Maybe it was time for me to move again?

Spanish Caravan

Shortly after I finally accepted that Monkeyman was over and that the guys in the band had really had enough of me and my failed attempts to stay clean, I took myself and my resentments along to my local substance misuse worker in the hope of getting a date for another stint in detox. This was not an appointment I could keep without some chemical assistance and so it was that by the time I'd begged enough money to score I was running late.

'I'm really sorry, Karen,' I lied. 'I thought it was 11 a.m. you wanted to see me.'

The lie was not that I'd got the time wrong; the lie was that I was sorry for being late. I was rarely capable of feeling sorry for anyone except myself. I may well have felt pangs of guilt from time to time but 'sorry' was not a concept I understood. It implies I took time to consider other people's situations, which by now I'm sure you realise was usually beyond me.

It was only due to the fact that her 11 a.m. client was in all probability cut from a similar cloth to me and therefore also late and full of shit that she agreed to see me.

'I need to go back into detox, Karen. I'm fucked, really in a bad way again . . . wife's left me, band has split up. I'm begging on my own street each morning, injecting in my legs . . . feel suicidal . . . sob, sob, sob, sob . . .'

'What do you want me to do this time, Simon?'

I looked up from my bloodstained jeans with something akin to incredulity.

'I need help, Karen . . . I need funding for detox and rehab.'

She looked at me and then said something that ultimately saved my life.

'No, Simon, not this time.'

I stared at her with the most pathetic, self-piteous face I could summon up and, let's face it, I was a gold medallist at this particular discipline.

'But . . . I'm fucked, Karen . . . I'm going to die if I don't sort myself out.'

'I know that, Simon. The problem is you don't.'

The weighty 'bag' of resentment I'd arrived with seemed to weigh considerably more as I plodded back towards my flat 20 minutes after being told that, 'If you can stay on a methadone prescription for four months without regularly using any heroin, I may consider one more detox for you but I have to say I doubt you'll manage it. Come back same time next week and we'll make the necessary arrangements, so that's 10 a.m. next Tuesday, OK, Simon?'

She was, of course, correct. I didn't manage it – didn't even come close.

Seven days later I'd sub-let my flat to a friend of a friend and at the time I was supposed to be meeting Karen I was waiting anxiously on my doorstep for him to arrive with the remainder of the moving-in deposit so I would have enough money to score the required amount of drugs to get me to the airport and onto a plane to Granada in Spain.

As I waited I got rapidly more agitated about Jimmy, who was late and therefore obviously trying to ruin my entire fucking life. I hate waiting for anyone, which is a bit of a bummer for a junkie who spent much of his time waiting for people to turn up with something to slow time down.

I'd been up to the phone box and back about ten times to unsuccessfully call his mobile and was about to consider a kamikaze-style shoplifting spree in Woolworths on the high street when Jimmy finally turned up with my cash. I gave him the keys and a vague story about going to Spain for a while to 'build a recording studio in the mountains near Granada. Pay the rent into my account every week on a Monday morning, please, Jim. Don't let me down, man, I'll be needing it to survive.'

As it turned out, for once I was right.

He handed me £300 and I gave him the keys. He went inside, I took the bag I'd packed five hours earlier and my guitar and trotted off to the nearest crack house to sort myself out.

'Look after yourself, Simon. Don't worry about the rent. I'll sort it out. Stay in . . .'

I was already on my merry way to my local crack/smack emporium and didn't hear the rest of his sentence.

Ryan's flat was less than 15 minutes' jog/stop for breath/puke away and had become one of my regular sources of joy/despair as I ineptly steered the pathetic remnants of me and my life through the streets of Stoke Newington. The albeit brief sense of joy provided by the sight of his face appearing at the window after I'd rung the bell was entirely dependent on whether or not his wife Joy was also at home and therefore able to provide me with the drugs she peddled from the back room of their flat.

Joy was his wife purely on paper; the marriage was one of convenience, facilitating her legal residence in the country in return for providing Ryan with a dowry, the £20 of heroin and crack each morning bringing new meaning to the 'in sickness and in health' proclamation made during their hastily arranged big day out at Hackney town hall, a wedding that I assume was probably not covered by *Hello* magazine.

Joy routinely proclaimed herself a God-fearing Christian who felt saddened by her current career but said it was the only option if she wished to adequately provide for her three kids, aged between seventeen and six, the youngest of whom was currently placing six small baggies of heroin and crack into my sweaty palm.

I'd not seen her mother since scrambling up the stairs into the family home. Her husband had placed my order and a six-year-old girl had gone into the bedroom to fetch it as I sat between Ben and Big Damo on the sofa and waited to tuck in.

'Gi's a pipe, Si,' said Big Damo.

'Yes, let's have a pipe, please, Simon,' said Ben.

'Sort me out first,' said Ryan.

'Mummy, I want to go to the toilet,' said the six-year-old little girl.

'*I want to die*,' said my soul, or whatever it was that found the scoring of drugs from a child so reprehensible.

What part of me was that?

All of me, no matter how loud the 'give me the fucking drugs now' currently sounded from every other voice in my head, echoing the demands of my friends sitting alongside me as the festivities began for my going-away party.

Five hours later I was having another 'final' hit in the toilets at the airport; half an hour after that I was slumped in my seat with a half-empty bottle of Jack Daniel's and a head full of crack, heroin and bad memories from which I fully intended to escape in Spain by any means necessary.

Once again I found myself staring out of a plane window as England disappeared from view and seemingly from nowhere, nowhere I could remember anyway, tears filled my eyes.

Orgiva, Spain

Driving Over Lemons: An Optimist In Andalucía is the title of a book written by someone who'd gone in search of a new life and been willing to devote both time and effort pursuing it in the same region of Spain as I now found myself. He'd arrived with his wife and a dream, whereas I'd just abandoned mine, bringing just me and my ongoing nightmare for company, devoid of optimism, looking no further than the next opportunity to get some money from somewhere then go and visit Pedro, the most unpleasant drug dealer in the entire world.

A new life?

Nope, just more of the same shit in a better climate, the only lemons involved being those regularly squeezed into a burnt spoon to cook heroin with.

Sharky had collected me from Granada airport after a journey I had very little recollection of other than fixing the last of my heroin in the toilet at the airport, buying a bottle of Jack Daniel's and passing out somewhere over France as I cradled Jack in my arms and wondered if the small bottle I had in my washbag contained enough methadone to get me through the next few days.

I'd had the strange notion that I might actually be able to detox myself gradually by drinking decreasing amounts of the sickly green liquid and increasing amounts of cheap local brandy – as ridiculous a notion as anything I'd previously entertained in a long history of deluded ideas about myself and what I was capable of doing or, more pertinently, not doing

'You look fucking awful, Si.'

'Thanks, mate. I've brought some methadone with me to get through the cluck, so I should be OK.'

Five minutes later we were sitting in his car, sniffing lines of cocaine off a CD cover before he steered us out of the parking lot and onto the road that, hopefully, would take us to Orgiva. It wasn't that he didn't know the route; it was just that he hadn't slept for a couple of days and wasn't really in much of a better state than I was. Snifffffffffffffffffffffffffffffffffffffffffffffffff.

He was now.

I explained my plan.

'So, yeah, I reckon I'll be OK in a week or so, mate. Got some juice with me, a few Valium, bit of cash, fuck it! I've done it before enough times, eh?'

'Green Dragon Festival starts next week, Si.'

'Oh?'

'There'll be loads of people doing lots of drugs, you think you'll be OK?'

Sniffffffffffffffffffffffffffffffffffffffff.

'Yeah.'

Just to be clear, what I have just learned is that at approximately the same time as I run out of methadone, roughly 3,000 drug-gobbling, Techno aficionados will descend upon my doorstep for a week's revelry and unbridled debauchery. There will be drugs, lots of drugs, and certainly the kind of drugs I am 'attempting' to get away from.

Sniffffffffffffffffffffffffffffffffffffffffff.

'You sure, Si?'

'Yeah, I'll manage.'

Anyone fancy a flutter on what happens next?

I fucking hate Techno.

At that point in my life it would have been safe to say that I hated Techno as much as I hated myself, which was a lot.

I had had a near-death experience due to Techno on the side of a mountain in France many years before but that is not why I hate it. I hate it because, like me, it is shit and very, very annoying, particularly when you are withdrawing from heroin and you feel like you want to die. It was also, as soon as the various generators and sound systems started up, relentless and very loud. It sounded like a lot of final nails going into the coffin masquerading as a bed in which I lay, thrashing about, not having slept for days and rapidly becoming too weak to get up and go and do something to remedy my situation.

Did I say 'too weak'?

I meant 'almost'.

You're never too weak to score.

Did I say remedy?

What I meant was go and make it worse in the long run but considerably better than it was when the Techno started. And it was bad even before the first sound system started up. A French sound system.

Cunts.

How did I know they were French? *Un moment s'il vous plaît.*

I looked over at my shoes and asked them if they would consider trotting over to the 'bag shop' for me to get some smack from Pedro.

Not surprisingly they didn't respond.

I had a quick puke onto the floor of my abode and ten minutes later was rattling down the hill on my way to try to either sell my digital camera or find something to steal, then score. As I stumbled on I had to pass the French people who were currently just adding to my discomfort but not actually the source of my misery. You can hardly stumble towards yourself, can you?

I saw the tinfoil.

From 50 yards I also saw the face of the person clutching it just inside the cab of the truck that was attached to the sound system.

I saw myself, a French version of myself.

Fanfuckingtastic.

From ten yards I smelt the smell.

Burning heroin, yummy, yummy, yummy.

I love French people.

They were a bit cagey at first until I showed them a recently acquired abscess on my arm and heaved up some sick on their firewood, after which they decided I was cool. They then took my camera as payment for a few grams of what turned out to be very weak but just about strong enough to stop me from shitting myself heroin. I was invited into the back of their truck, which stank to high heaven but allowed me an opportunity to get stuck in to the gear while my French chums started taking photos of us all with their new expensive digital camera.

Twenty minutes later I loved Techno and French people with equal vigour.

Heroin turns you into such a dickhead.

They rapidly got bored with me banging on about the recording studio and record label I was going to start up here. It didn't take a great deal of intelligence to figure out that some skinny English smackhead who was reduced to selling his possessions for a bit of shit heroin was probably not the next Richard Branson!

As the French people carried on with their preparations for the upcoming festival I stumbled off to annoy anybody I came into contact with, figuring I'd head into town to get a drink or ten at the Metal Bar. After sticking out my thumb in the hope of getting a lift from the numerous vehicles heading my way, it soon became apparent that nobody wanted to stop and pick me up. What the fuck was wrong with these people?

Eventually a couple of 'normal' British tourists en route to a week's walking holiday in the mountains pulled over and offered to drop me in Orgiva. The ride took less than ten minutes, by which time I'd convinced them to 'lend' me thirty euros so I could get a bus to Malaga in order to catch my plane and fly home to visit my sick mother.

'But you'll miss the festival, Simon.'

'Family comes first, Jean. We have to keep our values intact these days, don't we?'

I bade them farewell, thanking them profusely before throwing away the address I'd insisted they gave me to allow me to return their kind donation and trotting into the Metal Bar to see if I could find someone to talk to and buy them a few drinks in the hope they'd like me.

Why wouldn't they?

Outside the caravan into which I have just scuttled with a recently acquired used syringe and the last of my French Techno smack, there is a festival taking place. The Green Dragon is in full spate – the annual gathering of pan-European shabbiness with facial piercings, dreadlocks, kids on Ketamine and dogs on string that descends upon Orgiva for up to a week. Caravans, trucks and sound systems are parked up on a dried riverbed, as people with shaved heads and Oakley shades, unshaved legs, armpits and faces, unwashed clothes and chemically saturated minds are battered by the incessant sound of gabba-techno, drum and bass, and the obligatory dub-reggae system. A Spanish DJ places another slice of industrial nosebleed noise onto his decks as he plays host to a crowd of white, middle-class gap-year students off their tits on skunk, acid, cheap Spanish booze and recently cooked Ketamine. They fling their limbs up and down, dancing on the spot, bending low, hopping from side to side and generally having the time of their lives.

Inside a small marquee a few feet from my current hiding place there is a band bashing out well-intentioned but quite frankly awful versions of classic ska tunes to an audience of middle-aged hippies who grin inanely while trying to dance, wearing expensive sandals and lurid, ill-fitting clothes. They all stink to high heaven and I fucking despise the lot of them.

I attempt to sharpen the needle on the side of a matchbox while simultaneously trying to prevent a torrent of sweat dripping from my face into the burnt spoon that contains my crack and heroin cocktail, nestling between my knees while I hover over it.

Vinny is staring at the spoon, then the needle in my hand as he spits on the back of his own arm and slaps the reluctant veins in an attempt to persuade one of them to make an appearance.

'Fucking hippies, eh, Si? Useless bunch of cunts. You got that needle sorted yet, mate?'

Vinny has recently become my best friend in the whole wide world, or to put it more accurately he has taken me hostage, having decided that the two of us have bonded and as such need to stick together like some sort of parasitic, opiate-drenched mould that anyone with half a mind would do well to avoid for fear of catching something nasty.

Is he really my best friend in the whole wide world?

Of course not! He's just one of the last people on earth who will tolerate my presence for more than a few seconds. He is also a knife-wielding psychopath permanently out of his mind on heroin and crack, for which he has an appetite that makes my own look somewhat frugal, in my humble opinion at least, although I suspect I am the only person who holds that belief.

Finally, after years spent arrogantly deciding that I was not as fucked up as whoever it was currently dribbling into their lap in front of me, I had achieved the unenviable status of being the person that one of the most drug-crazed lunatics on the planet could point his skeletal finger at and think, *'I'm fucked, but at least I'm not as much of a mess as that prick.'* So, yeah, in some respects we were made for each other.

I'd arrived. Made it! Now what?

Something drastic is clearly required, which will in all likelihood involve me doing whatever it takes to finally get off the skag, stay off the skag and try to reassemble what remains of my life.

It is a plan, at least notionally a plan, and one I should have been trying to see through instead of deciding I had a more exciting one for years.

My latest life-coach also has a plan.

'For fuck sake, you got that pin ready yet? I've got people to see out there. I'm planning a trip up north tomorrow to score. If you want to drive as well we can be there and back in three days.'

When he says 'up north' he means Holland, and when he says 'score' what he is suggesting is that the two of us steal a car, drive approximately 2,300 km, hook up with some Hells Angels he apparently knows, buy a job-lot of high-quality smack then make the return journey to get back here at roughly the same time as all the local junkies run out of gear themselves.

'We'll fucking clean up, Si! Make a fucking fortune, mate. You in?'

When he says 'clean up', he is not referring to the plan I was almost considering considering again.

As I hold the newly re-sharpened syringe up to the candlelight to check it is now ready to visit the hole in my left forearm, then draw up the potentially fatal concoction in the spoon, I have serious doubts as to whether the two of us will make it out of the caravan alive, let alone get to fucking Holland. I swiftly wave the needle over the flame to 'burn off any germs', then deposit the speedball into the vein currently covered in the blood weeping from the abscess in which it is hiding.

Ten seconds later I'm considering jogging to Holland if we don't manage to steal a car, as Vinny flushes out the works with some water (bottled) then sucks up the remaining fluid from the spoon, passes the needle over the candle to 'burn off the germs' then plunges it into the back of his arm as he joins me in our own caravan-sized version of Mount Olympus.

I am now feeling omnipotent despite looking like death warmed up and not smelling too good either.

'Holland, eh? Yeah, maybe, mate, sounds like a plan and I ain't really got much on over the next few days. How much money you got to score, mate?'

'Depends how much stuff I can nick off those smelly cunts outside before we leave, mate. Right, I'm off. You're staying up by your mate's place, yeah? I'll swing by later; I gotta get to work, unless you wanna come with me now?'

'Nah, man, it's cool. I'd only cramp your style.'

'Yeah, that's probably true. You're a proper useless cunt, ain't ya?'

Si, señor.

Man in the Corner Shop

My 'plan', such as it was, was not going to plan and neither was the one recently proposed by my Stanley-knife-loving partner in crime. The previous night's enthusiasm for a potentially 'fortune-making' trip to the Netherlands had somewhat diminished in conjunction with the departure of the drugs from my bloodstream, and Vinny had not returned from wherever he'd slithered off to upon leaving the caravan. As I stared out over the early-morning carnage of the festival site from my observation point halfway up the hill that overlooked it I was not feeling even remotely like God any more, although my beard was coming along quite nicely.

The sound of a generator spluttering as it ran out of diesel signalled temporary relief from the continual onslaught of French Techno from the system it powered and within a few seconds what sounded to me like people using a pneumatic drill to break up large boulders, with added bass frequencies and high-pitched screeching, was silenced.

Vive la France! Despite my unbridled admiration for the way our continental chums had dealt with their monarchy and more recently provided me with some much needed heroin, I was currently not feeling much Francophile love. The remnants of a human being that sat there hating himself and the world in equal measure did not want his morning's self-hate/self-pity session sound-tracked by French or indeed Techno of any origin, but there was apparently nothing I could do to stop it – not the Techno nor the self-hate, self-pity and self-destruction.

Or was there?

As I sat there plunging into my latest cesspit of opiate withdrawal and contempt for the world and all its creatures, French or otherwise, I suddenly came up with a sneaky plan that if successful would go a long way to address my current dilemma. A twisted smile cracked across my face as I trotted off to 'borrow' Sharky's car, the boot of which would be required if I was to make good the first part of the ruse I was already convinced was the greatest idea I'd ever had. I was going to sort this fucking mess out right now!

'Bien sûr, salaud anglais! Allons-y!'

'He's saying he doesn't want the fucking generator, he's already got one.'

Pedro was speaking in some sort of heavily accented Spanish gypsy dialect, Vinny was translating and it wasn't the response I was hoping for.

'But it's a good one, it's French, tell him they make the best generators in the fucking world, Vinny. Come on, mate, it's worth at least £200!'

Pedro was standing just inside the doorway to his *cortijo*, otherwise known as the 'bag shop', from where he supplied pretty much every baghead/smackhead/crackhead in the area; at least he did when you'd run out of better options.

Vinny continued to try his best to convince him he needed to purchase the recently liberated Gallic generator as Pedro stood spitting at our feet wearing his pants.

He was not wearing any other clothes and neither did he apparently want another generator, as he shouted back at us from behind the partially opened door. My Spanish was poor but I think I understand 'Fuck off, you junkie cunt' in most languages.

Vinny tried again. He'd not originally been part of my cunning plan but I'd almost run him over as I'd sped away shortly after being delighted to discover my earlier hilltop calculations were indeed correct and I'd been met with the sound of French snoring rather than French Techno. I'd quickly unhooked the cables that ran from the generator to the now silent speakers and with the strength that only the fear of imminent heroin withdrawal can provide, relieved my European smack-dealing, noise-polluting friends of their high-voltage electricity supply.

Until this present gypsy/junkie stand-off, much of which actually required no translation whatsoever, my stroke of genius had been working out just fine, despite the unforeseen inclusion of my translator and his ever-present Stanley knife.

You didn't think I'd been planning to stop taking smack and sort my life out, did you?

If you were surrounded by thousands of tree-hugging, soap-dodging, foreign crusties, you'd surely want to get as off your tits as possible, too?

'He says he'll give us 50 euros' worth of mix for it, take it or leave it, mate.'

I looked at Pedro as he coughed up half a lung before depositing it in the dust at my feet. He had the twisted strips of tinfoil containing the mix in one hand; the other was either scratching his cock or about to pull the pistol from his pants. I couldn't be sure, nor did I really want to find out.

'Tell him he's a cunt.'

'You fucking tell him. What am I, stupid?'

The generator was retrieved from the boot of the car and Pedro summoned one of his lackeys to carry it through into his house, only handing over the drugs once it had crossed the threshold. Vinny and I then repaired to the abandoned chicken shed just up the road to have breakfast.

Mix, or *polvo* to give it its Spanish name, was what Pedro called the pre-mixed deals of crack and heroin he sold alongside pretty much anything else someone like me might require in the ongoing rituals of day-to-day junkiedom.

I don't know about you but I generally prefer more opiate than coke in my intravenous speedball; Vinny was inclined the other way. Scoring polvo from the Spanish pikey lent a soupçon of uncertainty into this already somewhat dangerous pastime. You basically had no idea of the percentages of the two drugs combined in the deal you were about to dispatch into your bloodstream, which possibly suggested some caution should be applied to the process. There was the serious risk of having a heart attack if there was more coke, a possible OD if he'd been more generous with the smack. If he'd got it right it was the most perfect solution someone like me could wish to molest himself with.

'Stick the fucking lot in the spoon, Vinny. That cunt's really pissed me off, so I wanna make this a decent hit, OK?'

'You sure? That's a lot of polvo in there, dude, and I'm not gonna call you a fucking ambulance if you go over.'

'Just fucking do it, eh? His gear's shit anyway. Fuck it, I can think of worse ways to die.'

We cooked up the drugs, squatting together in the abandoned poultry shed, surrounded by discarded crack pipes and used tinfoil, with just each other and the stench of decaying shit for company as we poked about in our arms to find a vein. The notion that there might in fact not be many worse ways to die, or certainly not many less pleasant locations, briefly entered my head. However, in hot pursuit of that somewhat disconcerting train of thought were the contents of the syringe now hanging out of my arm, so my current company and surroundings rapidly ceased to be important, despite the fact that Vinny suddenly looked like he was about to have a heart attack.

'You all right, mate?'

It was clearly a coke-heavy mix. Vinny's face had turned scarlet and he was almost squirting sweat from behind his eyes, eyes that were scary enough at the best of times but currently seemed to be trying to dislodge themselves from their sockets.

I was silently praying to anything that remotely sounded like god as I was assaulted by the double-whammy of coke-induced projectile vomiting and the thrilling/terrifying thought that there might not be enough heroin entering my bloodstream to prevent my heart from exploding. My head felt like someone had just climbed inside it with a flame-thrower as the drugs incinerated my cranium, my arms started twitching involuntarily and I struggled to breathe. Suddenly, something resembling a B-52 bomber taxied along the base of my spine before opening its throttle and climbing up to the inside of the back of my skull, then doing a victory roll as the opiates slammed home. I wiped the puke from my mouth and allowed myself a smile in recognition of the fact that that I wasn't about to die in a pile of chicken shit and vomit.

'Nice hit that, eh, mate?'

'You're fucking mental, Simon. You're a very dangerous person to be around. You really don't care any more, do you?'

What sort of question was that to ask someone who'd just nicked and sold a generator then shared the resulting drugs with you?

He was right, though. I didn't really care about anything, certainly not right now as the B-52 carpet-bombed my nervous system with its payload of pikey polvo.

Killing Me Softly

'Soft' targets were a speciality of mine, people who were easy to manipulate and unlikely to attempt to permanently disfigure me after I'd managed to relieve them of any possessions, money or drugs.

The permanent residents of the riverbed that had hosted the festival may have been somewhat smelly but they were not 'soft' or stupid. Within a few weeks of my descent into their community it was made perfectly clear that my presence was not welcome. They had enough causalities of their own, so when they spotted Vinny and me forging our drug-dustbin dream-team, words were spoken to my hosts up on the hill.

Sharky, who'd tried his best to help, had finally had enough of me. He'd spent his fair share of time chasing the shadows of prolonged substance misuse himself back in the day. We'd actually met and become mates in one of the treatment centres I'd attended but my scummy, lowlife, one-man band of self-destruction was now too much even for him to tolerate any more.

He had a young family and was trying to make a new life for them all as he sweated his bollocks off under the often relentless

Spanish sunshine, renovating a long-abandoned farm building and slowly, lovingly turning it into a home.

'You gotta go, Si. I can't fucking have this here, you're a liability, mate. I've got a wife and kids to think about. Sorry, mate, but you're just too fucking messy.'

Too messy to co-exist in a community made up of people who had made getting messy a way of life? But there's messy and there's my kind of messy, and my particular strain infected anyone with whom I came into contact. Sharky knew all too well that if I could not find a soft target from which to procure the funds needed to score, his family would quite possibly also be drawn into my torrid state of affairs and he was not going to let that happen. He was still my mate and as such did not want to find himself having to kick fuck out of me at some point; besides, I was doing a pretty good job of that myself.

The assortment of 'retired' criminals, drug dealers and various other dodgy characters that operated within the murky fringes of 'normal' ex-pat society in the local area did not take kindly to people such as myself wreaking havoc and disturbing the stoned tranquillity of their day-to-day operations. A series of burglaries from properties belonging to the indigenous population had forced the usually benign local Guardia to do some work, although when one potential suspect was brutally attacked by a baseball-bat-wielding mob, leaving him barely able to walk, it became clear that vigilante justice was always going to provide a faster reaction than anything the local cops might get round to doing.

Was I involved in any way? Put it this way, I certainly did not ever enter anyone's house to steal their possessions but had I been interrogated by the local cops or, more worryingly, the locals themselves I could have provided them with the name of the person they were looking for. It goes without saying that I would have done so too, in an instant.

There are plenty of junkies I have known over the years who had a mental list of things they would never get involved with in the pursuit of drugs; after less than a month in Spain my own list had been reduced to the sort of behaviour I now cannot even bring myself to type, let alone do. The local polvo had sent me into a semi-permanent state of psychosis as I crept from one abandoned building to another, leaving a trail of blood, sweat and often my own shit, my inability to escape from myself made all the more difficult as I tried to hide from everybody else as well.

The weekly rent from my flat back in Hackney would be withdrawn from the cashpoint in the middle of the town within seconds of it arriving in my bank account, before I clung to the early-morning shadows en route to see Pedro, hopefully managing to avoid the various people I'd somehow managed to convince to lend me money. I'd already made a desperate, tearful phone call to my mum, telling her I had been framed and arrested on some sort of 'bloody ludicrous charge, Mum. I've done nothing wrong but they're saying they are going to put me in jail unless I pay a bribe of some sort. These people are real peasants, Mum. I really need your help. I can't access any of my own money here. It's all tied up in the studio I'm building.'

Soft targets often don't come much softer than a worried mother and she'd transferred enough cash into my account to keep me annihilated by the bag-shop B-52 pikey polvo bombs for almost two weeks, after which it was back to driving my 'friend' about as he went about his business.

'We're going up to see the hippies in Beneficio today, Simon. You'll like it up there, they all live in fucking tepees, smoke too much weed and shit in the woods. Lots of solar panels to liberate there, though. They're all fucking middle-class idiots who think they're gonna change the world by giving their kids acid and growing their own fucking vegetables. Bunch of cunts if you ask me.'

I wasn't asking. I was permanently far too scared and psychotic to say anything and it had already been made clear to me that our 'partnership' was not something I had an option of leaving, thanks to my knowledge as to the whereabouts of many of his recent acquisitions and the fairly strong suggestion that as far as he was concerned we were a good team, on a roll and as long as I was under his protection no harm would come to me. We headed off towards the 'commune of cunts' to un-install their solar panels and 'maybe steal a bit of weed, too'.

Within a few minutes of reaching our destination my

hippy-loving amigo bumped into an old acquaintance of his and they shuffled off to have a 'quick chat', leaving me to wander about the car park that sits at the bottom of a track leading up into crusty Nirvana. My current accommodation situation left something to be desired, consisting as it did of whatever abandoned hovel I found myself nodding out in at the end of my 'working' day, so my attention was soon caught by the 'for sale' sign stuck on the windscreen of a tiny motorhome, sitting outside of which was someone that sent my 'soft-target' indicator flying off the level.

'Is that yours, then, mate?' I enquired of the sandal-wearing hippy currently snacking from a bowl of vegetables that probably contained more nutrients per mouthful than my shattered body had seen in years.

'Oh, hi, man, yeah, she's mine all right. Why, are you interested in buying her?'

I hate people who refer to cars, etc. as 'she' almost as much as I think I hate hippies, particularly when they're wearing sandals and seem to be happy and content with their life.

'I might be. Why are you selling it? Do you live in it?'

'Oh, wow, right, well, I drove her down from Blighty a few months ago and I've been living in her ever since, but I've just found an empty cave over the back of that hill there and I'm going to move into that now.'

There was part of me that suddenly wanted to break down and cry, hug him and beg him to take me with him so I could hide from my current employer and everybody else while I let him feed me bowl after bowl of healthy, life-giving vegetables to help purge the nasty, soul-destroying drugs from my system.

Me being me, or to be more precise the 'me' that I was currently pretending to be, I also wanted to stab him in the face with a rusty tin can, tie him up and drive off in his plastic fantastic motorhome.

'I'm Nigel, very nice to meet you, by the way. What's your name?'

He's called Nigel; he's fucking asking for it!

'Banksy, my name's Banksy. I'm an artist.'

Why did I say that? It's not as random as it may sound.

Years previously, when I was yet to demolish my friendship with Luke due to the encroachment of my nasty habit and associated behaviour on our previously enjoyable relationship, he'd introduced me to his then best friend and flatmate.

The paint-splattered ball of creative energy munching on his breakfast of scrambled eggs and bacon glanced up at me from across the kitchen table.

'You must be that dodgy geezer from London Luke's told me so much about, then?'

Luke looks at me and shrugs.

'Pleased to meet you, Dodgy. Do you want some breakfast?'

We had some breakfast and I had a new name, at least as far as the good people of Bristol I hung out with were concerned.

As well as sharing a house, they also rented a studio together in Easton and over the following years, whenever I was passing through, we'd all hang out, either at the workspace, The Plough pub or various free parties and festivals.

My dirty secret did not stay a secret for very long but I have to say that aside from a well-deserved punch in the face after too much cider and the correct assumption I'd been involving Luke in my trips to St Paul's to score smack, Banksy remained of the opinion that what I got up to was none of his business.

Whether or not this position was informed by the fact that what he did for a living was also a secretive though rather more productive way to spend one's time, I don't really know. Either way, we became good friends to the point that when he decided he was going to move permanently to London, prior to the new millennium, he asked me to become his manager.

My thinking at the time, preoccupied as it usually was with whatever bit of unpleasantness I was required to do that day in order to score, decided that there was no money in street art and so I declined.

Yep! That's right. I said no. I was far too busy chasing the next £10 bag of smack to get involved with Banksy, his boxes of aerosol paint, ladders and the bits of cardboard he kept trying to make stencils with. (Can you all please excuse me while I go and smash my face into the wall of my flat for a few minutes?) So, freeing myself up to eventually devote much of my time to running in and out of the nearest supermarket clutching stolen cuts of meat and bottles of whisky, we decided to keep our relationship on a more informal standing.

We hung out, drank lots of cider, went to watch his beloved Bristol City FC, painted some walls, bridges and cows, ate lots of scrambled eggs on toast and when he moved to Stoke Newington I took him Christmas shopping in the various pound shops of Dalston. We were mates but heroin was not welcome at any time. If I was busy with that he was too busy to see me. He devoted his time to spraying paint on walls, whereas blood from a syringe was more my stock in trade.

Our friendship had somehow survived up to the point where I now found myself pretending to be him as I attempted to persuade my soon-to-be cave-dwelling, sandal-wearing friend Nigel that I could be trusted to take his vehicle for a test drive.

'So you're really Banksy, then? Wow, I don't know why but I thought you'd look different.'

Hmmmmmmm.

'Look, Nigel, let's get a beer and have a chat about this, eh?'

We were about 20 minutes into our test drive, I was at the wheel and Nigel had decided on the sale price. I had convinced him the money wouldn't be a problem but he might have to wait a few days for me to get 'one of my people' to transfer it into my account. We parked outside the roadside bar and a few large glasses of calvados later we had a deal. The fact that he was now seemingly convinced I was a somewhat famous graffiti artist might also have helped to cement our arrangement.

Nigel was not a stupid man, far from it, but he seemed thoroughly convinced that because we had met in an area populated by salad-munching hippy idealists such as himself, I could be trusted. In truth, the tranquil valley of kind, ethical, peace-loving, caring folks he now considered to be his neighbours represented nothing more than a soft-target supermarket to skag-hungry scum like me.

Of course the 'real' me, the person I was more scared of than Vinny or anyone else, would have enjoyed nothing more than to spend some time here, at peace with himself and the world, tree-hugging hippies included.

Does everything really happen for a reason? I don't know, but what I do know is that the 17-year-old kid who'd stood and watched

The Waterboys at Glastonbury all those years ago would have given almost anything to be as at peace with himself as the people I was stealing from apparently were. This was the same part of me, still just about intact, that wanted to give Nigel a hug and show him some respect for having the courage of his convictions. The me that admired him for being of a similar age to myself and still being brave enough to pursue his dreams, unlike the skeletal junkie currently plying him with cheap brandy and about to steal his motorhome.

So does everything happen for a reason? Because all of a sudden it started to occur to me that amongst all the crusty travellers, new-age idealists, drug casualties and alcoholics that made up the numbers in Orgiva, I was often shown examples of remarkable human spirit, morality and kindness. People taking pride in what they were trying to create, having a go at life, rather than injecting mountains of shit drugs in the vain attempt to escape from an existence littered with hurt and destruction.

There were plenty of other people just as desperate as myself in the vicinity, I was far from the only drugged-up waste of space polluting the climate, but they were just a mirror of what I'd become. I understood what I'd become and being reminded of that on a daily basis was little more than an annoyance, whereas Nigel was in many respects the person who most reminded me of someone I once thought I could be, minus the fucking sandals, of course.

I was free to move into my new home immediately, on the promise of half the agreed sum being paid within the next few days, the remainder just as soon as I'd sold my latest canvas to 'a good friend of mine, Pedro. He's a local artist. He makes and sells bags, really lovely bloke. I'll introduce you to him one day. He also keeps me supplied with the materials I need for my work here.'

When I dropped Nigel back at crustyville my sidekick was nowhere to be seen, so I drove off to look for some Welsh drug dealers Vinny had recently introduced me to, who were apparently looking for someone with a vehicle to drive 50 kilos of hash from Spain to Ireland, where the consignment was to be delivered to some semi-retired paramilitaries.

I'd have Nigel's money in no time, either that or I'd be getting my kneecaps blown off, but having just relieved an obviously intelligent if not a little naive hippy of his motorhome, I was feeling lucky and clearly on a roll.

Everything Must Go

'Listen, I'm totally fucking up for it, lads. My campervan looks the part, there's no way anyone's going to suspect it's loaded with gear. It looks like the sort of thing a couple of old-age pensioners would be driving about in, eh?'

'Yeah, it does but there's a slight problem, though.'

'Really? C'mon, lads, you can trust me. I'm originally from Weston-super-Mare, I'm practically Welsh myself!'

The 'entrepreneurs' I was trying to offer my services to, known locally as 'the Taffia', seemed reluctant to entrust their goods to me and my new mobile home but for the life of me I could not see what the problem was.

And there you have it, probably the single most significant factor in this whole sorry business, certainly the root cause of almost every situation so far described. Certainly the reason why I was now living in a stolen campervan, parked up on some wasteland in the middle of nowhere, permanently strung-out, emaciated and covered in abscesses. It's without doubt also why I was currently pleading with a couple of possibly very dangerous drug dealers to give me 50 kilos of hashish to drive halfway across Europe for little more financial gain than I'd get for doing an honest bit of work for a few weeks.

A slight problem?

I think that's being generous in the extreme, because the problem, although slight in weight, was the very thing that had been crushing the life out of me for years. The problem, of course, was me.

'We'll think about it, boyo. Where can we find you over the next couple of days?'

'I'm parked up down by the dry river. I'm not going anywhere, lads. Leave a note on the door if I'm not in. I probably won't be too far away.'

Three weeks later and there had been no knock or note, nor could I find my prospective employers anywhere in the town. At least they didn't ever answer the door to their apartment on any of the numerous occasions I'd called by.

Vinny had found himself a new playmate and expanded his operations further afield, and the only people who would have anything to do with me were the raging alcoholics who drank by the fountain, probably because they were too pissed to notice what a fucking liability I was myself and also because they were in no danger of getting fleeced by me because they no longer possessed anything worth stealing.

The weeks passed, the list of things I'd never do to get money for drugs got shorter, resulting in growing feelings of self-disgust, guilt and shame that required more desperate trips to the bag shop, more lemons and blunt syringes and more foul-tasting cheap wine, as my world was reduced to an horrific single-occupancy existence with only Pedro or one of his associates providing any intrusion.

The 'dry river' in the centre of Orgiva was a polite way of describing what was really nothing more than a dumping ground for whatever useless bits of shit people discarded there, so it was as good a place as any for me to call home. It also ran, or didn't to be more accurate, right past the bag shop.

Convenient as it was, my current semi-permanent location was always going to be more of the permanent variety while I was left with the daily conundrum of whether to spend any funds I had acquired on drugs or petrol. I might as well have been living in a real house, as obviously this decision was made for me the minute I was woken each morning by the sound of a cockerel squawking about outside and the onset of cold turkey and subsequent urgency to empty my bowels in the chemi-toilet at the back of the van.

My financial affairs were in the same malnourished and desperate state as the rest of my existence and if buying petrol was off limits, finding the necessary funds to top up the chemicals required to make the toilet function properly was way down my shopping list. They say the Queen has been greeted with the smell of fresh paint everywhere she has gone; she'd obviously never been for a dump at mine, where everything stank of rancid junkie sweat and shit.

My guitar had been handed over to Pedro, along with the few bits of decent jewellery that had previously adorned my wretched body, in exchange for drugs weeks ago. My tenant back in Hackney had gone on the missing list and neglected to pay the outstanding rent, my mum was now totally off-limits and I'd run out of 'friends' from whom I could borrow/steal any money.

My wife had recently flown over to visit Sharky and Amber. They were also her friends and as such they'd felt the need to call her to disclose that from what they'd seen and heard it seemed likely I was going to die, if not of my own doing then quite possibly at the hands of any number of people who were now of the opinion that I was to blame for the spate of recent burglaries. Stealing solar panels and motorhomes from benign soap-dodgers was one thing but relieving serious dealers of their product was another altogether.

Was I guilty of extreme stupidity in the pursuit of funds with which to purchase the drugs I then used even more recklessly?

Yes, I was.

Was I stupid/desperate/brave/deranged enough to steal from the sort of people who would come looking for me with baseball bats or a gun?

Yes, I was.

Did I?

No, I didn't, but the blurring of fantasy and reality was by now almost impossible to distinguish, not just from my perspective but also by anyone else unfortunate enough to be involved at this particular juncture.

I could easily have been guilty and dealt with by the aggrieved locals, and perhaps the saddest aspect of that would have been that I wouldn't have cared. Sure, I'd have bawled my fucking eyes out in terror and pleaded for forgiveness, but only for my family's sake and not my own.

There was seemingly no point whatsoever to my existence, so

there was really nowhere left for me to go except a mortuary but I could not stop using, despite or perhaps because of that fact.

My situation and behaviour suggested there was apparently no hope any more, or certainly not enough to allow people the luxury of believing there was a chance of a happy ending.

The difference between reality and fantasy, good drugs and bad drugs, the people who took and sold them, was by now indistinguishable to the man who as a kid once thought he understood all that. The same person who'd now become a rotten, half-dead excuse for a human being, crying himself to sleep every night in a stolen campervan littered with dirty needles, blood-stained clothes, empty cartons of cheap wine and the stench of impending death.

My wife flew home after her short stay at Sharky's, during which time we'd attempted to do something 'normal' for the last time. Whether or not she thought she'd ever see me alive again was not something we talked about as we walked along the beach but as we parted before her flight home her eyes contained more hurt than almost any I have seen. The fact that neither of us realised we'd just spent our wedding anniversary together until we were at the airport was perhaps a subconscious mechanism that allowed us to try to focus on the present, no matter how painful, rather than the past and our highly improbable future.

I'd driven her to the airport myself. Sharky, in spite of everything but possibly because of his own experiences, had still just about managed to remain on speaking terms with me and had lent me his car, and my wife had in turn agreed to entrust me with some money with which to repay him for the fuel. Thus I was given the opportunity to demonstrate some respect to my long-suffering friend, who, despite being regularly derided for his loyalty towards me, still clung on to the notion that I was his mate and perhaps still capable of behaving as such.

I was but I didn't. The petrol money went to Pedro for a hit, a hit that didn't even touch the sides despite containing enough drugs to kill most people. This was a final act of betrayal that provoked a long-deserved punch in the face when my utterly exasperated and deeply offended mate caught up with me a few days later in the car park.

'Just fuck off, Simon, you fucking junkie piece of shit. We've tried to help you, you scummy cunt. You've no idea what I've had to do to stop people from battering you, you selfish prick. Just fuck off out of our lives, eh?'

'Mate, I'm sorry, I'm really sorry, I . . .'

'Sorry? You're fucking sorry? You don't know the fucking meaning of the word any more, you cunt. The only person you're sorry for is yourself. If I ever see you again I'll fucking kill you.'

He drove off in his car, the spinning wheels throwing up a cloud of dust that then settled onto what remained of me and the debris of my life as I sat, staring into space, silently drinking a carton of cheap, nasty, gut-destroying wine.

There was obviously something wrong with my guts as well as every other aspect of my existence, as even I could no longer stomach using the toilet inside the campervan and during a pre-scoring visit to the nearest foliage the following morning I noticed that what was being deposited onto the ground was not anywhere near the colour it should have been and also had blood in it.

As I was attempting to swallow the remaining mouthfuls of Vino Tinto from the carton that I had somehow left unfinished the previous night I spotted one of the part-time junkies I knew trundling along the track towards the bag shop in his van.

Nick lived a few miles out of town and as such avoided much of the lunacy surrounding those of us who were attempting to survive from day to day, under the relentless Spanish sun with an unforgiving habit and no discernible source of income.

He also had a job that paid well and meant that when he came into town to score he spent a lot of money. This fact was not lost on me, particularly after seeing orange and red liquid trickling between my legs as I'd done my morning ablutions, suggesting as it did all manner of potential ailments, the solution to which was obviously more heroin.

The wheels of his van had barely come to a halt before I'd launched myself upon his sense of compassion and begged him to sort me out with a bit of gear, just until I got my outstanding rent money in a few days, of course.

We retired to 'mine' to do what was required and while I was struggling to find a vein in the back of my arm, Nick enquired as to my plans.

'Mate, to be honest I was thinking of selling this and going back to London. Things ain't really worked out for me here, you know?'

'It's funny you should say that, cos I bumped into Nigel the other day.'

I let go of the belt/tourniquet on my arm and unleashed the polvo into my bloodstream, exhaling smoke from the fag clenched between my teeth and struggling to figure out if I actually cared in the slightest about what Nick had just said.

'What? Nigel from the cave, Nigel?'

'Nigel who doesn't live in a cave as yet and wants his fucking campervan back Nigel, actually.'

'I like him, I've been meaning to get up there to see him, but you know . . . I've been busy down here, mate.'

'So I hear. Certain people seem to think you've been taking liberties. I'm surprised you've not had a visit yet.'

'I, er, listen, Nick, I swear to fucking god, mate, none of that is true. I'm not like that, really.'

'Do you think I'd have scored for you and be sitting in your stolen wagon sharing my drugs if I thought you were?'

He looked me right in the eye. Normally I hated it when people did that because they'd see what a shyster I really was but at that precise moment it felt like I had no choice.

'Do you know what your problem is, Simon?'

Remarkably and possibly for the first time in my entire life, instead of nodding my head and preparing to explain exactly what my problem was, I remained silent.

He took another hard lick from his crack pipe, not, in my experience anyway, normally the precursor to a deeply profound but beautifully simplistic piece of advice, and exhaled.

The words that followed quite possibly have had as significant an effect on my life as the crack/heroin contained in the smoke that accompanied them out of his mouth.

'Your problem is that you keep running about saying, "Help me, help me, help me," but you won't fucking help yourself.'

He began to sweat like a lunatic then handed me the pipe.

'I'm sitting here because I can choose to, Simon; you're fucking dying here because you can't choose not to.'

Was Nick the first person to have ever relayed this crucial piece of information to me? Of course he wasn't, but he was the first person who'd said it with a crack pipe in their hand and even more bizarrely than that the first person who'd made me believe it.

Of course acceptance is one thing, actually making decisions based on that point of understanding, another thing altogether.

Bringing it all Back Home

Nick decided he wanted to buy the campervan and we went in search of its rightful owner up in hippy valley. I was free to continue residing in it until I figured out my next move, which by now was reduced to what seemed like three options: stay in Spain and die; go somewhere else and also die; or perhaps attempt to find a new way to live.

Nigel cheerfully accepted the cash offered by my new landlord and we drove up into the mountains to park it up on Nick's land, where, in between his work commitments and visits to the bag shop, he was attempting to build a house.

I should have been attempting to construct some sort of plan as to what exactly I intended to do next, as my latest vantage point of the world was only a temporary reprieve from the incessant carnage back in Orgiva and my host, despite his remarkable generosity of spirit thus far, had also made it clear I had not 'moved in' on a permanent basis.

Whatever course of action I was about to attempt, money would be required. Nick was currently preventing me from the onset of cold turkey in exchange for my somewhat pathetic attempts to act as housekeeper, housemaid and gardener, my inability to perform any of the basic tasks involved soon becoming apparent.

'Simon, I can't keep supporting your habit, mate. I'm not exactly flush right now. I just gave Nigel almost all my money for that wagon you're rotting to death in. Sorry, mate, you're gonna have to come up with something by the end of the week. I'm heading up the coast for a job, so you need to be gone by the time I get back, please.'

Lingering about like a parasitic, toxic bad smell was always going to have its sell-by date and when I 'borrowed' the campervan to drive into town to watch the Liverpool v. West Ham FA Cup final, somehow managing to return pissed out of my tiny mind, van intact but carrying some 'passengers' I'd invited along to celebrate the victory, Nick had no choice but to show me the red card.

'You are a fucking nightmare, Simon. I don't fucking believe this. I've tried to help you and in return you invite the only other junkie scumbags on the planet that make you look almost respectable back up to my house. The reason I live up here is to avoid people like that and now they're sitting in my fucking van, dripping blood all over the seats.'

He stared at me with a look of pure disgust, his facial expression suddenly aggravated further by the sight of one of my 'guests' attempting to have a shit in the bushes that lined the path up to the house.

'You've got 24 hours. If you're still here after that I won't be responsible for my actions.'

Nick decided to personally return my friends to Orgiva, locking them in the back of the van before speeding off down the track towards town.

I was left alone with a half-empty bottle of brandy and a loaded syringe, my cup-winning hit, the potency of which I hoped was as mindblowing as the goal Steven Gerrard had scored in the 90th minute of the match to level the score and force extra time.

As I'd driven into town earlier looking for something to steal, more out of pure desperation than any real hope, I'd checked my bank account to see if the tooth fairy had made a deposit. To my utter disbelief and subsequent delirium it appeared my tenant had paid in two weeks' rent money. Surely this was a sign the day was going to witness a famous victory?

Within minutes I'd been hammering on the metal shutter at Pedro's. Shortly after that I'd rounded up a few hostages to come and watch the game and give me someone to be nice to for a few hours. Drink and drugs on me because I'm a fucking rock 'n' roll star and also such a generous human being, of course.

The fact I was no longer able to tolerate my own company either with or without drink and drugs was soon obliterated by two weeks' rent money's worth of both.

So the mighty Liverpool Football Club lifted the cup, everybody, including myself, pretended to like me for a few hours, until the point where I found myself halfway up a mountain with just a needle and some cheap brandy for company.

As far as my own prolonged attempts to salvage some sort of triumph went, it now appeared the clock was ticking, we were into the final few seconds of extra time and the game was apparently lost.

Where the fuck could I get some more money from now?

I chewed at what remained of my fingernails, blood dripping from the raw, exposed flesh as well as from the abscess on my arm. The battered site had recently been disturbed by my blunt needle as I attempted to deliver my celebratory hit – a speedball containing so much crack that it had tipped me into a state of paranoid psychosis the like of which I'd rarely experienced before.

I paced up and down the track dementedly, swigging the remnants of the brandy in a forlorn attempt to slow down my heartbeat, convinced that I was about to have a seizure.

It was pitch black and I was alone, halfway up the side of a mountain in the middle of nowhere, strutting about clutching my chest, sweat pouring down my face, arms and legs, crying my fucking eyes out. I was also terrified, paranoid and at a point of desperation previously unimaginable even to someone like myself who had researched the subject thoroughly for years.

A miracle was required if I was to get the one thing that would help. I needed money because I could then go and score some more heroin, but where would I get it from?

As I wiped the noxious sweat from my face with my filthy, blood-stained Liverpool shirt I had a thought – as insane a thought as anything that had ever entered my frazzled brain before.

What had Nick said to me recently about not being willing to help myself? Yeah, that's it! I need to help myself and it suddenly dawned on me what that currently required.

'I just gave Nigel almost all my money for that wagon.'

I thought about the football earlier and a smile slashed across my face as I recalled the commentary:

'The ball comes to Gerrard. He shoots, scores!!! He's done it, just when he looked injured and out of it, he's equalised. It's 3–3 in surely the best cup final of modern times.'

I knew Nigel didn't have a bank account; he'd asked Nick to pay him in cash. I also knew he lived a few miles away on the other side of this fucking mountain, in a cave of some sort.

The cash was in all likelihood hidden somewhere inside. It was a long shot and there was a fucking mountain in my way, but I'd just whacked up a speedball, so fuck it! It was time to go and start helping myself a little bit. Surely even round here a posh hippy in a cave couldn't be that hard to find?

Singing possibly the most demented rendition of 'You'll Never Walk Alone' ever heard, or not heard considering I was alone on the side of a mountain in southern Spain, I trotted off to snatch an unlikely victory from the jaws of defeat.

A few hours and countless renditions of 'You'll Never Walk Alone' later I was quietly ransacking Nigel's little patch of tranquillity, getting increasingly frustrated by the apparent absence of the cash I'd convinced myself would be there.

Had I been attempting to steal a month's supply of chickpeas, lentils, ill-fitting sensible clothes and incense, I'd have been dancing for joy by now but the likelihood of Pedro wanting to exchange any of that stuff for a few wraps of smack seemed remote to say the least.

Nigel was nowhere to be seen, probably knocking out a few late-night versions of Cat Stevens' songs on some bongo drums in a tepee somewhere, while I was dripping blood and sweat all over his clothes and groceries.

There's only so long you can ransack what amounts to little more than a hole in the ground covered by a tarpaulin before accepting that it doesn't contain anything of value, certainly nothing of value to the demented vile excuse for a human being currently engaged in that process.

There was clearly nothing there I could persuade the possibly even more vile pikey smack dealer to accept as payment for what my bowels were rapidly beginning to tell me they required in order to keep functioning and not leave a puddle of blood-flecked shit as a calling card.

An hour later and once again minus my translator I was outside Pedro's trying to convince him to buy the generator I'd liberated from a nearby Buddhist yoga centre shortly after abandoning my search for the cash at Nigel's.

'*Polvo, Pedro, por favor, amigo, mi generator, bien, English generator, bien bien. Polvo solo, nada crack, amigo, eh?*'

In what was surely the most miraculous event of the day, if not even my entire life, Pedro smiled and nodded his head.

'*Si, no hay problema.*'

He was giggling and looked about as off his fucking head as I'd ever seen him. Maybe one of his goats had relented and let him have sex with it, I have no idea, but he was obviously in a good mood and within seconds I was back in the chicken shed cooking up a wrap of polvo solo – just heroin, no coke – having decided I'd had my fill of injecting crack for the time being.

The following morning, having nodded out amongst the fossilised chicken shit and more recently deposited human excrement, I headed up to the fountain in town and sat down to consider my next move as I supped my breakfast of cheap wine and bread.

Gazing into water as I perched on the side of the fountain I saw my reflection, possibly the last thing I wanted to look at, but the bearded, emaciated, yellowing face that stared back at me was the only company I was likely to have that day – until Nigel appeared, that is.

'Hello, Simon, I think this must be yours?'

He was holding a syringe.

'I'm assuming you left it during your visit last night. Surely even you aren't stupid enough to think I'd leave all that cash lying about? I had a feeling you'd come looking for it, you know.'

I stared at him, not really able to fathom the situation.

'I suspected you were in trouble from the minute you tried to convince me you were that artist chap, Banksy, but I'm generally of the opinion that if people are willing to make such fools of themselves there must be something seriously wrong somewhere. I gave you the keys to the van because I knew you wouldn't be going anywhere. You can't leave because you're too bloody scared to.'

I kept staring, unable to speak, as befuddled by the words I was hearing as I was by the remnants of the opiates in my system.

'You're not very well, are you, mate? But I think you need to go back to London or wherever it is you're from. Here's some change, go to the phone box over there and call whoever you need to to get home before you kill yourself, eh?'

He handed me a few euros and the syringe that had obviously dropped from my pocket as I'd searched his cave the previous night, smiled at me and walked off. I never saw him again.

Had Nigel given me the kicking I so fully deserved, perhaps what happened next might not have transpired, I'll never know. He didn't, he assaulted me with the truth in the same way Nick had done recently and the truth sets us free, or so they say.

The truth can only settle on fertile ground, not the chemically devastated vista that I awoke to each day, regularly obliterated as it was by the substances I had been devouring for so long. Now, however, the seeds of kindness thrown at me by those two individuals had somehow taken root, no matter how many drugs I took. In effect, the drugs had stopped working!

As if in some sort of daydream I shuffled over to the phone and dialled the first of only two people I knew that might still speak to me. One was the artist I'd tried to convince Nigel I actually was, the other, my sister. Between them and in what turned out to be the last conversation I ever had with Banksy, they agreed to put enough money in my bank account to get me a flight home. In fact they both independently transferred enough cash to make this possible, as I neglected to inform either of them I'd been speaking to the other. One deposit was spent on the plane ticket, the other on the drugs I felt I required in order to get everything done before I left and actually got to Granada airport. I proceeded to get paralytic on brandy as I paid off Pedro, retrieved my guitar and jewellery, and scored my final few wraps of polvo. In a final act of utterly undeserved kindness Nick agreed to drive me to the airport. Five hours later I was scoring some smack from Bishop in Stoke Newington before heading over to Ben's to attempt to go cold turkey, again.

The End

There are very few things less likely to occur in life than two junkies living under the same roof with access to cash successfully attempting to endure heroin withdrawals and stop using. It pains me to say it but Liverpool are probably more likely to win the Premiership some time soon than Ben and I were to not score the minute my tenant paid in another two weeks' rent money on day three of our hastily agreed detox regime.

By then I'd managed to empty the contents of both the bottle of methadone I'd procured and the drinks cabinet of his sister's flat, the sofa of which I currently occupied as she was away working for a while. We both agreed it would be better for me to live elsewhere after we'd devoured the blue baggies of smack I'd returned with after my trip to the cashpoint. His sibling had no idea I was staying there and was due to return shortly anyway. My window of opportunity had disappeared again.

Much of what occurred after I'd decided this actually wasn't a 'good time' to get clean anyway is something of a mystery. At the same time as I'd purchased the methadone I also stumbled into someone who'd got their hands on a bottle containing 200 Pakistani Valium, the contents of which, when not dissolving in my rotten stomach, I was now selling to every smackhead I knew in Hackney.

There are a lot of junkies in Stoke Newington and I knew many of them. Show me a junkie who says they don't enjoy goofing out on Valium and I'll show you a liar. There is a reason why so many people enjoy using them, particularly on top of strong lager and gear, despite being quite possibly the hardest of all drugs to get off. The withdrawals can sometimes last for months and are horrific, but if there's a better way of pretending you don't exist on a daily basis, I've yet to experience it.

The Valium haze or 'cloak of invisibility' as many shoplifters describe it, as well as making watching daytime TV seem to be the most culturally enlightening experience available to mankind, also does a remarkable job of erasing the memory of any amount of Jeremy Kyle you might wish to be exposed to.

All I know is that at some point I had conversations with both my sister and my wife. My sister made me an offer, my wife agreed to assist.

The deal was thus: my eldest nephew was shortly to turn ten and had asked that his uncle Simon come and visit and take him and his mates ice skating for the day. He also said I wasn't allowed to be on drugs of any kind.

He was still an innocent child yet he felt he had to say that about his uncle. It hurt and cut through all the Valium and street drugs swimming through my system. Like some sort of smart bomb of truth it exploded into my consciousness, momentarily stunning, then exposing the reality of my situation like never before. There was no way I was ever going to get clean. Despite the gnawing revelations exposed by the final few days in Spain, I'd failed again.

Ben didn't want to stop using, at least not yet, whereas I needed to if I was to survive any longer. But the thought of having to deal with life without drugs while facing up to the years of hurt and suffering I'd inflicted upon almost everyone who'd loved me seemed too much to bear.

To raise people's hopes? Family, friends, whoever and then snatch all that back yet again? No! This had to stop for good and the only individual who could halt this continual procession of false dawns and disappointment was me.

Help me, help me, help me?

Fucking right it was finally time to really help myself.

I went to find hardcore Dave and hopefully score enough drugs to then kill myself or both of us, I didn't care. I tracked him down and you've already read about what happened next in the prologue to this book.

There is a particular low-rise council block just off Nevill Road in Stoke Newington, as unassuming and nondescript as you will find anywhere, so much so that I would struggle to point it out to you today should you ever care to take a stroll though the area with me.

It has, of course, hosted its share of life's dramas over the years – newborns arriving and loved ones departing. Days and nights expanded with joy, weighed down with tears, punctuated by hateful damaging fists and life-affirming laughter. Such is life here, stacked up and divided into boxes on the Shakespeare Estate as it is anywhere, tiny compartments arranged neatly in the misguided belief they would bring people together. Yeah, they brought people together; the dividing walls are only an inch or so thick!

It is 30 May 2006, the exact time of day roughly five minutes after I've given a teenager on a stolen bike some money in exchange for some drugs that I hope will comprise my last hit ever.

A gram of heavily cut heroin and half a gram of equally fraudulent crack cocaine are being dissolved on the top of a discarded Coke can currently in the tremulous grip of the desperate unwashed hand connected to what remains of the rest of the mess that masquerades as a human being squatting at the top of the stairwell.

'Simon, you're gonna fucking kill yourself, mate.'

My audience of one suddenly seems a bit concerned.

'Doubt it, Dave, but if I do you can have my can of Special Brew. It's still cold.'

'Thanks, but I prefer Skol.'

'I've got a quid left over in my pocket, fucking take that if I go over and get yourself one of them, then, OK?'

'Ta, mate, nice one.'

The contents of the Coke-can cooker bubble and quietly hiss their disgust as they turn the requisite colour not too dissimilar to that of the nicotine-stained fingers now dropping the filter from a cheap cigarette into the tiny puddle of liquid self-hate rapidly cooling on the top of the can.

On the floor below us we hear a voice.

'Don't forget my fucking fags, you prick,' is the parting comment from whoever has been left shut inside that particular box as a door slams behind the prick in charge of buying the cigarettes and whatever else has been ordered to help alleviate the monotony of another day on the Shakespeare Estate.

I draw up most of the contents of the Coke can into my syringe and spit on the back of my left arm in preparation as I attempt to obliterate myself from the monotony of another day in my life. This stairwell, a public toilet, a crackhouse, my old flat or a campervan in Spain, it makes no difference to me. I can't escape myself any more, so hopefully this hit is going to finally send me somewhere I might get some peace.

My audience is restless.

'C'mon, Simon, don't take the piss. You got most of that in your works, you've not left much for me, you cunt.'

'I paid for it.'

'Yeah, yeah, true, but I sorted us out yesterday.'

'That was yesterday, Dave, and yesterday you got the bigger hit, a bigger hit of a lot less fucking gear too, mate, so shut the fuck up or I'll put the rest in my works and you'll get fuck all.'

'Dickhead.'

'Whatever.'

'You really gonna do all that in one hit? You're off your fucking head, mate.'

He's starting to really get on my tits, so I put my syringe back onto the filter and draw up some more of the shit-coloured fluid.

'I strongly suggest you shut your fucking mouth, Dave, and take what's left before I have the fucking lot, OK?'

'Proper dickhead you, eh? All right, get out the fucking way, will you?'

I am hopefully about to get myself permanently out of his way, everybody's way in fact.

There is a small abscess on the back of my left arm, slowly seeping blood, somewhere inside of which is the remnants of a vein that hopefully will be able to receive the blunt needle of the three-day-old syringe I am about to start prodding it with. In a life long since devoid of any hope these few seconds of optimistic intrusion into the hole in my arm are as good as it gets. Think about that!

This is it. I hate God almost as much as I hate myself but offer the scruffy twat a little thought as I beg for this elusive vein to show itself by flooding the barrel of my syringe with my poisoned blood and allowing me to release the belt I have wrapped around my arm so I can relieve the syringe of its contents and myself of the heavy burden of being alive.

Freedom is what drugs strongly suggested was on offer all those years ago. Freedom from feelings I struggled with then and still do now as I squat, trying to not puke prior to getting the drugs into my body. My inability to exist within my own skin in a world I have struggled to make any sense of is the double whammy to which eventually, after working my way through every other substance I could, only heroin seemed able to provide a solution.

Now, as I am about to bow out for the final time I'm convinced that as I overdose and check out permanently, my audience might possibly rifle through my clothes, take anything he can sell and leave me there for some other unfortunate resident of the estate to find. I accept this as par for the course but a small part of what remains of my soul hopes it's not a decent human being who'll discover me, someone who has no choice but to exist alongside all the scumbags like me who use their stairwells to inject drugs to try to avoid feeling like an utter cunt all the time.

Why do I feel this way about myself?

Do I actually know what I think about myself any more?

Who knows? Who cares?

Certainly not me as I rejoice at the miniature tidal wave of blood that suddenly washes up inside the barrel of my syringe and tells me the end is nigh. I release the tourniquet and prepare to take my final bow.

Maida Vale, London, five days later

'I'm going to work. If you go out and use don't bother coming back. If you steal anything I'll call the police. If you're still here when I get home tonight I might cook you some food. You've got 12 days to get clean before you take your nephew ice skating. I suggest you call that number for Narcotics Anonymous on the kitchen table. Good luck.'

I am lying, wrapped in a sweat-soaked duvet on the floor of my wife's flat in west London. My 'final hit' in Hackney had been as successful as every previous attempt I'd made to either die or stay clean and now, having decided I couldn't even kill myself properly, I began considering the notion that I might try to stay alive.

Dave had dragged me out of the stairwell shortly after it had become obvious, despite my best efforts that day, that the world and I still had some unfinished business. He propped me up outside an off-licence while he went in to get another can of Skol Super, before depositing me on the sofa at his mate's place a short walk/stumble away and throwing six Dexedrine tablets down my throat.

The pharmaceutical speed had kick-started my respiratory system and saved my life, much to my apparent exasperation and very shortly to the obvious annoyance of the sofa's owner, who now had to listen to my amphetamine-induced babble while I castigated Dave for forgetting to get me a can of Brew en route to our current location.

'Selfish ginger prick, I'm spitting feathers here. Hey, does your mate wanna buy any Valium?'

Four days and four Valium, heroin and Special Brew-induced overdoses later, not surprisingly I was asked to vacate the latest sofa I had taken to calling my home.

'Simon, I'm going to ask you politely, please fuck off and try to kill yourself somewhere else, eh?'

Ungrateful bastard. I'd been sharing my Valium with him all fucking week and this was how he repaid me?

So now there really was nowhere left to go. Getting thrown off the last sofa in town seemed to finally convince me it was time for me to give up trying to die and so I made the call to my wife and told her I wanted to try, one more time, to get clean, stay alive and go ice skating.

The door slams shut behind her as, choking back tears, she walks out into the street below and off to the job she hates, leaving me lying on the floor with the thing I hate the most: me.

It's come down to a bottle that contains a few drops of methadone and a silence that grows, echoing with 20 years of memories, some good, most not so as I exhale the smoke from another cigarette I don't want and watch as it flows in front of the early-morning light invading the room in which I am being strangled by the present moment and the memories of what seems like every fucking day that has led up to this point.

The silence is in stark contrast to the cacophony made by the stream of eager reporters from self-pity TV that are currently broadcasting inside my head.

The news they fervently deliver in the toxic soundbites currently battering my mind is turned up to full volume and not exactly the sort of story saved for the 'and finally' section of news broadcasts worldwide.

I stare up at the ceiling. I know every inch of its surface by now, having been staring at it for the past few hours. It's just another unremarkable interior to have come under my scrutiny during the insomnia that has accompanied the departure of heroin from my system every time I've lain down to try to wave that shit goodbye over the years.

I can't do this. There's no fucking way I can do this. I'm a junkie, always have been, always will be. I don't know why, but I am.

I crawl over to the window and, three floors up, I sit on the ledge and try to convince myself I actually have the courage to jump off.

Who am I fucking kidding? What the fantasist inside me would really like is for someone to come bursting through the flat door and beg me to reconsider and climb back inside but even I apparently know the difference between fantasy and reality now, because this time it seems the truth is all that remains as the heroin departs.

As for the difference between good drugs and bad drugs?

None of them seem to have ultimately done me any favours. Yeah, there were good times but all that seems like such a long time ago.

The CD player in the corner of the room blinks, its display lights indicating there is a disc on pause contained within its chrome exterior. Music? I remember music, I remember when the purchase of the latest offering by The Jam, The Smiths or The Stone Roses filled me with a sense of excitement beyond anything a trip to Pedro's, or indeed anywhere else like that, had done for a very long time.

I cry. I cry more tears than I knew I had within me as my gaze darts from the CD player to the methadone beside me. There are soon more tears running down my face than there is liquid contained in the bottle of green futility I'd brought with me to aid me in my attempt to get off heroin.

Crawling back across the floor, I turn the volume up and press play. The CD inside spins into life and as the opening bars of 'The Whole of the Moon' beautifully shatter the silence in that flat in west London, I remember Glastonbury 1986.

I had been 17 years young and full of the drugs I clearly required because without them I could not seem to generate any hope, acceptance or self-belief. I was convinced that without some sort of substance inside me I would disappear and fall apart, when all I really wanted to do was exist and be part of . . . Part of what? Part of that crowd who'd stood listening to the band on stage that day in 1986, part of the city I'd fled to from my home town, part of the friendships I'd witnessed over the years but had never been able to truly participate in.

Why?

I had no idea. The overwhelming sense of emptiness I felt in that moment provided no answers, just questions.

Too high, too far, too soon?

Perhaps?

I looked up out of the window and spoke out loud to my long-departed dad, provoking a torrent of tears and an involuntary shudder as I cried out to him for help.

'Daddy, I love you. I miss you so much. Please help me. I need you, please make this stop.'

The song on the CD player ended and there was silence.

I had a moment of clarity, a peculiar notion emerging from the barren mental wasteland of my desperation, stunning in its simplicity but smart enough to outwit the deviousness of my self-piteous, truculent, smackhead methodology.

I never have to use again, no matter what. But clearly I was going to need a lot of help to stay clean.

In that completely unexpected but deeply profound moment of truth, I felt a sense of relief far greater than anything previously provided by something I'd injected, snorted, swallowed or drunk for longer than I could remember.

Fuck it, it's time to stand up and be counted. It's time to empty the void rather than continue to try to fill it.

My daddy was right there with me. He'd never been away – just as he'd promised in the letter he'd sent me a few weeks before he'd died.

My face is a mess of tears and snot. I shake uncontrollably like a terrified child, then smile, stagger to my feet and try to dance, stumbling into the kitchen to get the phone number my wife had mentioned earlier.

The next song continues, as does my deranged jigging about while I sing the words I'd listened to but never really heard as I'd wandered out in the world for so many years. Despite there being no witnesses to my tearful, spasmodic frugging, I suddenly, incredibly, feel like I'm not on my own any more and maybe never really had been, despite so many years trying to escape myself and evade anyone who tried to get close.

Replacing The Waterboys with *Exile on Main Street* and turning up the volume even more, I went into the toilet and flushed the methadone away, as the beautifully drug-soaked songs from many years ago drowned out the voice in my head saying I'd just made a big fucking mistake.

Then it was time to ask for some help about how I could help myself.

'Hello, is that Narcotics Anonymous?'

'Yes, it is, how can we help?'

'I'm fucked. I need help or I'm going to die.'

'OK. Well, I'm really glad you called. Have you been to a meeting before?'

'Yeah, a few. Never really listened to much of what was being said, though.'

'Ha, ha, I was the same, always too busy thinking about myself to hear anything of value for years!'

If I'd had any doubts about going to another NA meeting that fucking sealed it. How the hell did he know that about me?

Three hours later I fell down the stairs of a meeting in Ladbroke Grove. Someone offered me a cup of tea and asked me if I was OK.

'Yeah, I'm fine,' I lied, and then tried again.

'Thanks for the tea. No, I'm not fine; I'm absolutely fucked. I have no idea what to do but I'm desperate to stay clean. I've got to go ice skating in a couple of weeks.'

Epilogue: February 2013

I am currently sitting on a very small chair attempting to write the 'what happened next' chapter of my story. The reason the chair is so small is that its owner and sometime occupant is a little girl – my daughter, Tabitha Honey Mason.

Tabitha was born in April 2008, by which time, a day at a time, I'd managed to avoid ingesting any drugs or alcohol for nearly two years; at the time of writing this it's approaching seven.

I was driving her to school recently and as we drove past a phone box in Stoke Newington she chirped up from the safety of her booster seat, 'Daddy, can we have Rolling Stones on the CD, please? I like rock 'n' roll.'

I glanced back at her in my rear-view mirror and smiled as she started bopping up and down in her seat. A tear of unrestrained joy then fell from my eye as I remembered the countless hours I'd spent standing by that anonymous phone box we'd just passed, waiting for a dealer to turn up and deliver something that, at best, might bring me temporary relief from the pathetic day-to-day existence my life had become.

'Actually, no, no, no, Daddy, Stone Roses, 'Waterfall'; it's my favourite.'

Another tear, another wave of happiness, beautiful in its purity and simplicity as Tabitha and I sing along together at 8.45 a.m. while we travel through the streets of London N16 before I drop her off at school then head off to work. I've got a busy day ahead of me trying to help people trapped in the misery of their own addictions, many just as helplessly lost as I once was.

So, yeah, seven years of recovery, seven years of life, some of it beyond my wildest dreams, much of it, I'm pleased to report, much the same as anybody else's!

So what happened next after that NA meeting I attended?

I went to another and another and kept on going, two, sometimes three times a day as my body reflected its displeasure at the sudden lack of heroin, booze and methadone coming its way by refusing to let me sleep for days on end, rejecting any food I tried to eat and generally doing a convincing impression of a battered, confused and terrified human being with no idea of what to do next other than keep going to those meetings, crying my eyes out and refusing to succumb to the intense cravings to score.

People who shall remain anonymous walked with me almost every step of the way during those first few months, nodding their heads with identification when I opened my mouth to speak at the meetings, after which they brought me coffee, fed me and let me sleep/lie awake all night on sofas and in spare rooms.

They told me I was not alone, that they cared about me, that I was an inspiration as I went through the hell of raw cold turkey but refused to give in to the sometimes incessant urges to score or drink. They picked me up and drove me to meetings when I was too weak to walk, put credit on my phone so I could call them day or night when I just needed to talk or cry to someone as the drugs came out of my system and my true feelings resurfaced.

Feelings?

What the fuck was I supposed to do with them?

'Just talk about them, Simon. Feelings ain't gonna kill you but you're going to have to get used to them, mate.'

A simple truth but something I needed to hear every day back then and often still do now.

People cared, they cared about me at a time when I could barely do so myself. They told me all would be well just as long as I didn't pick up the first drink or drug.

I got 30 days clean, started to sleep again, kept walking to meetings, hanging out with people who knew me better than I knew myself, always made me feel welcome, were always prepared to listen to the torrent of confusion and self-doubt, the bad jokes, the fear, the hope, the questions, the remorse and guilt, *never* judging me, always ready to suggest a simple way forward, always a day at a time.

Got 60 days, then 90, still sleeping on friends' sofas and spare rooms, still walking to meetings but now with a real spring in my step, Walkman clamped to my ears as I stomped about west London, singing songs as I went, the songs I'd forgotten even existed, the songs of my youth, the music I'd first fallen in love with at the same time I'd begun my doomed romance with drugs.

At six months clean I moved back to Stoke Newington where often, sometimes on a daily basis, I'd see old dealers and people I'd used with.

'You look well, Simon. You want my new number? Got some good . . .'

'No, no, I don't. Bye.'

I kept walking, kept singing along to the songs on my Walkman, started to play the guitar again, began to do some voluntary work, kept going to NA meetings, connecting with people.

At a year clean my wife and I decided to give our marriage one more go and she moved back in with me. I celebrated a year clean with a party and the purchase of a 1963 Lambretta TV175, which meant I could scoot to meetings rather than walk!

Some friends and I then started an NA meeting in Stoke Newington, almost directly opposite the kebab shop I once begged outside of.

At 18 months, I started a band with some of my new friends in recovery called The Should Be Deads.

At two years clean, the greatest gift I could ever have came into this world as my beautiful daughter Tabitha was born. They cut her out of her mother's belly, wrapped her in a towel and placed her in my arms. I held her tightly next to my heart, where, of course, she will always remain.

Two years of recovery also saw me go back to City Roads detox, a place that had saved me from myself on numerous occasions. Walking back through the doors as a volunteer, then a few months later as a part-time paid member of staff, was and always will be one of the most rewarding experiences of my life. I continue to work within the drug-treatment system to this day.

As the months and years passed I kept walking, singing and sometimes even dancing or at least trying to as the band were lucky enough to play in front of thousands of other recovering addicts all over the UK, Spain and Israel.

The Should Be Deads live at the Dead Sea? You couldn't make it up, huh? But you could make it happen and we did.

There are many more significant events I could list as the months became years, some utterly mind blowing and joyous, some, like the break-up of my marriage at four years clean, unfortunately not so. Such is the stuff of life, as they say, so I try not to forget the many people I knew who didn't survive their own addictions and therefore, I also try, not always successfully I might add, to consider each day a gift.

I've not yet witnessed Liverpool FC win the Premier League, but if you consider the remarkable changes that have recently occurred in my life, you'll forgive me for living in hope of witnessing that one day too!

So, yes, almost seven years ago I did manage to take my eldest nephew ice skating for his tenth birthday. Admittedly I sat and shivered at the side of the rink because of the state of me at only a few weeks clean, but he didn't seem to care. The fact is I was there. Yesterday I drove him to Liverpool and back as we went to watch the football together, something I'd initially promised him years ago before I got clean, but unlike the promises made during active addiction this was one I knew I could keep.

When I call my mum or sister on the phone these days there is no sense of dread from them when they hear my voice any more. They know I am OK and are proud of me, as I am also to be their son and brother. I am a daddy to Tabitha and a good daddy at that! I am a loving uncle to four and a friend to (hopefully) many.

Writing this book has itself been a journey, from the initial badly constructed sentences purloined from the diaries I somehow managed to keep hold of throughout the years of addiction, hostels, homelessness and rehabs, to the story you have hopefully kept reading up to these final words. If you or anyone you know has been through or is currently experiencing the hell of addiction I sincerely wish that, by whatever method works for you, there is also a happy ending. I am by no means in any way special; my recovery has and continues to involve the support of many, and there are many similar stories to my own, of addiction and recovery, that I have witnessed, each just as extraordinary in its own way.

Thank you for reading my story.